Bloomberg
— BY —
Bloomberg

WITH INVALUABLE HELP FROM
MATTHEW WINKLER

JOHN WILEY & SONS, INC.

New York • Chichester • Weinheim • Brisbane • Singapore • Toronto

Published by John Wiley & Sons, Inc.
Published simultaneously in Canada.

Library of Congress Cataloging-in-Publication Data:

Bloomberg, Michael.
    Bloomberg by Bloomberg.
      p.   cm.
    Includes index.
    ISBN 0-471-15545-4 (cloth ed.)
    ISBN 0-471-20888-4 (paper ed.)
    1. Bloomberg, Michael.   2. Capitalists and financiers—United
States—Biography.   3. Investments—United States.   4. Businessmen—
United States—Biography.   5. Telecommunication—United States.
I. Title.
HG172.B56A3   1997
384′.06′573092—dc21
  [B]   96-53327

Printed in the United States of America

20

Preface

O n the night of November 6 last year, my family, friends, and colleagues at our company, Bloomberg LP, gathered at a midtown restaurant and waited for the results of New York City's mayoral election. Five months earlier, I ignored the warnings of so many wise men and women and took the plunge by running for office. I had always said that if I ever got the chance to go into politics, being mayor was at the top of my list and a natural extension of my experience as the chief executive of Bloomberg.

It had been 20 years since we started the company in a small room on Madison Avenue—refugees from Wall Street motivated by an idea that we could build something new that just might make a difference in the world of money and investing. We were too young and too insignificant for anyone to warn us then that we were crazy to think we could create a company that could challenge the giants of financial media. So we didn't hesitate. Within a year, we had our first customer and five years later, our first overseas office. By 1989, our annual sales were approaching $100 million and there were now more than 400 of us selling a machine that had a small, growing following.

We kept building. From a bond product, we branched out into stocks, commodities, and news. We added magazines, radio, and television—all tethered to the 24-hour machine—that made us unique as a multimedia company catering to the people with the most at stake. Within Bloomberg, we were never satisfied and that drove us to work harder and build more. Whether we made our luck or luck made us, by May 1997 as *Bloomberg by Bloomberg* hit the bookstores, we were able to install our 75,000th Bloomberg computer terminal, bringing our annual sales to $1.3 billion.

Even as the dot-com boom became a bust and the economy soured in 2001, we continued to grow, bringing the paid-up number of Bloomberg users to 164,000 and our annual sales to nearly $3 billion. Our staff climbed to 8,000 in 108 offices, serving customers in 126 countries. But our success continues to be derived mostly from one thing: our own people. They will always be our most important asset and, if there is anything that defines our company, it is an awareness that nothing is more important than customer service. The only way to have the best customer service is treat our people the best.

That's what drove me in business and that's what motivated me to consider public service an extension of my career as a chief executive. An hour after the polls closed on Election Day last November, I still didn't know who the winner was. Win or lose, I was glad to have made the race. It is only by doing what many say is difficult or impossible that we achieve.

There is no substitute for the simultaneous sense of humility and inspiration that I enjoyed when I took the oath of office and became the 108th mayor of New York City. There are difficult times ahead. September 11th will forever be remembered for the unprecedented sorrow and destruction visited on New York. But it also will become part of a new chapter for the city and the nation in which freedom emerges from this tragedy stronger than ever.

Whatever I have achieved until this point, I like to think that it helped prepare me for the challenge of uniting our public sector, corporate community, labor force, academic institutions, and philanthropic and cultural organizations. The story that follows is about building partnerships, shared vision, and, ultimately, sharing the rewards.

Bloomberg by Bloomberg is about becoming the best and I want to assure every reader of this book, the best is yet to come.

MIKE BLOOMBERG
New York, New York
February 2002

Contents

The Last Supper

The Thrill of Getting Fired:
Tarrytown 1981

So there I was, thirty-nine years old and essentially hearing, "Here's $10 million; you're history." One summer morning, John Gutfreund, managing partner of Wall Street's hottest firm, and Henry Kaufman, then the world's most influential economist, told me my life at Salomon Brothers was finished.

"Time for you to leave," said John.

On Saturday, August 1, 1981, I was terminated from the only full-time job I'd ever known and from the high-pressure life I loved. This, after fifteen years of twelve-hour days and six-day weeks.

Out!

For a decade and a half, I'd been an integral part of the country's most successful securities trading firm, even of Wall Street itself. Not just in my head. If my press was to be believed, in everyone's. Suddenly, though, needed no longer. I was a general partner. An owner rather than an employee. Nevertheless:

Fired!

I wasn't going to know what was happening, wasn't going to be making decisions, wasn't going to share in "my" company's profits and losses, wasn't going to be part of it at all. "We" had become "them and me."

"What do you think about us selling the company?" asked Henry.

"If I'm being thrown out, better now than later," I replied.

Of course, there was the $10 million I was getting. America's a wonderful country.

*　　　*　　　*

The Salomon Brothers Executive Committee had decided to merge the seventy-one-year-old partnership with a publicly held commodities trading firm, Phibro Corporation (previously part of Engelhard Minerals and Chemicals). We found this out on a hot, summer Friday night at a hastily called, "mandatory attendance, utmost-secrecy required," mysterious partners' meeting at the Tarrytown Conference Center, the former New York estate of society hostess Mary Duke Biddle. Security guards surrounded the complex, checking in each participant as he arrived. (Unfortunately, security missed seeing a *Fortune* magazine photographer who'd been tipped off and was hiding in a tree. So much for confidentiality!) For sixty-three of us, it was our last meeting as Salomon partners and the occasion when Gutfreund and Kaufman told me my time at Salomon Brothers was over.

We got together in a big conference room before dinner. Expensive lawyers and accountants, being paid at overtime rates, hovered to the side. Exchanging furtive glances, they oozed a nervousness, perhaps in fear that some prewritten script would go awry. Tables and chairs were arranged in rows with the Executive Committee seated in front, facing "the troops." At each partner's seat was a dark gray personalized leather folder. I sat at my assigned place and, though we had been told to wait, like everyone else I immediately opened the book in front of me. The first enclosures were financial projections for our company after a proposed merger with Phibro, this almost unknown oil, metals, and agricultural commodities dealer. Pro forma income statements, balance sheets, legal documents, and other corporate gibberish were attached.

But the second presentation in the book was infinitely more interesting: the effect of the deal on me as an individual. It meant millions of dollars in my pocket!

The pointless speeches went on and on. The Executive Committee was determined to sell the assets of the Salomon partnership. This transaction was a foregone conclusion: The process, a jury trial parody, where witnesses saw the accused pull the trigger, no mitigating circumstances are entered as evidence, and the judge instructs the jurors to deliberate. Everybody walks into the jury room and the foreman asks, "Did he do it?"

Twelve people instantaneously answer, "Guilty."

"Let's go back."

"We can't. We've got to give the accused some consideration. Let's sit around and talk for an hour."

So at Tarrytown we talked for sixty minutes. We were solemn. We were serious. Some asked about differences in corporate culture, others about earnings potential, a few about management structure and duplication of staff functions.

Irrelevant! The Executive Committee wanted this merger and could have voted it through on its own. Yes, we were presented with a fait accompli. But, make no mistake. There was 100 percent approval from the rest of the general partners. Nobody in that meeting gave a moment's thought to rejecting the sale, including me. It was such a lucrative deal for us, as owners.

By the time we sat down to eat, everything was said and done. We were all as serious and businesslike as we possibly could be while trying to stifle the enormous grins on our faces. Everybody attending this meeting was now wealthy beyond his dreams. Previously, partners' money had just been numbers in a capital account ledger book, "funny money." We could give it to charity, or retire, and wait another ten years to get at it. Other than that (and 5 percent interest paid out to us yearly), our fortune was only on paper. That was then. But this was now. All of a sudden, it was real. And ours. In our pockets. In cash!

We were told not to tell anyone until the public announcement the coming Monday. Nobody, inside the company or outside, had known that a sale was even being considered. (Still, my friend and partner Bob Salomon guessed, the day before, that whatever was brewing involved Phibro Corp. He showed me the company's symbol on his stock monitor before we drove to the Tarrytown meeting. Smarter than the rest of us!) The Executive Committee hadn't told the retired limited partners. Not even Billy Salomon, the grand, old man of the company. He was informed personally in a much criticized surprise helicopter visit to his Southampton summer home two days later.

Strict instructions to the contrary notwithstanding, some partners did telephone their wives that Friday night. I thought it was nonsensical to make your spouse a possible leak suspect. What difference would it make if she didn't know for an extra day? Others didn't share my view. One partner called his wife while she was at their country club. She ran back into the club's dining room screaming, "We're rich, we're rich!" Fortunately, nobody paid any attention to her.

After the meeting, we ate greasy steaks and drank hard liquor. We shot pool, smoked Cuban cigars, played poker, and laughed uproariously. It was a great big wonderful fraternity party. Boozing and carousing into the wee hours. No thoughts of others. A moment just for us. We had worked for it; and whether or not we deserved it, we got it!

*   *   *

The next day, Saturday, with enormous hangovers evident all around, each partner sat down with two members of the Executive Committee. My meeting was with Gutfreund and Kaufman. Most of the sixty-three partners were asked to stay on as employees of the new company. Not me, though. A half a dozen other guys were pushed out at that time as well.

"Since you don't need me anymore, I'm going home."

There was no reason to stay for the meetings with the new owners. I wasn't going to be involved.

Was I sad on the drive home? You bet. But, as usual, I was much too macho to show it. And I did have $10 million in cash and convertible bonds as compensation for my hurt feelings. If I had to go, this was the time. I was getting my money out of the firm then instead of ten years later. With Phibro paying a merger premium, I was doubling my net worth. Since somebody else had made the decision, I'd even avoided agonizing over whether to stay at Salomon—a timely question, given my then-declining prospects in the company.

Still, it was unsettling that future discussions would be about someone else's company, a firm that until then had been mine. If they'd said, "We have another job for you"—say, running the Afghanistan office—I'd have done it in a second, just as I did at an earlier career turning point in 1979, when Billy Salomon and John Gutfreund told me to give up my sales/trading responsibilities and supervise the computer systems area. I was willing to do anything they wanted. It was a great organization and I would have been happy to stay. I'd never have left voluntarily: There'd be no reason to in good times, and I couldn't have abandoned them in bad times. Unfortunately (or fortunately for me, as it turned out), staying wasn't an option.

Afterward, I didn't sit around wondering what was happening at the old firm. I didn't go back and visit. I never look over my shoulder. Once finished: Gone. Life continues!

*　　　*　　　*

Although Phibro technically bought Salomon, Salomon soon ran the combined companies. The power shifted with record speed. Phibro took over when the transaction occurred, and Phibro became Phibro-Salomon. As the securities business boomed, the commodities business collapsed. Soon the entity became Salomon Inc., with Phibro Energy and Philipp Brothers as subsidiaries. The

Philipp name went back to the obscurity it had had five years earlier. The acquirer never knew what hit it. The acquiree dominated almost from day one. A total mismatch.

With the merger, the Salomon partners got their freedom and their fortunes, but in the process, they ended their own firm as it had existed for decades. By losing control of its key employees, Salomon destroyed its greatest strength. Until then, partners had a long-term, firmwide perspective insured by the golden handcuffs of a ten-year capital "lock-in." After the merger, everyone was just a hired gun. Today, at Salomon, as at Phibro, virtually all who were there at the time of the merger are gone. The then-partners may have gotten rich, and today the resulting combined organization may be doing very well, but both old-line companies "lost" in the end.

*   *   *

I went to see Billy Salomon a week after the merger was announced. "So long, thanks for everything, and goodbye" was the purpose. He was not happy. He was, in fact, furious and embittered that "his" firm had been sold and that he had had no part in the decision.

"You screwed me," he said.

"Billy, these were your rules. You dictated years ago that nonexecutive general partners and all limited partners [as he had then become] had no say. You decided that the Executive Committee ruled absolutely. You personally picked every one of its members. Rightly or wrongly, they're your legacy. They made this decision to merge, not the rest of us."

I never thought Billy had a real bitch. One of style maybe, but not of substance. John and the Executive Committee had a responsibility to do what they thought was right for the firm—which is to say, for its owners. Billy had selected the people who made the decision. They followed the rules he had set. He just didn't anticipate or like the results.

Although I did say "So long" to Billy Salomon, my recollection is that John Gutfreund didn't say goodbye to me. The next time I saw him was seven years later at the surprise fiftieth birthday party for Jack Kugler, our former partner. "Hello, young man, and how are you?" he said to me.

"Fine, and younger than you."

"You always were a wiseass."

That was it. Thanks, John. He had hired me as a fresh MBA when I needed a job—and he had fired me when my era there had really passed. In both instances, his timing was impeccable.

Even though my Salomon career ended involuntarily, I owe a great debt to William Salomon and John Gutfreund. They were my mentors. They taught me ethics, philanthropy, hard work, and to take care of others. They encouraged me to strive for success and supported me fully, even when I failed. They gave me the opportunity to prove myself, not to mention the chance to walk away with an almost unseemly fortune, which I used later to start my own firm. Given all the people Salomon Brothers employed over the years, there are myriad others who must feel the same about both of them.

Though their careers ended very differently, Billy (who retired voluntarily) and John (forced out when an underling cooked the books) have both made their respective contributions. Wall Street is a better place because of their efforts—and I'm a smarter, better (and richer) person because of them. To this day, I consider them both friends.

*   *   *

During the week after the Salomon partners' last supper in Tarrytown, I went to a furrier on Third Avenue and ordered a sable jacket for my wife, Sue. We had been married for five years at that point, during which time I was a Wall Street star. Unfortunately, from that Tarrytown dinner onward, when she met somebody in the street and was asked, "What does your husband do?" she'd be tempted to answer something like, "Well, he *used to be* a very important Salomon Brothers partner." The sable would be a surprise to get her mind onto something else.

While I was never embarrassed to say that I'd been fired and was now running a small start-up business, I'm tougher than many others (or, perhaps as a psychological defense mechanism, I have convinced myself not to care what others think). But I was worried that Sue might be ashamed of my new, less visible status and concerned I couldn't support the family. A sable jacket seemed to say, "No sweat. We can still eat. We're still players."

I asked the furrier to stay open until 7:30 P.M. on my last day of work, September 30, 1981, and I put in my normal twelve hours. On the way home, I picked up the jacket. Sue was delighted. We drank a bottle of champagne, gave our daughter, Emma, a kiss, and went out to dinner. Next morning, I started Bloomberg, the company. The rest is work in progress.

2

Capitalism, Here I Come

School, Work, and Hard Knocks

It was a long way to that Tarrytown conference center from the place I began my journey. The child of hard-working middle-class parents—my father was an accountant at a dairy, my mother a woman of liberal views and independent mind—I wasn't exactly preordained from birth to make a big success of myself on Wall Street or anywhere else. But as a child, from them I learned hard work, intellectual curiosity, and the ambition to strive relentlessly for the goals I set—all of which would serve me in good stead at school, during my capitalist education at Salomon, and in creating my own company later on.

The town of Medford, Massachusetts, was a blue-collar community outside of Boston. Its city-run high school (I was class of 1960) had 250 students in each grade. Very few went to college. Vocational training was the main mission. I was totally bored until my senior year, when the school started two "honors" courses—one in history and one in literature. For the first time, I was interested in and challenged by my studies.

The history teacher made current events come alive, especially those politically controversial events in America's past that he told

9

us had never before been taught in government-supported education. One event was the labor struggle in the 1920s, exemplified by the trial of anarchists Sacco and Vanzetti. He described how his mother went each day to the courthouse to listen (the predecessor of today's Court TV), how some thought them heroes and others thought them the Antichrist. But by bringing his own family into it, the instructor made history real and relevant, not just something to read and memorize. Similarly with literature: The English teacher helped us analyze the world's great books instead of teaching spelling and grammar (two things I never did learn thoroughly). Discussing the meaning of the story versus memorizing the plot made the difference—fascinating versus boring. Both classes broadened my perspective: The exposure to non-politically-correct history and culture opened my eyes to a whole new world. What a shame all the preceding time was partially wasted. Somehow, we as a society must find a way to better engage our children in the joys of learning. Generation after generation of functional illiterates we don't need.

Outside of school, in my early years, I remember reading *Johnny Tremain*, a novel about a teenage messenger and spy for the Yankee rebels in Boston in 1776. I must have read it a hundred times and often took the subway downtown to visit the Revolutionary War sites the story mentioned. I thought of myself as the hero patriot, sticking it to old George III—a maverick role I still try to emulate. I developed a sense of history and its legacy, and remain annoyed at how little people seem to learn from the past; how we fight the same battles over and over; how we can't remember what misguided, shortsighted policies led to depression, war, oppression, and division. As citizens, we continually let elected officials pander for votes with old, easy, flawed solutions to complex problems. As voters, we repeatedly forget the lessons of others who didn't hold their chosen officials accountable. God help us if George Santayana was right and we're doomed to repeat it all again.

Being a Boy Scout brought together my sense of community with my ambitions of personal accomplishment. I loved it. I savored earning every merit badge, took pride in achieving every rank. I was one of the youngest Eagle Scouts in that organization's history. Boy Scout summer camp was the highlight of the year. I paid for my lodging there by selling our troop's Christmas wreaths door-to-door (my first selling experience). Accommodations were two-man tents under the stars for six weeks in the wilds of New Hampshire. A bugle blew reveille in the morning. We showered under ice-cold water. The food was hot dog and hamburger fare in a big mess hall where everyone took turns peeling potatoes, setting the tables, doing the dishes. I remember loving meals, particularly the grape-flavored punch called "bug juice." Daily, there were riflery, archery, rowing, canoeing, swimming, art, ceramics, and dozens of other games and skills. Hikes and river trips were the highlight of the week—and parents came to bothersome visiting days only once or twice in the whole summer. It was the time I learned both to be self-sufficient and, simultaneously, to live and work with others.

On Saturday mornings in the winter, I went to the Boston Museum of Science for lectures that introduced the natural and physical world in a way my school could not. Each week, for two hours, I sat spellbound as an instructor brought snakes, porcupines, and owls for us to hold; demonstrated the basic laws of physics with hands-on experiments; and quizzed us on every museum exhibit. All the kids—including me—tried to show off by having every answer. This competition taught the value of precise observation, attention to detail, and careful listening. Once the question concerned the age of a tree whose five-foot cross section was displayed in the museum upstairs. The exhibit had great historical events marked by a light bulb at each appropriate tree ring, from the current-day outside circle back to the tree's germination, centuries earlier, at the center of the display. The question was asked about "the redwood tree." We were suitably frustrated by an instructor who refused to accept what we all knew was the "right" answer, until someone realized the tree cross section was not from a redwood at all, but rather from a giant sequoia—a related but slightly different variety. Listen, question, test, think: Those instructors taught me the value of intellectual honesty and scholarship years before college.

*　　　*　　　*

While in high school, I worked after class, on weekends, and during summers for a small electronics company in Cambridge, Massachusetts. The technical genius of the company recommended Johns Hopkins University in Baltimore. I was interested in science, and she knew people at the school's Applied Physics Laboratory. Since I had to go to college some place, why not? I sent in an application and was accepted in due course. The way things worked out, Hopkins probably isn't sorry it gave me a chance. And I was never sorry I matriculated there.

Academically, I was a mediocre student in college, more from a lack of motivation than natural aptitude, or so I hope. Mostly, my grades were Cs (average) in engineering, but during my senior year, I took double the normal course load and earned almost all top-of-the-class As. Nevertheless, I did little more than read the books, listen to the lectures, understand what was said, and parrot it back. Never did I think I could have gone out and originated the material. I hadn't the interest or intellect to be a real engineer, physicist, or mathematician. What I really liked doing—and what I was good at—was dealing with people. I became president of my fraternity, president of the Inter-Fraternity Council, class president, and all-around Big Man On Campus. I learned how to campaign for office while seeking elected school positions. I developed organizational abilities when I planned school dances and fraternity parties. I practiced building consensus and getting people to work together as I ran various school-related extracurricular organizations. All these skills helped me later at Salomon Brothers on Wall Street and eventually with my own company.

When I began thinking about life after graduation, it was obvious that administration was the career for me. I probably would have looked for a job straightaway but for the fact that most people at Hopkins went on to get graduate degrees. Under this communal social pressure, I applied to business school. When the acceptance arrived, I was with friends in the campus mail room and noticed a large brown envelope from Harvard Business School in my mailbox.

"Great. Got in. Let's go get a cup of coffee," I said.

"Don't you want to open it?" someone asked.

"What's the point?" I responded. "They're not sending me a thick package if it was a rejection. That comes in a very thin letter."

*   *   *

My two years at Harvard were well spent. I learned the basics of accounting, marketing, production, management, control, finance, and behavioral science. Harvard's "case method" teaching honed my analytic skills and sharpened my communications abilities. There's nothing as educational as the instantaneous feedback of a hundred classmates shouting you down when you're caught unprepared or can't justify a position.

The academic standards there were superior, but not what I'd call outstanding. There were some very bright students in my class, some classmates I thought "not exactly intellectually gifted," and a few that I considered total frauds who could only talk a good game. From today's vantage point, thirty years later, those whom I thought were smart generally did well later in life; those whom I considered dummies did less well. The bullshitters faded away. Street smarts and common sense, it turned out, were better predictors of career achievements after graduation than academic success. Given that I received average grades at "The B School," I don't exactly mind.

Embarrassingly, I remember being more impressed by whom I was matriculating with than by their abilities. As a kid from working-class Medford, never before had I met people as close to the limelight. Many were the sons of famous business leaders I'd read about in the newspapers. Did I think they'd rise to the top just because their dads did? (Generally, they didn't.) Was I secretly hoping for a career-enhancing introduction to their parents? (Few of their fathers' companies even survive today.) Was I looking for glamour by association? (Now, around our offices, "celebrities" are a dime a dozen.) In fact, although many Harvard relationships have helped me to this day, almost none are with those who impressed me so much back then.

*　　　*　　　*

Preparing to finish The B School with a Master's in Business Administration in 1966, I really hadn't pondered where my life and work would take me. Like most young men of my generation, I expected to go straight to Vietnam after graduation. Nobody I knew was actually in favor of the war, and I certainly didn't relish the idea of getting shot while walking through the jungle, but in those days the thought of rebelling against our country never entered our minds. Virtually no one went to Canada to avoid the draft, in spite of what the press said. Home, school, Boy Scouts, sports, politics, newspapers—everything in life taught us duty, loyalty, responsibility, sacrifice, patriotism. A handful marched, got riled up, and wrote about civil disobedience. But generally, Uncle Sam called, and we went.

I had a commitment from an army unit that would make me a second lieutenant after Harvard. Three months before graduation, I went for my standard-issue military physical. It was a pro forma thing; I was in perfect health. To my great surprise, the doctor told me, "You have flat feet. You're not going."

Now, not having to go and possibly get killed was good news. But I was given a draft classification that didn't disqualify me. Instead, it would let the government change its mind later if the war effort needed those of us with this dreaded podiatric deformity.

And down the road, who knew what unit I'd be conscripted into or how my career would be going? So I tried hard to secure a 1A classification that would get me into the military right away. I wrote my senators and congressmen for assistance, trying to do the right thing—serve my country—but also trying to maintain a measure of control over my own life. The legislators' offers of help were my first taste of politicians' promises that never seem to arrive. Other than the form letters written by staffers ("We'll try to help"), none of them ever appeared to intervene on my behalf. And as it turned out, even though in the mid-1960s everyone under age twenty-five was potentially marching off to war, I never heard from my draft board again. Eventually, we declared victory, and lost the war.

*   *   *

What would I do with my life? With twelve weeks until graduation, I had no plan for how I'd turn an expensive education into a living. I hadn't given it any thought, nor had I signed up for recruiting interviews. My good friend, Steve Fenster, a Harvard classmate who later would become a member of my company's board of directors (five years before he died of cancer), told me to call the firms of Salomon Brothers & Hutzler, as it was then named, and Goldman, Sachs & Co., and to say I was desperate to be an institutional salesperson or equity trader.

"Who are they?" I asked. "What would I be doing?" Busy as I was learning the details of Keynesian economic theory and the intricacies of textbook finance, I wasn't exactly familiar with the jobs and people of Wall Street. I had always assumed I'd go to work in general management for some engineering or manufacturing company, or perhaps even into real estate as my best friend from Harvard, Ron Burks, was doing. (Wall Street did not become the magnet for newly minted MBAs until the 1980s.)

"Don't worry about it," Fenster told me. "Just do it."

Steve had worked at the Pentagon as a Robert McNamara "whiz kid" and then at Morgan Stanley for a summer. My resident expert

15

on both the military and the Street, he said I'd fit in and be happy at either place, doing either thing. Not having any better ideas of my own, I made the calls.

Fortunately for me, as someone who hadn't exactly hobnobbed with Rockefellers during his wonder years or had a mogul for a father, securities trading and sales were considered second-class occupations in those days. Relatively few Ivy League graduates wanted them. Unlike investment banking or research analysis, they were definitely not the prestigious jobs; not the kind of work that the more privileged kids would deign to do. Both involved getting your hands dirty by actually picking up the telephone and talking to customers. Forget the fact that almost all occupations have a big selling component—selling your firm, your ideas, yourself. Never mind that the deans of investment banking depend on their Rolodexes as much as their analytical skills. Overlook the fact that a good trading mentality is synonymous with the ability and discipline to compartmentalize, focus, and compete for success. In those days, no self-respecting research analyst or banker ever thought of working the phones, actually bringing in business. Soliciting was undignified. Trading and sales jobs were going begging. The "swells" were heading elsewhere.

But I came from a background where none of those class distinctions mattered. I didn't know better, and I wouldn't have understood if someone had tried to explain the social niceties. I grew up with the civics-class traditional American ethic, with my parents as role models: Work hard, value education, and do things yourself, whether the labor was mental or physical. For me, with college loans to pay off, a good job was a good job. And, as I would learn later on in my life—at Salomon Brothers and in my own company—it's the "doers," the lean and hungry ones, those with ambition in their eyes and fire in their bellies and no notions of social caste, who go the furthest and achieve the most.

As a Harvard Business School graduate willing to go into the Wall Street trenches, I got an interview at both firms that Steve had suggested. Invited to New York as one of those relatively few MBAs wanting a Goldman, Sachs sales/trading position, I was introduced to Gustav Levy, managing partner of the firm and a true legend. "Mike, this is Mr. Levy."

Standing in front of me was this ordinary guy, at once cordial and distant, whose circle of friends and acquaintances, while including world political and financial leaders, until then hadn't included me. I shook his hand and exchanged the usual pleasantries. Ignorant of his true importance, I wasn't as impressed as I should have been. Gus, as he was called, really was somebody and had done great things as one of the Street's top arbitrageurs and philanthropists. Decades after his death, he's still revered as an innovative banker, trusted adviser, and brilliant risk taker. I wish I'd had the smarts to ask him a few questions and, later in my career, spend some time with him before he died. But I didn't.

Then I trotted off to my Salomon Brothers & Hutzler interview. I was the only one at Harvard who'd signed up to meet the folks from this little bond trading firm that lacked the high-and-mighty profile MBA types typically sought. While being shown around by their personnel manager, Stuart Allen, I started talking to some man named Billy whose full name I didn't catch. We talked about school, New York, the weather, whatever. He seemed friendly, like a distant cousin at a family wedding.

"What did you think of Billy?" my escort asked after the guy had ambled away.

"Who was that?" I asked.

"Well, that was William R. Salomon."

I didn't know. He was just some easy-to-talk-to, nice person. But since I was now on a first-name basis with "Billy," the managing partner at one firm, and I had encountered "Mr. Levy," the senior person at the other, I knew where I fit in.

My actual job interview at Salomon was not with Billy, but with three other people: the sales manager, Harry Nelson; the head of equity trading, Sandy Lewis (son of Bear, Stearns's, then-managing-partner, Cy Lewis); and the number-two partner at Salomon, John Gutfreund. It took place in a windowless conference room that opened into the firm's Partners' Barber Shop, a standard owners' perk in those days. Equally impressive was the art (all rented, it turned out). I can still picture the massive famous oil color of the Dempsey–Firpo prize fight hanging in their lounge. I'd never seen real art outside of a museum before. When I went back for the obligatory second interview with the same group, they offered me a job for $9,000 a year. In the meantime, I'd been offered employment at Goldman, Sachs by its sales manager, Dick Menschel, starting at $14,000 a year—the going rate in those days for a Harvard MBA graduate.

"Look, I can't afford to work at Salomon," I told Nelson, Lewis, and Gutfreund. "I want to. I'd love it. But I don't own another suit of clothes." For those who sat back row in a Harvard class, the dress was jeans—called dungarees in those days—and your college jacket. "I don't have an apartment to live in. I have no cash in the bank. All I've got are outstanding National Defense loans I took for tuition when my part-time campus job as a school parking-lot attendant didn't pay enough."

"How much do you need?" Gutfreund queried.

Instantly, I decided asking for $14,000 it would look greedy. Requesting less would get them to give me more. They'd obviously see that, with enough money, I could focus on the job rather than on paying for three meals each day.

"I need $11,500," I blurted out.

"Fine," said Gutfreund. "That's $9,000 salary and a $2,500 loan." He got up and left the room. So much for my trading ability.

"Well, that's done," said Sandy Lewis.

"But I didn't say yes or no," I protested.

"It doesn't matter."

And that was that. I signed the loan agreement (at least it carried no interest). The first year, my bonus was $500 forgiveness of the loan's principal, followed twelve months later by forgiveness of the remaining loan balance. In 1973, I would frame the note with Gut-freund's signature showing it had been paid off, along with the news-paper announcement of my entry into the firm as a general partner.

*   *   *

To say that I fit into Salomon and loved the industry is an un-derstatement. I reveled in it, every minute of the day. In 1966, Wall Street wasn't the impersonal, corporate business it is today, where it's not uncommon for someone to change jobs six times in ten years. People then didn't move around. They were, or quickly became, a "Morgan Stanley type," an (A.G.) "Becker person," a "KL-er" (Kuhn Loeb), and so on. People were not only identified with their employers, but actually picked up the personalities of their firms, which ranged from haughty and pedigreed to breezy and disarming. The firms in turn were a collection of their staffs' characteristics. From the moment I was hired, no question, I was "Salomon." While many of the top firms coveted distinguished lin-eages, manners, accents, and Ivy League educations, Salomon was more of a meritocracy that prized go-getters, tolerated eccentrici-ties, and treated both PhDs and high school dropouts disinterest-edly. I fit in. It was me.

There was a reason each of us took on the protective coloration of our employer: What mattered on Wall Street in those years was not the individual but the organization. We never used the first per-son singular. (Billy Salomon once overheard a stock trader saying to a customer, "*I'll* buy 50,000 shares." In a very loud voice, Billy asked him how he got that kind of money in his personal account.) Today, with many companies having lost the family attitude, hiring and firing hundreds of people at a stroke, company spirit has dis-appeared and personal ambition is rampant. Employees are out for "Number 1." Everybody's a cowboy. Even the most junior-varsity assistant traders consider themselves individual, self-centered su-perstars. Today's Wall Streeters admit little value from their sup-port people, their company's balance sheet, the franchise name, or

19

their colleagues. Rather than join an organization, they "accept" employment. The company is merely a vehicle, something that offers them a venue for their irreplaceable (and always undercompensated) talents; they declare their free agency status almost on day one.

But when I began, if you could get into an investment banking firm—not an easy thing to do for a nondirect descendant of the founding family—you thought of it as a job for life. You would work your way up, eventually become a partner, and die at a ripe old age in the middle of a business meeting (that's how both Cy Lewis and Gus Levy left this world). You may not have liked all your coworkers and/or partners, but success was "joint and several." Their success helped ensure yours; your achievements abetted theirs. And when that important rule was forgotten by the end of the 1970s, the community that was "The Street" shattered. Charles Darwin told us what would happen: It may be survival of the fittest as nature meant it to be, but lots of good and worthy creatures die in the process.

*　　　*　　　*

The Salomon partnership was a unique organization. It didn't have the normal politics and infighting of the typical commercial enterprise. It was the ultimate "what you see is what you get" environment. Everyone important worked in the same room, sitting shoulder to shoulder, trading or selling stocks and bonds. Disagreements flared, as they did with any group of excitable Type A employees. People who were adversaries on an issue screamed at each other. Then compromises would be made, and the squall was over. Alliances were formed anew. Enemies in the last battle would become allies in the next. Tempers didn't simmer behind closed doors, with staffs encouraging animosities and constructing barriers. Here, it was open, quick, and NOW!

Nor did so-called corporate democracy get in the way. "Empowerment" wasn't a concept back then, nor was "self-improvement" or "consensus." A managing partner presided at the top, with an Executive Committee below, followed by the general partners and everyone else. (The partners thought they had more power than nonpartners, but in reality, most didn't.) The managing partner in those days made all the important decisions. I suspect that, many times, he didn't even tell the Executive Committee *after* he'd decided something, much less consult them before. I'd bet they never had a committee vote. I know they never polled the rest of us on anything. This was a dictatorship, pure and simple. But a benevolent one.

The boss when I joined in 1966, William R. Salomon (WRS as we referred to him behind his back, or Billy as he preferred to be known), made the culture at Salomon Brothers special. He was decisive and consistent as a leader. If he ever harbored doubts after making a decision, I never saw it. And although he was easily approachable and willing to listen to everyone's views, when he said we were going left, we went left, and when he said right, right it was. We didn't have to prepare for both directions. He set the rules and even he conformed to them. Was it a rule to conduct one's personal affairs so as not to embarrass the firm? His own private life was exemplary. When he thought another's wasn't, we had an instantaneous partners' meeting to remove the offender—no matter how important that person was to the immediate bottom line. Did he decree each of us should be accessible to all? Anyone could come up to his desk, anytime. He was on a first-name basis with as many people at the bottom of the corporate ladder as at the top. Did Salomon have a mandatory retirement for partners at age sixty-five? Billy retired voluntarily at sixty-three, when he felt he was slowing down. There was no different set of rules for him. He led by example. What he said, he did. And the rest of us did as well.

John Gutfreund was a great leader too, but I always thought he listened to too many people. The final guy to see him often carried the day. That was fine when I was desperately trying to save my career. As long as I saw John last and persuaded him of the virtue of my position, he'd back me versus the entire Executive Committee. But in retrospect it made running the firm much more difficult for him. Smart people prepared for both left and right when John succeeded Billy as managing partner. This event split resources and made it harder to lead when the going got tough. Unlike Billy, John consulted all interested parties before making a decision. No matter how noble the motive, that resulting apparent indecisiveness eventually destroyed his constituency and led to his downfall. Comparing John Gutfreund to William Salomon on leadership, I always thought John was as principled, as honest, as caring, more egalitarian, less effective.

The real difference between Billy and John was that John was smarter with securities, Billy with people. Neither man will be happy with this distinction, but I always believed the firm was best off when they ran it together. Each had different strengths. Without John, I think Billy would have had trouble running the financial engineering side of the company as the securities world grew more complex with derivatives, swaps, mortgage securities, and so on. And John certainly did have trouble running the people side of the business without Billy, when the organization ballooned to thousands of employees around the world. As a team, until Billy retired in 1978, they were the best.

After their partnership ended, as my career in running equities was waning and I needed something new to do, I tried convincing John that he needed an aide to tell him when the emperor had no clothes—someone to stand up and fight him a little. Someone to test his resolve and let him hone his responses. But he wouldn't sign on. Maybe John didn't think I was competent. Maybe he just didn't want someone looking over his shoulder. In any case, my proposal for a chief-of-staff, a gatekeeper—and me being it—didn't fly.

* * *

I got to Salomon's run-down building at 60 Wall Street in June 1966, and I worked my first summer there in "the Cage," physically counting securities by hand. It was a pretty lowly start for a Harvard MBA. We slaved in our underwear, in an un-air-conditioned bank vault, with an occasional six-pack of beer to make it more bearable. Every afternoon, we counted out billions of dollars of actual bond and stock certificates to be messengered to banks as collateral for overnight loans. Then, every morning, when those certificates needed for delivery to customers were returned by a group of disheveled old men who blanketed the streets of lower Manhattan carrying "bearer" bonds and stocks door-to-door, we checked them back into the firm's inventory. By the 1980s, such practices would be as quaint as the horse-drawn carriage, eliminated by the computers of the information age. Not then, though.

Three months into my career, I was promoted to the Purchase and Sales (P&S) Department. One day, when good weather caused us to dawdle outside, the former longshoreman who was my manager explained at the top of his lungs (embarrassingly and deliberately, in front of the entire department) that a one-hour lunch didn't mean more than sixty minutes away from one's desk, even, or rather particularly, if one was an HBS prima donna. Working in P&S under this guy's eye was not much of a step up from working in my underwear in the Cage. There I was, a Johns Hopkins and Harvard Business School graduate, toiling in a slum with worn-out linoleum floors and broken wooden chairs, putting little paper slips in alphabetical order all day long, and getting berated by someone I probably should have respected, but didn't. When my friends asked what I was doing at work, to save face I told them I was "studying methods and procedures to simplify the work flow." After all, my friends were research analysts and investment bankers with lush, private, windowed, and carpeted offices, and I was what can only be called a clerk. Why didn't I quit? Too embarrassed.

Eventually, though, my big opportunity came. At the end of my first year, I got picked to be a real "Clerk" on the trading floor at the Utilities Desk. Here was where the action was—and the high-paying jobs. In this particular area, the bonds of electric and gas companies were bought and sold. It was run by two Salomon partners, Ira Lectman and Connie Maniatty. My main function was to keep the position book updated with our current inventory as we traded. After a partner signed each transaction ticket (big trades got both partners' signatures), I stamped them with a consecutive number and updated our records. The tickets then went zipping down the conveyor belt to the Back Office from whence I had just escaped. At last I had become an integral part of capitalism. Stamping and updating: I was so glad I'd gone to graduate school!

The execution of my only other Utilities Desk task proved to be my downfall—or my salvation, depending on your perspective. I was charged with the grave responsibility of having six sharpened No. 2 pencils in front of Ira and six sharpened No. 3 pencils in front of Connie each morning when they arrived—or maybe it was the other way around. Anyway, one day, to relieve the boredom and express myself, I deliberately gave them each other's pencils and broke off all the lead tips. Connie took it well. Ira, though, stood up and started screaming to John Gutfreund that I should be fired. Pencils were important to Ira.

John summarily removed me from that department (thus changing the fate of the utility bond business forever) and installed me temporarily in his Syndicate Department, but seated in back of a pillar alongside his second in command, Jay Elsas. From then on, Ira didn't have to have his field of vision ruined by my face. A little anarchy at Salomon in the form of a practical joke was fine, but I had pushed the envelope too far.

A month later, I moved to the Equities Desk and the rest is history. No more bonds. I was in the stock side of the business for good. The firm had just brought in Jay Perry, a glib, fast-talking salesperson from the St. Louis office, to build up our new block trading business. For decades, Salomon had been buying and selling thousands of bonds in single trades, away from any listed exchange, thereby avoiding sudden price fluctuations. For stocks, block trading fulfilled the same function, enabling big institutions to acquire or unload in bulk, without market disruptions. Salomon would become the biggest in this field. And I was part of it as Jay's right-hand man—or he as my left-hand man, as I was known to say on my more modest days.

Actually, Perry and I were a dynamite team. We could sell anything to anybody. If you wanted to dispose of a block of stock, we probably could have even convinced your spouse to buy it. Salomon wasn't a multifaceted full-service firm in those days, so we had to do without what our competitors had and took for granted—research, analysis, contacts. We just did what all great salespeople do: We presented everything we had, and then highlighted whatever facts enabled customers to convince themselves they were getting a good deal.

"It has a strong specialist behind it," I'd tell one buyer who might not have the slightest idea why the specialist mattered. (Specialists are people on the floor of the New York Stock Exchange who are obligated to buy and sell a company's shares, thereby ensuring an orderly market at all times.) "The chart pattern looks like a breakout," Perry would declare for those who believed "The trend's my friend." I'd add, "Look at who the buyers and sellers have been," for the "misery loves company" crowd. Or, "You buy this and we'll help you sell that," we'd say, as if we wouldn't do either separately.

Often, when we worked on one of the big, critical, risky trades, Billy and John would stand over me, watching silently while I was on the phone with a customer, head down, totally focused on making the sale, talking, explaining, cajoling, pleading. I felt a great thrill when they saw I had closed the deal. "Done," I'd say matter-of-factly with a straight face as I hung up the phone and tossed the completed order slip to the trader with a studied nonchalance. And they'd walk away without a word. There weren't any congratulations. They weren't needed. I was the up-and-coming star. I was expected to make big trades. I (and they) knew!

And if our other strategies didn't work to close a deal, we had the ultimate weapon: the firm's capital and five smart guys with the knowledge and decisiveness to "pull the trigger" when needed. The two traders on the desk, David Healy and Robert Bradley (Perry and I called ourselves traders, but we were really just salespeople), along with Michael Meehan, David Kirkland, and Hans Kertess on the New York Stock Exchange floor, could always threaten to buy the stock for Salomon's own account. This would force the buyers to act, even if they wanted to wait. "Buy now or risk buying never" was the message. They always bought.

It was great. This mega trading was a new concept. We developed it as we went. Cy Lewis from Bear, Stearns, and Gus Levy from Goldman, Sachs had started it—trading stocks like bonds. One large transaction going "over the counter" at a single price. It was an entirely revolutionary business compared to the old way of accumulating or disposing of many shares through small individual transactions executed over time on the stock exchanges. Through these pioneering efforts with block trading, we created a bigger, faster market for the gigantic new institutionalized money pools that were more and more coming to be stock market players: pension funds, mutual funds, hedge funds, and insurance annuities. In doing so, we changed the buy-side/sell-side relationship from the "old-boy" concept of doing business based on whom you knew to open, fair competition based on price. It was new, different, initially lucrative, and fun, and I was proud to be one of the young turks making it happen (along with contemporaries Ginny Clark, Bruce Hackett, and James Massey, who all became Wall Street luminaries later in their careers).

Over time, Billy and John, while not the hands-on traders Cy and Gus were, actually had more to do with making the concept fly than the other Wall Street leaders. Salomon and Gutfreund knew the value of consistency in customer service. They also knew the value of publicity, of getting out the word regarding

Salomon's proficiency and aggressiveness in this new field. They encouraged us to do every trade, profitable or not. Before Billy ran Salomon, the bond partners invested in B&O Railroad bonds rather than Haloid stock (which eventually became Xerox). After Billy took over, equities dominated. Later, when the same Salomon partners complained that Perry was crazy, John excluded them and pushed block trading and stock underwriting as the firm's future. When they demanded that Salomon's capital—their money—not be jeopardized by nonpartners like this kid Bloomberg, John just ignored the lot and let us build a whole department of aggressive traders who would provide the service, take the risk, and get everyone together. "Never let the customer go down the street to another store—he might find they sell the same thing there and not come back," Billy always told us. "Do the trade today. Figure out how to make it profitable tomorrow."

*   *   *

I didn't love Wall Street just for the money, I also loved it for the lifestyle it provided. The Street promised vast riches—although in fact I've read of few great fortunes having been made there. From John D. Rockefeller to Sam Walton (and ultimately to Mike Bloomberg, I hope), great financial success comes from starting businesses with concrete products in the real world, building jobs, creating value, and helping people. But in those years, the practical comforts of prosperity, together with the delights of the job itself, kept me engaged and happy.

As a kid from the provinces, I had a lot to learn, not only about the Street, but about the amenities of high-style Manhattan living. I still remember the first time I went to a fancy New York French restaurant, La Côte Basque, in 1967, with Dave Osborn, a cosmopolitan salesperson who started at Salomon the same time as I did. (He became a general partner the same year as I, and got thrown out of the company, years later, on the same day yours truly

27

met his demise.) I couldn't stop gawking. It was my first time in such opulent surroundings. A dozen people were seated around a table featuring the largest flower centerpiece I'd ever seen.

The woman seated to my right talked to me only when she had to, and in an accented English I couldn't readily understand. Her topics of conversation were equally incomprehensible, and certainly as inapplicable: Where did my family have vacation houses in Europe? In what country was our yacht registered? Where did we keep our plane? My late father, who never earned more than $6,000 per year, would have chuckled. And in front of me was more silverware per place setting than my family owned in total. I'd never seen forks and spoons set across the top as well as down the sides. Needless to say, I waited for others to start each course and just followed along.

In addition to showing me the life of high society, Osborn taught me about expense accounts. We took customers to the theater, to sporting events, to breakfast, to lunch, to dinner. We even took them to conventions, to golf outings, and to ski resorts out West, all on the firm's money. Everything was always first-class as we went about cementing those "vital client relationships." Yes, it was legitimate business, but it was whatever tickled our fancy, when, where, and with whomever we chose.

Sometimes, I thought I'd gone through the looking glass into another world. Once, we cruised uptown in a big black limousine. The only other time I'd been in such a car was at my father's funeral. At our destination, someone tossed the driver fifty dollars—for what would have been a two-dollar ride in a cab! That amount of money would have covered my entire week's personal, social, and food budget. Funny world. Funny money. And different from everything I'd ever known.

*   *   *

Back in reality, I took the subway to work and read the office copy of the *Wall Street Journal* upon arrival, to save the fifteen-cent newsstand cost. I came in every morning at 7 A.M., getting there before everyone else except Billy Salomon. When he needed to borrow a match or talk sports, I was the only other person in the trading room, so he talked to me. At age twenty-six, I became a buddy of the managing partner. I would stay later than everyone else except for John Gutfreund. When he needed someone to make an after-hours call to the biggest clients, or someone to listen to his complaints about those who'd already gone home, I was the someone. And I got a free cab ride uptown with him, the No. 2 guy in the company. Making myself omnipresent wasn't exactly burdensome—I loved what I was doing. And, needless to say, developing a close working relationship with those who ran the show probably didn't hurt my career either.

I've never understood why everybody else doesn't do the same thing—make himself indispensable on the job. That was exactly what I did during the summer between my first and second years in graduate school, when I worked for a small Harvard Square real estate company in Cambridge, Massachusetts. Students would come to town just to find an apartment they could move into in September; they were always in a rush, eager to get back to their vacations as soon as possible. We ran generic advertisements in the newspapers for three or four different sizes of rentals; each ad would fit twenty of our apartment listings. Every day, the newly arrived would-be renters got up early, grabbed the newspaper at their hotels, looked at the real estate section, made a phone call, scheduled an appointment with "the next available agent" to see housing that sounded appropriate, and went back to bed. Later in the day, they'd go out and actually look.

I went to work at six-thirty in the morning. By seven-thirty or eight o'clock, all potential renters visiting Cambridge had called our company and booked their apartment-viewing visits with whoever was there. I, of course, was the only one who bothered to come in early to answer the phone: The adult "professionals" who worked for this company (I was "the summer kid") started work at nine-thirty. Then, all day long, they sat in wonderment as person after person walked into the office asking for Mr. Bloomberg.

Woody Allen once said that 80 percent of life is just showing up. I believe that. You can never have complete mastery over your existence. You can't choose the advantages you start out with, and you certainly can't pick your genetic intelligence level. But you can control how hard you work. I'm sure someone, someplace, is smart enough to succeed while "keeping it in perspective" and not working too hard, but I've never met him or her. The more you work, the better you do. It's that simple. I always outworked the other guy (and if I hadn't, he or she would be writing this book).

Still, I had a life. I don't remember being so driven or focused that my job got in the way of playing in the evenings and on weekends. I dated all the girls. I skied and jogged and partied more than most. I just made sure I devoted twelve hours to work and twelve hours to fun—every day. The more you try to do, the more life you'll have.

Although I was serious about my career, I never had a "budget" for my future. Unlike so many of my classmates, I didn't set out to be a partner or vice president at age thirty, or a trillionaire at thirty-five, or President of the United States when I turned forty. Make a comprehensive scheme for the rest of my life? I had trouble filling out the part of the college application where you're asked to write fifteen hundred meaningless words about what you're going to do for the next ten years. Both at business and at home, I've never let planning get in the way of doing.

Life, I've found, works the following way: Daily, you're presented with many small and surprising opportunities. Sometimes you seize one that takes you to the top. Most, though, if valuable at all, take you only a little way. To succeed, you must string together many small incremental advances—rather than count on hitting the lottery jackpot once. Trusting to great luck is a strategy not likely to work for most people. As a practical matter, constantly enhance your skills, put in as many hours as possible, and make tactical plans for the next few steps. Then, based on what actually occurs, look one more move ahead and adjust the plan. Take lots of chances, and make lots of individual, spur-of-the-moment decisions.

Don't devise a Five-Year Plan or a Great Leap Forward. Central planning didn't work for Stalin or Mao, and it won't work for an entrepreneur either. Slavishly follow a specific step-by-step strategy, the process gurus tell you. It'll always work, they say. Not in my world. Predicting the future's impossible. You work hard because it increases the odds. But there's no guarantee; much is dependent on what cards happen to get dealt. I have always believed in playing as many hands as possible, as intelligently as I can, and taking the best of what comes my way. Every significant advance I or my company has ever made has been evolutionary rather than revolutionary: small earned steps—not big lucky hits.

And I stay "flexible." A couple of years ago, long after Salomon had abruptly given way to my forming my own company, a reporter asked me what we at Bloomberg had failed at, as opposed to the successes that get all the attention. My answer, after some thought, was, "Nothing; but what we accomplished wasn't always what we set out to do." Often, in the process, things worked that we hadn't planned on; unforeseen uses arose for our products; customers appeared whom we hadn't known existed—and exactly the reverse occurred for those we had been dead sure of. Planning has its place; the actual thought process sometimes leads to great new ideas. But you can only accomplish what's possible when you get there.

Then, whatever your idea is, you've got to do more of it than anyone else—a task that's easier if you structure things so that you *like* doing them. Since doing more almost always leads to greater accomplishments, in turn you'll have more fun. And then you'll want to do even more because of the rewards. And so on. I've always loved my work *and* put in a lot of time, which has helped make me successful. I truly pity people who don't like their jobs. They struggle at work, so unhappily, for ultimately so much less success, and thus develop even more reason to hate their occupations. There's too much delightful stuff to do in this short lifetime not to love getting up on a weekday morning.

*　　　*　　　*

I expected to be at Salomon for a year or two while I looked for a job in manufacturing. Even though I thought I'd just date the company, not marry it, my romance with Salomon ended only when they threw me out after fifteen years. Thank goodness, every time another firm came to hire me away, I said no. I always found a reason to stay, some fresh outlook on my Salomon life that made me recommit myself to the firm. Maybe I lacked the guts to try someplace new. Maybe I possessed the resolve and foresight to ride with the best. In any case, in retrospect, staying was always the right decision—as I would find out in 1981, at the very end of my Salomon tenure, in a conference center in Tarrytown, New York.

Young people starting their careers today are too impatient for current compensation, at the expense of continuing their education and giving their jobs a chance. Get back to work. Forget the money today. There's plenty of time for that later. Novices should go to the best firm they can get into—and then shut up and learn those few things they don't happen to know already.

The best example of reward for patience (perhaps the best in the history of the world) was when I wasn't made a Salomon general partner at the time I thought I'd be, and didn't quit over it.

Things were going great six years after I was hired. I was the fair-haired boy, the block-trading superstar in the most visible department of the trendiest firm on the Street. I was the pet of its two top executives. I greeted all important visiting customers, got interviewed by every newspaper that mattered, and had a great social life playing the role of Wall Street power broker to the hilt.

More than "a legend in my own mind." When the other young turks sat around and predicted who would be anointed with the ultimate reward of a partnership, I was on the top of the list.

Money wasn't the issue. I'd long since paid off my loans and was living a respectable if not extravagant life. I took the subway to work, I went to free concerts in Central Park, and my most romantic dates were beer and pizza with a girlfriend late at night on the Staten Island Ferry (five cents round-trip, food and drink extra). I lived in the same one-room studio for ten years and didn't bother to own a car. I never spent a lot, but I also don't remember wanting anything I didn't just go out and buy. Good times, great friends, fantastic job, lots of cash: I had it all.

Still, the prestige of the partnership mattered more than everything in the world to me. It was the in-your-face statement to the world that I was the best, that I could go to the top in the most competitive environment there was. The B School kid had used his smarts and skills to work his way up the ladder. I'd earned this partnership, and now I wanted the public acknowledgment of my value once and for all, as a big fish in *the* big pond. Maybe it was all in my head, my private inferiority complex. But, no question—becoming a general partner in Salomon Brothers was my holy grail!

And then, the day came, in August 1972. The list of new partners came out—and I wasn't in! Everyone, just *everyone* else was on that list. All those people who deserved it less than I were there, even those who, according to company gossip, had no chance. I had been passed over and, with such a big group accepted, humiliated as well. It was so bad, there wasn't even anyone left with whom I could commiserate. I was devastated. To this day, no one has ever explained why I wasn't chosen.

With tears in my eyes, I at first denied the truth. Then I thought up wild schemes of revenge. I searched for someone to blame. "I'll quit," I told myself, in the first of many crazy mutterings. "I'll kill 'em." "I'll shoot myself." How would I face anyone ever again?

They would all be looking at me and laughing behind my back. I knew I shouldn't have been so arrogant. Damn it, I never learn.

Fortunately, after work, my normal evening jog alongside the East River let me take my anger out on the pavement rather than on management. The next morning, I went to work and did one of the largest trades the firm had ever done up to that time. I dotted every *i*, crossed every *t*. I focused. I worked. I smiled. I dialed. Was I stronger than everyone else? No one would come close. I would be as good at not making partner as I was at aiming to be one. "Screw 'em!"

Three months later, with no warning, the firm had an unscheduled partners' meeting in Billy Salomon's office. The participants came out stern-faced and silent. My boss, Jay Perry, walked over to my desk and stood behind me with his back to the others.

"What do those idiots want?" I growled without picking up my head.

"They're going to make you and Don Feuerstein general partners," Perry said.

He never could keep a secret. At that instant, someone yelled over to me, "Mike, Bill Salomon's secretary, Margarette Wilson, is calling on line one."

I picked up the phone. "Yes, Margarette?" Margarette always liked me.

"Mr. Salomon wants to see you."

"Does he want Feuerstein, too?"

"Oh, yes. How did you know?"

Billy never gave me an explanation for why they'd made me a partner then and not three months earlier. He was, as I have become, a member of the "never apologize, never explain" school of management. Asking him would not have been good form. And there was no chance I would have gotten an answer anyway. So when he gave me the good news, I didn't ask why they'd waited. I said, "Thank you," politely but not profusely. Even when I got what I wanted and deserved, I would be tougher than the rest.

*   *   *

Someone once said, "Be nice to people on the way up; you'll pass the same ones on the way down." I believe in treating associates well, but not for that cynical reason: Having been both up *and* down repeatedly, my experience says you pass different people as you go through the inevitable cycle.

From the high of the anointment as a general partner, to the low of being fired in 1981, life at Salomon was a constant roller coaster. In 1973, my career was skyrocketing. I had just been made a partner. Next, I was given responsibility for all equities. It happened when Dick Rosenthal, the partner running the arbitrage department, and Jay Perry, the partner supervising stock trading and sales, had a fistfight. Perry was sent to run the Dallas, Texas, office; Rosenthal was ordered to an out-of-the-way area off the trading floor to "do deals," and I got promoted to run all stock trading, sales, arbitrage, and convertible bonds combined.

Although technically I was Jay's boy, nevertheless the three of us—Rosenthal, Perry, and I—conducted a multi-year battle for supremacy. Even Jay and I, who had worked together for years as one of the world's great sales teams, competed against each other, particularly in the last twelve months before his banishment to the Southwest. By then, he was having serious emotional problems. At one point, he became a recluse, actually not leaving his private office or taking any business calls during the day for weeks. Then one morning, while I was upstairs breakfasting with our two biggest customers, he stormed into the trading room and in a fit of pique over some imagined slight, emptied my desk drawers all over the floor before disappearing back into his sanctuary. Called out of the dining room by the desk clerk, I gave

35

instructions to put my papers back before the meal was over. The clients never saw the embarrassing scene and Jay never mentioned the incident, ever. Nor did I. But one month later, after the famous Perry/Rosenthal brawl, I was in charge.

In 1979, my career at Salomon reversed its magical upward climb. Negotiated commission rates and increased competition had made the block-stock business unprofitable. While we were dominating the transaction volume on the NYSE, my administrative and trading skills were constantly being questioned. We certainly weren't making money. Then a surprise administrative message was hand-delivered to all employees, announcing that Richard Rosenthal would join the Executive Committee and from then on would oversee the firm's equity efforts. I walked over to John Gutfreund's desk, which was literally four feet behind me. Billy's was another ten feet away. "I need to see you both, now!"

We went into Billy's conference room. I held up the announcement. "I'm not going to work for Rosenthal, and he won't want me anyway."

"We know that," Gutfreund said. "We want you to go upstairs and run the computer area."

*   *   *

So I started what was to be my last job at Salomon, running Information Systems. This group was responsible for both keeping the firm's books and providing the analytical tools the traders and salespeople needed. I reported directly to Gutfreund in this position, as in the last; but from the beginning, the Executive Committee—particularly one member, my old nemesis, Rosenthal—made my life miserable. Dick, who constantly bragged about his business success in spite of never having finished Erasmus High School in Brooklyn, was jealous of anyone who had a college education, particularly someone who had added an MBA from Harvard. Rosenthal and I had started as friends in the mid-1960s. (I once took his sister-in-law out for a date.) We stopped being friends around 1968 when I was assigned to work with Perry, who became my mentor and Dick's archenemy. Now, he was determined to keep his battle with Jay Perry and "Perry's boy" going.

So, even though I was out of equities, and computers weren't his area of responsibility, the guerilla warfare continued. It wasn't a fair fight. Truth never got in Dick's way. If the facts didn't fit, he just made them up. Over the next two years, he was an instantaneous expert on everything in my domain as well as his—and everyone else's, too. Determined, and armed with that great advantage lack of knowledge gives one, Rosenthal was a winner: Our rivalry was preordained to end in my divorce from the company.

Sure enough, by early 1981, he had persuaded everyone that I was incompetent. Many mimicked his ridicule of my insistence on one firmwide computer system to facilitate cross-department cooperation and multiple-product risk management. It didn't help my situation when I argued vociferously that the firm was going down the wrong path with the adoption of profit-center accounting I thought ill-suited to a complex, totally integrated business. Maybe I shouldn't have criticized the changing of our employment strategy away from promoting in-house producers to managers and toward acquiring outside, transitory, superstar "rainmakers" as department heads. It might have been smarter politically not to have focused computer development toward the newly fashionable minicomputers (which forced me to battle the entire IBM sales management team as well as Dick). Mythology also says I shouldn't have claimed I could run the firm better than the Executive Committee, although I don't remember ever saying that.

I had stirred the pot, lost the battle, and was paying the price. And though John Gutfreund supported me almost to the end, eventually the consensus in the Executive Committee would be unanimous. They won. I lost. It was time to go. The only questions left were when, how, and with what: I would receive all three answers unexpectedly at the 1981 "Last Supper" in Tarrytown.

*   *   *

Perry and Rosenthal have since died. Perry succumbed to leukemia after leaving Salomon Brothers and enjoying only mediocre success elsewhere. Rosenthal died later, and more quickly. On a rainy Good Friday in 1987, I was sitting in the car and listening to the radio while my family was shopping. A pilot from Briarcliff, New York, had been killed, crashing a new Beech Baron aircraft into a house on his approach to Westchester Airport. And I thought to myself, "I'll bet that's Dick Rosenthal." (Barons are very expensive twin-engine private planes. There aren't very many people who can afford them, and whoever it was came from the town where Dick lived. Too much of a coincidence.) They didn't announce the name until the next morning. Was I happy, or sad? After all the years of bitter fighting, I guess I'm ashamed to say that the right word was *ambivalent*.

I had nine great years at Salomon as a general partner, fifteen in total. I loved going into the office every single day for the entire decade and a half I worked there, even those days I knew would be tough. I made an unconscionable amount of money. I got some (but not all) of the acceptance and prestige I thought my due. And what I learned—not to mention the money I made—would provide the foundation for the company I created after I left.

3

I Love Mondays

Entrepreneurship: Vocation and Avocation

I had spent my first twenty-four years getting ready for Wall Street. I had survived fifteen more years before Salomon Brothers threw me out. At age thirty-nine, the third phase of my life was about to start. With whatever values my parents had taught me, $10 million in my pocket, and confidence based on little more than bruised ego, I started over.

A month after the 1981 meeting in Tarrytown, I realized that Goldman, Sachs, the firm that had offered me my first job in 1966, wasn't going to call and offer me a partnership. If they had, I'd probably have accepted it just for ego reasons. But when they didn't, I had to knock on doors looking for a job, stay unemployed, or start my own company. The prospect of working for someone else wasn't exciting. Perhaps no one would hire me. Besides, I'd already done that. As to retiring, I've always been too restless. I'd go crazy just sitting around. So the last option, chasing the great American dream, seemed all that was left.

Resources weren't a problem. I didn't have to worry about feeding my family. That gave me the luxury of time. I had capital to fund a new business (thank you, Salomon Brothers). I knew how to manage and always thought both names on my old business card

(Bloomberg and Salomon) mattered. Thus, I could be an entrepreneur rather than an employee if I wanted to.

Did I want to risk an embarrassing and costly failure? Absolutely. Happiness for me has always been the thrill of the unknown, trying something that everyone says can't be done, feeling that gnawing pit in my stomach that says "Danger ahead." Would it be nice not to have uncertainty, to sit back and "veg out"? When the phone rings constantly, when people keep demanding attention, when I desperately need time to myself, it seems an attractive notion just to "chuck it all." But then nobody calls, nobody stops by, and soon I'm nibbling my nails and getting irritable, and I realize that's not what I want. It sounds good. In reality though, I want action, I want challenge.

Work was, is, and always will be a very big part of my life. I love it. Even today, after toiling for thirty years, I wake up looking forward to practicing my profession, creating something, competing against the best, having comradeship, receiving the psychic compensation that money can't buy. Whether you're in business, academia, politics, the arts, religion, or whatever, it's a real high to be a participant rather than a spectator. Not everyone gets the chance. But to have that opportunity and not use it? What a sin! (I was once quoted as saying, "Sunday night was my favorite because I knew when I awoke the next morning, I'd have five full days of fun at the office.")

Think about the percentage of your life spent working and commuting. If you're not content doing it, you're probably a pretty miserable person. Change it! Work it out with those next to you on the production line. Talk to your boss. Sit down with those you supervise. Alter what's in your own head. Do something to make it fun, interesting, challenging, exciting. You've got to be happy at your job. Sure, being able to feed the kids is the first focus. But when layoffs and promotions are announced, those with surly looks on their faces, those who always try to do less, those who never cooperate with others get included in the layoffs and miss the promotions. This big part of your life affects you, your family, society, and everything else you touch.

So, while finishing my last month at Salomon, I decided to be an entrepreneur rather than an employee. After a decade and a half as a loyal corporate soldier, I'd be my own general. Great. Enough of concept, however. Specifics pay the rent. Unfortunately, until I actually stopped working at Salomon, I didn't have much time to plan my next moves—or even to worry. I worked my usual 7:00 A.M. to 7:00 P.M. twelve-hour shifts right up to the last day and seldom discussed my next career with anyone. The only time I searched for office space in which to start my new venture was on weekends. No one could say I didn't give Salomon my all, even at the end.

Still, I did think about it while running (the time I have my most creative thoughts). What would I do? Since I didn't have the resources to start a steel mill, I ruled out that possibility; in other words, I wouldn't go into industry. Having no musical abilities precluded starting a songwriting business; entertainment was out. Lack of interest in retailing excluded competing with Wal-Mart; Sam Walton's investment was safe. My impatience with government kept me away from politics; all elected officials could stop worrying. Should I start another securities trading firm and compete with my former colleagues? Been there. Done that. Maybe I could be a full-time consultant like so many forced-out executives. No. I'm not much of a bystander beyond watching my daughters Emma and Georgina ride horses. Doing rather than advising others is for me.

What did I have the resources, ability, interest, and contacts to do? The question led me back to Wall Street. It was obvious the economy was changing and services were taking a bigger share of the gross domestic product. My talents, my experience, my financial resources, the momentum provided by the American economy—everything fit. I would start a company that would help financial organizations. There were better traders and salespeople. There were better managers and computer experts. But nobody had more knowledge of the securities and investment industries *and* of how technology could help them.

All I had to do was find a value-added service not currently available. I conceived a business built around a collection of securities data, giving people the ability to select what each individually thought the most useful parts, and then providing computer software that would let nonmathematicians do analysis on that information. This kind of capability was sorely lacking in the marketplace. A few large underwriting firms had internal systems that tried to fill this need but each required a PhD to use and weren't available off the shelf to the little guy.

When it came to knowing the relative value of one security versus another, most of Wall Street in 1981 had pretty much remained where it was when I began as a clerk back in the mid-1960s: a bunch of guys using No. 2 pencils, chronicling the seat-of-the-pants guesses of too many bored traders. Something that could show instantly whether government bonds were appreciating at a faster rate than corporate bonds would make smart investors out of mediocre ones, and would create an enormous competitive advantage over anyone lacking these capabilities. At a time when the U.S. budget deficit (financed by billions of dollars of new Treasury bonds and notes) was poised to explode, such a device would appeal to everyone working in finance, securities, and investments— combined, a very big potential market for my proposed product.

At great expense, each of the largest securities companies collected data independently. Worse (for them but not for me), they were practically relying on abacuses and slide rules, or the modern equivalents, such as small handheld calculators, to manipulate that information. I could provide a far more sophisticated system at a fraction of the price. Sharing expenses over many users would give me a distinct cost advantage. And if most firms used my data and analysis, I would be creating an industrywide standard, something which, for competitive reasons, the insiders themselves could never accomplish. Equally important, the advantage I had of not being a broker/dealer, of being beholden to no one, would give my product an independence others couldn't possibly claim. And best of all, nobody was currently doing it.

*   *   *

If you're going to succeed, you need a vision, one that's affordable, practical, and fills a customer need. Then, go for it. Don't worry too much about the details. Don't second-guess your creativity. Avoid overanalyzing the new project's potential. Most importantly, don't strategize about the long term too much.

Consider banks and venture capitalists your worst enemies. They create doubt in entrepreneurs' minds with their insistence on detailed game plans before they lend. They want five-year projections in a world that makes six-month forward planning difficult, even for stable and mature businesses, and they insist on "revenue budgeting" when no one knows what the new product will look like or who'll buy how much. And worst of all, they think an originator will be helped by their oh-so-insightful views on how he or she should run the new business. Often, they kill off what's different, special, and full of potential.

A while ago, one venture capitalist who's on the boards of two successful companies came to see us. This guy was one of those self-entitled men who had been born on third base and thought he'd hit a triple. After telling us that everything we were doing was wrong, that we were too unstructured to survive and were stupid because we were unable to predict future growth with clairvoyant specificity, he left to advise his partners not to buy from Bloomberg. The reason? We didn't show much interest in his views on how to run our company. He sure was right on that account.

I once saw the classic cart-before-the-horse planning error during a presentation by a would-be competitor. He showed slides of his new company's shipping department. There were conveyor belts, packaging machines, truck-loading equipment, and a group of white-coated technicians ready to send out thousands of units each week. The only minor problem? They hadn't yet built the first unit. And they never did.

At Bloomberg, we've always built the product first. We think about accounting and shipping much later in the process, when those functions become important, at the point where we'd better stop and refocus or get into trouble. Selling is the only process we run simultaneously with development from the start. That gives us feedback as we build—and makes the customers part of the evolution process (they come to believe it's their product). This strategy may not be without risks, but I've always thought it ridiculous to make the wedding arrangements before agreeing to the marriage.

The classic consultant's model for success dictates building in controls at the beginning, but that kind of premature preparation is counterproductive; in fact, it's usually diverting enough to preclude producing anything at all. You don't know exactly what you're going to deliver. You can't predict in what order things will be done. You have no real idea who will purchase it. Why bother gazing into the crystal ball? If you're flexible, you'll do it when it makes sense, not before.

In computer terms, doing it whenever needed, on the fly, is working from a "heap," not a "stack" or a "queue." Working from stacks and queues is the rigid, bureaucratized method of operating; it makes you take out things in a predescribed order (i.e., last in, first out for a stack; first in, first out for a queue). But if you work from a heap, where input and output are independent, you can use your head, selecting what you need, when you need it, based on outside criteria that are always changing (e.g., what's needed *now,* such as responding immediately to a customer complaint or getting a gift for your spouse's birthday when that day arrives and you've totally forgotten). Look at your desk. Is everything in order? Or is it in a big pile like mine? Take your choice.

Don't think, however, that planning and analysis have no place in achieving success. Quite the contrary. Use them, just don't have them use you. Plan things out and work through real-life scenarios, selecting from the opportunities currently available. Just don't waste effort worrying about an infinite number of down-the-road possibilities, most of which will never materialize.

Think logically and dispassionately about what you'd like to do. Work out all steps of the process—the entire what, when, where, why, and how. Then, sit down after you are absolutely positive you know it cold, and write it out. There's an old saying, "If you can't write it, you don't know it." Try it. The first paragraph invariably stops you short. "Now why did we want this particular thing?" you'll find yourself asking. "Where did we think the resources would come from?" "And what makes us think others—the suppliers, the customers, the potential rivals—are going to cooperate?" On and on, you'll find yourself asking the most basic questions you hadn't focused on before taking pen to paper.

As you discover you don't know it all, force yourself to address the things you forgot, ignored, underestimated, or glossed over. Write them out for a doubting stranger who doesn't come with unquestioned confidence in the project's utility—and who, unlike your spouse, parent, sibling, or child, doesn't have a vested interest in keeping you happy. Make sure your written description follows, from beginning to end, in a logical, complete, doable path.

Then tear up the paper.

That's right, rip it up. You've done the analysis. You've found enough holes in the plan to drive your hoped-for Bentley automobile through repeatedly. You've planned for myriad what-if scenarios. You've presented your ideas to others. You've even mapped out the first few steps.

But the real world throws curveballs and sliders every day, as well as the fastballs you practice against. You'll inevitably face problems different from the ones you anticipated. Sometimes you'll have to "zig" when the blueprint says "zag." You don't want a detailed, inflexible plan getting in the way when you have to respond instantly. By now, you either know what you can know—or you don't and never will. As to the rest, take it as it comes.

*   *   *

So, I wrote out my analysis and then ripped it up. I rented a one-room temporary office on Madison Avenue. It was about a hundred square feet of space with a view of an alley, a far cry from my previous place of employment, Salomon's multi-acre forty-first-floor trading room overlooking the New York harbor. I deposited $300,000 of my Salomon Brothers windfall into a corporate checking account. And fifteen years later, I had a billion-dollar business.

Of course, it took a little while to arrive at Bloomberg's current offices on Park Avenue. And I really didn't start out all by myself. At the end of 1981, I recruited four former Salomon protégés, three of whom are still with us today: Duncan MacMillan, who helped assess what our potential customers might want; Chuck Zegar, who created our software infrastructure; Tom Secunda, who wrote many of the first analytics and now manages our several hundred programmers; and one other guy. In our broom closet of an office, we celebrated our start on day one with a bottle of champagne.

Much to my surprise, on day two, the fourth guy came back to see me. "I'm more valuable than the others. I deserve more than they," he told me.

"That's not true and that's not what we agreed."

"Yes, but I have kids to think about."

"This isn't about your children," I said. "It's you who has the problem."

"Mike, this is too much of a risk for me with too little a return. You're going to have to do better for me to join."

I've had several conversations like this with different people since then, as Bloomberg has grown from a handful of individuals to over three thousand employees in more than seventy cities around the world. They all end the same way, before they start. Either they believe in me, trust me, and are willing to take the risk that I will deliver success, or they don't. It's that simple. There's no haggling. I don't negotiate.

Years later, I told my wife I felt sorry for this guy because he hadn't swallowed his hubris and joined us back then as we got started. Since that day, he's had a mediocre career at multiple companies, never really making much of an impact on the world. Had he joined us, he would have done something important, had a great time, and become wealthy beyond his wildest dreams.

"Don't feel sorry for him. He didn't have the guts for it. The others ran risks. They alone deserve the rewards."

She's right, of course. At the same time, I do find myself more understanding, if not outright sympathetic. It's scary taking a chance. If I hadn't had the moneys from the Salomon sale bonanza, would I have made the leap? Funny, the older I get, the less simple life looks.

We rented a second temporary one-room office next to the original space and bought a small refrigerator for sodas and a coffee machine for survival. The first order of business once we were together was to go to our respective homes and make sure there were no papers there that arguably belonged to our previous employer. Since we'd all worked at Salomon, I worried someone would allege we were stealing software or ideas. That kind of accusation, however false, could make everything we were trying to do more difficult, from obtaining credit to building a reputation—the latter being especially critical, since our business was to be based on our collective reputation for probity.

Then, to maintain both the style and substance of independence and honesty, as we began getting some basic systems together and building the fundamental financial-information database, we took pains to differentiate ourselves from anything we had previously worked on. We used a different brand of computer. We wrote in a different computer language. We documented when and where we collected information. We even picked a different terminology and syntax for our entire system to use. After all that, it turned out that nobody ever questioned our honesty, but better safe than sorry.

The original four—Bloomberg, MacMillan, Secunda, and Zegar—got along pretty well from the first day (we still do). One time, though, I got annoyed at something they did that could have become a serious problem—so serious that I no longer remember what it was. It was infuriating enough that I stormed into one of our two office rooms and slammed the door shut behind me. I slammed it so hard, the catch broke. I was locked in. Having been an ass, I now had to humble myself and knock on the door until they came to let me out. They played with the handle for a while before it sprang open. I never asked whether the fumbling was deliberate or not.

In 1982 and 1983, we added some programmers: Tom Neff, your typical, brilliant, six-foot-two-inch gawky computer nerd; Mark Purdy, mustache and all, whose great claim to fame is that he is a synthetic music expert; Bob Ostrow, who worked on the Hubble telescope but claims no responsibilities for the incorrect curvature of its mirror; and Buddha-like Andy Wu, still as imperturbable as he was years ago. Later, Nick Failla joined to run our nonexistent "Computer Room." Mac Barnes would become our customer liaison person, along with Susette Franklin, who took over administration—even though we had no customers and little to administer. In 1985, before we had a product to sell, our first salespeople came on board—Stuart Bell, Dana Neuman, and Curtis McCool—followed by programmers Lynn Seirup, John Punturieri, and Fred Mitchell, for whom we had no desks and no computers. We hired operators Rodney Brown, Brett McCollough, James Rieger, and, for London (our first foray overseas), Laurence Seeff. These are people who joined before we had much of a business and have stayed through the tough times. That's the kind of loyalty that binds us together and earns a mutual respect that survives to this day.

*   *   *

Right after forming our company, we did some consulting. It brought in cash, gave us exposure, and helped provide us with Wall Street legitimacy that would later lead to work for more clients. And it brought our first sale: to Merrill Lynch & Co.

Three powerful members of that firm's Capital Markets Division—Sam Hunter, Jerry Kenney, and Gerry Eli—had convinced us to study Merrill Lynch's relationships with institutional customers. After a lot of traveling and research, our conclusions were the kind of insights we probably could have provided at the beginning based on just our Salomon experiences. Nevertheless, they seemed pleased with the report we wrote. We received $100,000 plus expenses for our six-month effort. That paid some real bills.

While Merrill was convincing us to undertake the study, we were told, "If you start to work for Merrill, you'll never leave." Well, the four of us didn't exactly dash back into standard-issue Wall Street life, but the comment was on target nonetheless. The contacts we made and the trust we built gave us our next big break: an introduction to the fellow running Merrill's Capital Markets Division, Ed Moriarty.

It was to Moriarty that I had to sell our proposed product. I finally arranged a meeting with him and his staff. It took place in an enormous corporate boardroom. At a forty-foot mahogany table, Ed was surrounded by accountants, lawyers, computer programmers, salespeople, traders, administrators—everybody in their company was represented. I went by myself, the way I always go into big negotiations, and was seated to Ed's left. Hank Alexander, who was running all their software development, was sitting on his other side. Speaking as confidently as I could, and making it sound as if our company, Innovative Market Systems, as we were then known, had exactly what Merrill needed (I implied with perhaps some minimal embellishment that everything but the packaging was completed), I made my pitch.

"We can give you a yield curve analysis updated throughout the day as the market moves. . . . We can show you the futures market

49

versus cash and graph it for you as it's changing. . . . For your traders, we'll keep track of every transaction as it's made and mark their positions to market instantly without any fussing . . . ." No one else had done any of these things—and neither had we—yet.

Moriarty turned to Hank Alexander. "Well, Hank, what do you think?"

"I think we should do it internally," Hank replied. "Build it ourselves."

"How long would it take?" Ed asked.

Then Hank made his fatal mistake. "Well, if you don't give us anything new to do"—which was clearly not a practical scenario— "we'll be able to start in six months."

And that was my opening.

"I'll get it done in six months and if you don't like it, you don't have to pay for it!" I practically shouted. "Since Hank can't even start for half a year, there'll be no time risk. And since you only pay if it works, no cost risk either."

Moriarty got up. "Well, that sounds fair enough," he said, and he left the room.

I don't think anybody had seen a decision made at Merrill that fast. Even I was surprised. But from Ed's point of view it was a "no-brainer." He didn't have any downside; it was win or break even for him. Hank just sat there, speechless, as did everyone else.

When I came back from the meeting with Moriarty, my colleagues were elated—until the reality of a six-month delivery for something that didn't exist began to sink in. As developers, we're magicians, not miracle workers. Fortunately, it took Merrill Lynch and Bloomberg two or three months to write a contract. That's when the six months we promised actually commenced—a little extra time to deliver something we hadn't yet started.

Month after month as we worked, our mood alternated between elation and a feeling of impending disaster. We weren't just putting out fires. We were adjusting to major earthquakes when some new software bug forced us to start over. But every day we got closer to building the machine we promised.

Our style then was pretty much the same as today. We took the problem and broke it down into little, manageable, digestible pieces. Then each of us took responsibility for the one we were best suited to do. We needed a proprietary terminal to give us a technology and marketing edge; we hired an engineer, Ron Harris, to build it for us. We needed a central information storage computer; Chuck Zegar analyzed which was the best and wrote a customized database package suitable for our specific application. We needed some data; Duncan MacMillan collected it, scrubbed it, and typed it in. We needed calculations; Tom Secunda sat at a workstation and did the programming. We needed customers; I went out and sold. We needed outside support; we retained a lawyer, Dick DeScherer, and an accountant/CFO, Marty Geller. It wasn't elegant. It was laughably simplistic by today's standards. But we did it, and it worked.

*   *   *

Most Wall Streeters don't understand the language of general-purpose computers. It isn't intuitive. A key labeled "Tab" on a regular PC doesn't mean anything to average folks. Other buttons labeled "Ctrl" (Control) or "Alt" (Alternate) aren't salespeople's or traders' terms. To be better, from the beginning we built things for real people. We changed "Enter" to "GO" on our keyboard. (Remember Monopoly? "Pass Go and Collect $200.") "Tab," "Alt," and "Ctrl" disappeared. Function keys were labeled in English— no technical gibberish, no F1, F2, and so on, for us. Making something practical ("user-friendly" in computerese) became our hallmark.

Merrill wanted its traders to be able to enter a transaction and automatically update the firm's positions themselves. That wasn't a big deal, you would think. But the only systems Merrill had for trade entry used massive, unreliable, and complex terminals that wouldn't fit on regular-size desks, much less in the typical, sales-person/trader's small cubicle. They connected these terminals to a single, large mainframe without backup. This wasn't what the market needed.

We built our own compact, low-priced workstations so we could give the reliability that a single-purpose, single-user machine pro-vides. (PCs and mainframes have to do everything with everybody. By comparison, we, with our own "closed," custom-built hardware and software, could focus on a single task with perfect machine compatibility.) We designed our own color-coded, easy-to-use, small keyboard for the limited space our customers had in front of them. We built a customized square enclosure for the display screens we'd chosen, so users could stack them up vertically. We engineered our electronics to support keyboards and screens over great distances; that way, the actual computer didn't have to be at the user's cramped, dirty desk (the way PCs have to be), but could be kept separate, "down the hall," in a life-prolonging, temperature-controlled, and dust-free machine room. Desk space doesn't sound important unless you don't have any.

We made mistakes, of course. Most of them were omissions we didn't think of when we initially wrote the software. We fixed them by doing it over and over, again and again. We do the same today. While our competitors are still sucking their thumbs trying to make the design perfect, we're already on prototype version No. 5. By the time our rivals are ready with wires and screws, we are on version No. 10. It gets back to planning versus acting. We act from day one; others plan how to plan—for months.

Then, as now, we had the resolve to see it through. We put to-gether prototype after prototype and scared up business again and again. We underwent a few very long years. In presentation after presentation, I guaranteed our product was going to happen. It was only a matter of time, I told the clients—and myself. Our ef-forts and my cash would carry the day.

Halfway through, I must admit I worried. I had committed nowhere near enough money to fund development. And it wasn't obvious that the customers would appreciate what we were attempting. In my own private world, maybe, just maybe, I questioned the wisdom of jeopardizing my wealth and our reputation. In fact, we were spending what would grow to be a $4 million investment of my $10 million Salomon Brothers windfall. Simultaneously, I was becoming responsible for the families of almost two dozen company employees. I had convinced these people to follow me, and if the venture had not succeeded, I would have failed them, their spouses, and their children, as well as our prospective customers. Fortunately, however, even had I wanted to leave this enterprise behind, there was no graceful way to exit (thank God for ego!), so we plowed ahead.

From the beginning, I was convinced we were doing something nobody else could do. Nor was anyone else trying. Our product would be the first in the investment business where normal people without specialized training could sit down, hit a key, and get an answer to financial questions, some of which they didn't even know they should ask. To this day, we still don't have a competitor. Although investors can get some of our data and analysis elsewhere, most features of our system are unique.

We give our clients the ability to select investments, do "what-if" scenario analysis on their securities portfolios, and communicate over a private, secure e-mail system with their customers, suppliers, and associates. It all occurs fast, accurately, and easily, without having to enter the complex, detailed variables, delimiters, limits, constraints, and so on, that most computer systems require. We allow them to study markets and securities in absolute terms and relative to alternative investments. They can research companies, buy and sell stocks and bonds, even create new financial instruments.

Our customers can calculate the exact cost of a mortgage based on existing interest rates and then obtain one from a broker in real time, all on the Bloomberg terminal. They can do this while simultaneously, on the same screen, watching our latest world and national television news, or purchasing brownies, flowers, teddy bears, jewelry, or clothing on-line, or selecting a flight for their next visit overseas, or checking their favorite company's latest quarterly report, or listening to the head of a central bank prognosticate on interest rates, even though he or she actually did it days earlier, in another language and on the other side of the world. All these are useful features that no one else provides.

*   *   *

After the meeting with Moriarty, I was adamant we were going to deliver a product when we promised. It became a joke at Merrill: Bloomberg would deliver the first on-time software project in history. Yeah, right! What chance did we have when, in addition to writing software and collecting data, we had to build our own hardware? (There was nothing commercially available that could do real-time, computational analysis and still let us be profitable. In the early 1980s, we built a multiuser PC, something manufacturers are still trying to do today.) What chance did we have when no one had ever designed a real-time interactive system that was user-friendly enough for nonspecialists? Fourteen-hour days became typical at Starship Bloomberg. At one point, when nobody in our little electronics sweatshop could remember time off, the entire firm marched into a theater to see a movie and unwind together.

Finally, the day arrived. Almost. The six-month promise ran out on a Saturday, so we could postpone delivery until Monday. And Monday didn't necessarily mean Monday morning; it could be Monday afternoon. We were constantly having to fix the software, rewriting it again and again to deliver the consistency needed for reliable real-time analysis. "We're out of control!" I would shout, as each software bug surfaced. "We're going to be out of business if this continues!" (I still say the same things today.)

Late on that fateful Monday in June of 1983, Duncan and I got into a taxi on Madison Avenue. I carried the terminal and Duncan carried the keyboard and screen. But it was hopeless. For reasons we couldn't understand, some newly introduced software problem kept the machine from starting up. Still, we took it down to Merrill while the others kept debugging the computer code. We installed the hardware in the office of the head bond trader, a smart, demanding guy named Danny Napoli. Everybody was standing around, astonished that the machine had actually appeared; nobody really expected delivery when promised. Were we going to be the first team in history ever to do so?

We plugged it in and turned on the power. As I talked, playing tour guide, I noticed out of the corner of my eye a flashing message on our screen saying "Loading Software." Instantly, I knew that the big software bug that had befuddled us all weekend had been fixed—*while we were in the taxi.* I could feel the tension ease out of me. It was going to work!

By that time, a bottle of champagne had been opened by a dozen traders. These guys were the most friendly people I had seen in six months. Everybody was laughing and slapping each other's back. I think we ran one function and the computer crashed. It didn't matter. It was the principle that we had delivered something on time (close to), something that worked (sort of), a machine that would be useful (somewhat). Then our entire staff went to a restaurant on the Upper East Side to continue the celebration.

When I saw that screen light up that day in the Merrill Lynch offices, I lost any residual doubt that Bloomberg could make it. We had picked just the right project. It was big enough to be useful, small enough to be possible. Start with a small piece; fulfill one goal at a time, on time. Do it with all things in life. Sit down and learn to read one-syllable words. If you try to read Chaucer in elementary school, you'll never accomplish anything. You can't jump to the end game right away, in computers, politics, love, or any other aspect of life.

*   *   *

The data we use in the analytical calculations we supply to our customers are dramatically better than anything the competition has. Collecting that information provides a case history for how our methodical, do-it-in-steps procedures really work. The problem lies in the data's complexity. Much of today's data is too sophisticated to be collected by a semiskilled clerk. But, to some extent, information collection is a repetitive mechanical function. If the people willing to do the gathering don't have the skills to understand what they have in front of them, you get garbage. Computer people have an expression, "Garbage in, garbage out."

One of the great contributions made to our success was by John Aubert, the man who started our data-collection facility in Princeton, New Jersey. When Mac Barnes introduced me to John in the Merrill Lynch cafeteria in April 1984, he was head of a three-person company consisting of himself, his wife, and his son. They collected sinking fund data (information about how companies and governments pay off the debt incurred from the sale of bonds) and put them into a book called *Sinkers.* As luck would have it, the day we met, John had just had a disagreement with his only customer and wanted to deal with someone new. We had a cup of coffee together, and by the time the meeting ended, a handshake. His company got absorbed into ours. He collected data better than anyone else and loved the process. His eyes still light up when he talks about information gathering. That's the kind of person we want in our company, somebody who loves what he does.

John devised a way to give the data-collection process an analytical component. The clerical part became minor. Thus, we got much smarter people to "scrub," categorize, and store each piece of data where it truly belongs—not just where it's convenient to put it. They're not automatons on an information assembly line. They're traditional analysts who can provide a detailed contextual understanding of a market or industry based on current and historical information assembled from a multitude of sources.

Take our collection of income statements and balance sheets from companies around the globe. Many countries define depreciation differently. We hired a consultant to teach us all the accounting systems in use around the world. Now our specialists understand each standard. Thus, unlike other databases, ours knows the important distinctions. Companies can be viewed from different locations on a comparable basis. If one company depreciates assets one way, and another company a second way, we'll highlight the discrepancies up front. At Bloomberg, a problem spurs a solution. That's what makes us successful.

*   *   *

For our first product delivery, we built twenty-two terminals, keyboards, and screens. Our plan was to install the twenty Merrill Lynch had ordered and then use the two others ourselves, for development and backup. Needless to say, we installed all twenty-two in their trading room. They wanted them. And who were we to argue? We needed the revenue. Of course, we had no reserves, but now we had the cash flow to build more machines for ourselves, for Merrill, and for other customers who would soon hear the good buzz on Bloomberg.

In the beginning, we had the inevitable reliability problems. But at least we had something. And that something was Merrill's system as much as ours. When we first installed it, Merrill assigned two traders to work with us. I thought they'd be real pains and second-guess us every step of the way. Was I wrong! It turned out both of them, Jack Delaney and Jack Meyers, were as responsible for our success as anyone. They were nitpickers, but not in a nasty way; they wanted us to succeed. When they said something didn't work, they could show us it didn't work, so we knew for sure it didn't work, and—more importantly to help fix the problem—under what specific circumstances it didn't work. Every day, our system got better as we fixed each problem they pointed out. I'd always rather have a smart, fair, honest, demanding client than a nasty dummy or an "I don't care" user.

The agreement with Merrill was that *if* we delivered on time and *if* they liked it, they would pay us $600,000, a one-time custom development fee, plus $1,000 a month per terminal for two years. We would receive no money until the entire system worked reliably. So, although Merrill didn't fund our initial development, they were invaluable to our start-up. We just knew that if we could give them something useful, there was no way they'd walk away. And having one happy customer would lead to the next. For example, the Bank of England, one of the world's oldest central banks, became a customer within two years (they still send me a Christmas card). The Vatican became a customer by the mid-1980s. (When their electricians seemed to take forever to install the wire needed for our terminal, a nun in their funds management office told us she'd have the Pope bless our cabling to make the installation process go more quickly. I don't know if he did, but the next day the installation was completed.) The World Bank, the Bank for International Settlements (the Central Banks' central banker), every Federal Reserve Bank—all became Bloomberg clients.

There was still a risk for Bloomberg after Merrill's first order. It was a long time before revenue exceeded expenses. But after building the machines for Merrill, we had money coming in and a product to sell. I remember calculating repeatedly on the back of an envelope, "Twenty-two terminals at Merrill at $1,000 per month times twelve months per year equals $264,000, plus $600,000. We won't make a lot of money, but we'll cover our costs and stay in business." Today, that amount barely covers our reception area's flower bill. But by starting small and working hard, we got where we needed to go, and Bloomberg was on its way.

Over time, along with the growth in our revenue, we've hired more employees and gotten more specialized. Fifteen years after we started, we have human resource professionals and accounts receivable and accounts payable people. We have a contracts department, a communications department, and an administration department. Currently, we employ controllers, lawyers, bookkeepers, consultants, accountants, tax advisers, and so on, just like any other big company.

Amazingly, for our first three or four years in business, I did all those functions. I also simultaneously worked full-time selling our services, negotiating all our supplier and customer contracts, and running the company. Never before or since did I have as much fun and as challenging a time. I'm not sure the company wasn't better off then either.

Today, Bloomberg has the very best service and installation professionals. But back when we started, the original half dozen of us, after finishing our regular jobs, would go into clients' offices on weekends and do these functions as well. During the summer, with the air-conditioning turned off in those sealed skyscrapers, the heat sometimes hit 100 degrees Fahrenheit under the new customers' desks where we crawled to lay our cables. Amid old McDonald's hamburger wrappers and mouse droppings, we dragged wires from our computers to the keyboards and screens we were putting in place, stuffing the cables through holes we drilled in other people's furniture—all without permission, violating every fire law, building code, and union regulation on the books. It's amazing we didn't burn down some office or electrocute ourselves. At the end of the day, ten or eleven o'clock at night, we'd turn it on and watch what we'd created come alive. It was so satisfying.

Today, we have shipping departments around the world with packaging machines, static electricity prevention devices, automatically printed-out customs declarations, tracking and ordering computers, even our own trucks with the Bloomberg name on the side. Back in the good old days, we transported the equipment in the back seat of a yellow taxicab. Import/export regulations? We just carried it into the next country in our luggage. Did we obtain passes to get computers and keyboards and screens into and out of buildings, past the security guards? "Hey, man. Going to get coffee. Want a cup?" They wave you through every time. Inventory tracking? "Did we install two or three at that last place? Beats me."

Banks and accountants do our payroll now; I used to write all the checks myself. I signed every contract. I paid every bill. I did the hiring and firing. I bought the coffee, sodas, cookies, and chips we nibbled on. I emptied the wastebaskets and dusted the window sills. I wrote and handed out the paychecks personally to each and every New York City employee, thus giving me the chance to follow up on project and people development, to offer encouragement, or to "bust a few chops" if need be. Today, there's a specialist for each of these functions and I don't recognize two-thirds of our employees, even in the home office.

Those were the best days, the first few years in the early 1980s. We all were involved in every aspect of our company. I helped design furniture, select equipment, demonstrate our capabilities to prospective customers, order phone lines, collect data. I used a screwdriver as much as a pencil. As we grew and turned these functions over to newly hired specialists, I felt like I was losing a child to adolescence. Good for the kid, but painful for the parent.

Moving from "hands-on" to "hands-off" management has been a gradual, and not all that pleasant, process for me. I'm an operating guy as opposed to a strategic person. I like doing things myself, getting my hands dirty. If we're to grow and not be dependent on yours truly, turn it over I must. But that doesn't mean I'm happy about it.

Often, when we "farmed out" a project to others, I'd be reminded of the difference in Bloomberg's pioneering culture compared to others' standards, and I'd wish we'd done it ourselves. A consultant comes in to do something and stops at 5:00 P.M. Everyone "inside" works till 7:00, 8:00, or 9:00 at night, until the project is done. Once, we hired an electrician to "pin" (put plugs on the end of) a bunch of 25-wire, color-coded cables. It was one of those things that had to be done perfectly (i.e., red into No. 7, blue into No. 19, green and red stripe into No. 24, and so on, as specified on some highly detailed schematic drawings) or the computers would crash. The electricians' union shop steward assigned us an experienced guy who was hanging on until retirement, arguing that his age gave him the patience to do this tedious task without error. A month later, after tearing our hair out trying to find the reason nothing worked, we discovered he may have had lots of good qualities and work habits—but he was legally color-blind. Every single connector was wrong. The waste in computer programmers' time diagnosing the trouble was enormous. (The next electrician just cut off all the ends and did the job again from scratch. Needless to say, we had to pay for both electricians.) Outsiders at best do only what's asked. Insiders do what's needed.

The differences between "us" and "them" persist to this day. When I watch a visitor throw a paper towel toward a wastebasket in the bathroom, miss, and just walk away, I want to scream. I react the same way when I see someone walking by a piece of scrap paper on the floor and ignoring it. Perhaps I'm compulsive, but I stop and pick it up, even at someone else's place. Your company is one of your families, and the office is that family's home. Do those outsiders live in pigsties?

*   *   *

America really is the land of opportunity and home to more start-up enterprises than any other country. In this country, banks, venture capitalists, and stock exchanges are all accustomed to funding new ideas. The United States has a culture that prizes innovation, its social hierarchy is built around merit, and it rewards the risk taker. Open borders for trade, publicly funded research, and favorable tax laws encourage entrepreneurship. The results speak for themselves: greater job creation, higher equity values, a diverse and constantly improving selection of products for us as consumers.

Not all ventures succeed here though. Myriad other companies started at the same time we did, many with capital, enthusiasm, and potential. Some had transitory success. Like a balloon, they expanded rapidly and eventually exploded. We think those that lasted were the companies with philosophies and management practices that were appropriate for the time, well articulated to employees and clients, and consistently applied. Through both good and bad periods, staying power, we believe, requires team leadership in a constant direction, one that the organization understands and accepts. The winners have this kind of leadership. We hope we do!

Bloomberg philosophy may sound strange to "outsiders," but not to those who matter—us. We've always assumed that even if we're paranoid, they probably *are* out to get us. While you're reading this, we're thinking about how our competitors are plotting to take the food from our children's mouths. They must be attempting to beat our quality, provide better functionability, undercut our reputation, and mislead us as to their direction. And if they aren't, they should be.

To counter this attack (whether real or imagined) in every way, we've got to improve just to stay even. Each of us at Bloomberg has to enhance his or her skills. Every element of all our products must be improved. All our expenses need reexamination. Our suppliers must be pressed a little harder for a better deal. Our marketing should be refocused and our customer service enhanced. The basic assumptions behind our business must constantly be reassessed, "off-line" and out of sight. When we say we'll do A, we've got to do A, but internally we've also got to prepare for B and C in case the world changes or we've erred in our judgment. We really believe we won't die, but that doesn't mean we don't buy life insurance just in case.

The difference between stubbornness and having the courage of conviction sometimes is only in the results. Since the first twenty-two terminals were installed at Merrill Lynch, we've developed into a global, multiproduct, entrenched company with tens of thousands of clients. Sure we're inflexible, if that means we don't react every time a news article claims a competitor's "to-be-introduced" product will be our downfall. But we change. We do things today we said "never" to years ago—and we no longer do others that were our sine qua non then. Our customers, resources, and opportunities constantly shift. Our policies do too—when and at the speed we want them to, not just because we're being goaded by some outsider who doesn't have to deal with human beings, pay bills, or suffer the consequences of a hastily made wrong decision.

To run our organization, we've got to be consistent. But that doesn't mean we have to have the same consistency forever. What's appropriate in one part of our development isn't necessarily so in another. Henry Ford's infamous, arrogant statement that "You can have any color car you want as long as it's black" wasn't wrong. It worked for his company when he was the only large maker of autos. But he ultimately switched to a multicolor strategy when others came along with comparable vehicles and changed the competitive landscape. My job is to recognize that time in our business in advance and lead the organization into the new world.

Another tenet of Bloomberg philosophy is that our main asset is not our technology, our databases, our proprietary communications network, or even our clients. It is our employees. Improving the rest is far less important than the care and feeding of ourselves—the maintenance of our culture, protecting it from the outside world. Physical plant, compensation politics, personnel policies, promotion, training, and so on—all of these at Bloomberg are designed with our culture in mind.

Nevertheless, we also periodically face the fact that our competitors started out lean and mean too. They may be overstaffed today, but they didn't get that way deliberately. People at those companies never sat around trying to hire mindlessly. Every time they added someone, it was done with good reason. Likewise with us. None of our managers has ever requested a "needless" addition. But our world evolves, and people change. If we always add—and never cut—why will we be different? We must have made some mistakes.

Infrequently we do have to face the issue of someone who just can't do the job. Very seldom do we have the stomach for the process. But that's what management's all about. What are we doing with the bottom 10 percent? Do we as managers have a plan to improve those employees' productivity? Are there better places for them in our company? Have we sat with them and attempted to address their problems, improve their attitudes, provide counseling, discover personal problems we can help with, retrain them? And if nothing works, after all that, while we're doing well and can afford to be generous, no matter how distasteful facing the inevitable may be, have we exercised our responsibility to upgrade our staff? Management's obligation is to all of us in the organization. We sink or swim together, and when someone's not carrying his or her weight, everyone in the company suffers. It's painful, but nature is filled with examples of extinct species that didn't improve the breed. We don't want to be one of them.

Most companies never upgrade until they are forced. When you read of a management's "decisiveness" in making large sudden layoffs, ask yourself what they've been doing all along. No change in labor requirements happens suddenly. If they'd been minding the store, they'd have stopped additional hiring years earlier, retrained their excess workers for other positions, and improved everyone's productivity so as to avoid the downturn and layoffs.

*　　　*　　　*

Doing things differently has been basic Bloomberg from day one. If the world's going left, we often go right. In football, going around the line when you are a light running back usually makes more sense than going up the middle through the heart of the other team's defense. For us too. If our competitors' strength is their balance sheets, we try non-capital-intensive strategies. If they concentrate on one part of the world, we focus on another. Letting them define the rules is a sure way to come in second. And in life, unlike in children's games, second place is first loser!

We will survive if we can control our own destiny. We've come a long way since Merrill's first order, but the challenge is still fundamentally the same. What's in our interest? Who's going to take us there? And most importantly, are we taking care of the current clients who got us this far?

Bloomberg has always treated its existing customers at least as well as its new ones. Not everyone else does the same. The next time a magazine subscription comes up for renewal, watch what happens. The first request asks you to pay full price. Don't sign. The second's at a lower price. Don't sign. The third's better still. Let it expire and they'll practically pay you to subscribe again. Why some companies give a better deal to their worst customers, I've never understood. What's the incentive to be a good client? When we introduce a hardware enhancement, we obviously can't retrofit all our thousands of clients overnight. But we try to do it as fast as we can, and we generally do it for as little as possible. When we reduce our prices for new customers, we simultaneously do the same for existing ones (for upward adjustments, the new users pay the higher price immediately; the old ones, when their leases renew). Treat your customers well and they'll stay with you forever.

Our pricing policy for all our products tries to reward the best clients over those not so good: the five-person firm with five terminals over the thousand-person firm with one hundred terminals. Size isn't everything. Intent matters, too. Sure we want the giant orders, but we don't forget that the Big Guys are with us because we're the small ones' champion.

The same with pricing. Want a special deal? If we give it to you, how could you be sure we're not giving your competitor an even better one? To publish one price and then negotiate secretly with those you want to favor or those who complain the loudest—that just encourages confusion, dissent, uncertainty, and unpleasantness, not to mention what it says about the seller's ethics. Favor one client over the other and, when the roles reverse, the favored client forgets and the initially disadvantaged one remembers.

At Bloomberg, we have a published price and generally stick to it. If we do make an occasional exception, it's for the small guy on the verge of bankruptcy. My sympathies have always been with the struggling up-and-coming firm anyway. We were once like that, and to this day I remember who helped us and who didn't. Besides, if a company chooses another's product over ours because of small price differentials, we don't have a long-term customer.

*   *   *

From unemployed to having my own going, growing business has been a lot of work. I loved every day of my fifteen years at Salomon Brothers. I've been just as ecstatic, in the past decade and a half, "doing my own thing." In both venues, I've worked six-day weeks and twelve-hour days. In both, I've cared about the company and other people there. In both, I've strived and thrived.

People always ask which I liked better: working for others or working for myself. Many assume the answer's the latter. But I'm not sure. Certainly I've made much more money being an entrepreneur, but I remember every day at Salomon as being just as challenging and just as much fun. Let's leave it that I'm a lucky guy. I've had two careers so far—and I've loved both.

4

We Can Do That

Elementary Journalism, Not Rocket Science

I first met Matt Winkler when he called me one afternoon at our New York office while I was making popcorn. I love popcorn and often make some in our food court to share with our customers and staff (an easy way to take everyone's temperature while we nibble together). A reporter for the *Wall Street Journal* who enjoyed the intricacies of the bond market, Matt was the first person in the news media to analyze the Bloomberg enterprise. Winkler was trying to figure out why we were actually starting to challenge Dow Jones & Co.'s dominance of financial news. He was to become a pivotal character in making Bloomberg a major contender in journalism and would help us not only to expand the utility of our on-line computer terminal, but to wrestle a way into news dissemination by other means as well.

Matt and I share a glass-is-half-full outlook, and that initially brought us together. When he called in February 1988, he said he was working on a story about me for the *Journal.*

"Come on up," I said. I liked the idea of getting interviewed for a story in the flagship enterprise of a future competitor.

Unbeknownst to me, Winkler had already come to see Bloomberg as a major threat. I would find out later, to my great pleasure, just how many of his Wall Street contacts, who were also my close friends and customers, agreed with that view. He was a well-connected reporter. In his ten-year career, he had written about financial markets for all the big Dow Jones media platforms—*Barron's,* the *Wall Street Journal,* and Dow Jones News Services.

It was as a Dow Jones reporter in London in the mid-1980s that he first learned of the Bloomberg terminal—then a beige box with a small amber computer screen that flashed "what-if" scenarios for the bond market. He was interviewing Merrill Lynch trader Mark Cutis, who had a rare ability to explain which bonds from the United States, Japan, or Germany were cheap or expensive on any given day.

"Mark," he asked, "Where do you get all this stuff? Nobody has all this information in his head."

"Oh, that's easy," he replied. "We get it from Bloomberg."

Our computer-based information terminal that let users determine the relative value of debt instruments based on their yield and price histories was by that time installed on fifteen hundred Merrill Lynch desks around the world. In the 1980s, bonds were coming to new prominence in the financial market, totaling trillions of dollars. Deregulation of the housing finance and the thrift industries, the repeal of withholding taxes worldwide, soaring budget deficits, and the high interest rates required to bring down inflation—all these events helped transform the government and corporate bond markets into Wall Street's hottest growth industry. Suddenly, the world's biggest fiduciaries were buying and selling junk bonds and Eurobonds. They invested in bonds created out of mortgages and car loans. Becoming the rage were "structured" securities that enabled borrowers to exchange the cash flows from bonds sold in different markets and different currencies. Although not as visible to the general public, as a business, debt had become bigger than equities. And for a firm like Merrill Lynch, doing everything it could to expand its offerings beyond service to individual investors, the Bloomberg system was indispensable.

In May 1987, after returning to New York to cover Wall Street and revise the bond tables for a new money and investing section, Winkler learned to his horror that I had just convinced the *Wall Street Journal* and the Associated Press that Bloomberg should be their sole supplier for daily U.S. government bond prices, instead of the august Federal Reserve Bank of New York. For decades, the Fed had been the authoritative, impartial source for U.S. Treasuries. The daily prices of United States Treasury bonds and bills help determine every company's borrowing cost, everyone's personal finance interest rates—and the perception of the United States as a strong or weak country. Every stock and bond trader around the world pays attention to U.S. Treasuries. Bloomberg, then a five-year-old company with less than 150 employees, would become the definitive source for the key market that told all the other markets what to do. That, needless to say, made me very happy.

We'd been able to beat the Fed at its own game by becoming a benchmark for yield information. The New York Fed had procrastinated for years on its promise to automate the delivery of its daily U.S. government securities price list. Each afternoon, a runner would show up at the New York Fed's downtown offices and be handed two or three legal-size sheets of paper with prices and yields on the front and back. The runner would rush uptown through end-of-the-day traffic to the Associated Press office in Rockefeller Center. Upon arrival, he'd hand the price sheets to some tired wire operator poised to type the prices under intense deadline pressure so newspapers could get them in time for the next day's first edition.

It was essentially the same pony express method in use for more than one hundred years. The fury of meeting the deadline with so many numbers with decimals invariably created typographical errors in the next day's newspapers. Readers complained. But Bloomberg could deliver, with perfect accuracy, more timely prices (reflecting the trading that continued after the runner left the Fed) in five seconds, at 5 P.M., electronically. We could even provide prices of zero-coupon Treasury bonds, a burgeoning new market—numbers that the Fed itself couldn't supply.

Matt, who at the time hadn't met me and whose "blood ran Dow Jones red" (something he would remind me of again, and again, and . . .), believed no one in his company understood that suddenly the *Wall Street Journal* was running a full-page, daily, free advertisement for Bloomberg, a direct competitor of the Telerate electronic bond information terminal, the only product of a company Dow Jones was in the process of acquiring for more than one and a half *billion* dollars. In a single stroke, this arrangement had made Bloomberg-delivered financial information the daily source for the most important market in the world. Freshly returned to New York, he wasn't in a strong position to convince anyone at the *Journal* that, from their point of view, this was a bad idea.

Further, to him at least, a Bloomberg-provided broadsheet-size page of the most important bond data from Merrill Lynch, a securities firm that sold bonds and actually set the prices we were reporting, was problematic. "How can we do this?" he asked his colleagues.

Because it was efficient and expedient and because no reader ever complained, he was told. But as long as Merrill was in the business of selling securities, commodities, and other forms of money to people, Matt thought, this arrangement where Merrill was pricing those same securities presented a potential conflict of interest.

*   *   *

The alliance of Bloomberg and Merrill Lynch was mutually beneficial. Merrill, which lacked a long history of institutional relationships, needed credibility with the biggest investment institutions, such as central banks and pension funds. It got a customer-service edge by putting its information on the Bloomberg system. Bloomberg needed real-time prices to provide timely analysis. Merrill, because it managed hundreds of billions of dollars and sold securities to several hundred thousand investors daily, had better, more accurate prices than anyone. A truly symbiotic relationship.

Merrill also assisted Bloomberg and its own cause by helping Bloomberg rent as many terminals as possible to Merrill customers. That way, the terminal users would have firsthand knowledge of what Merrill (as opposed to other securities firms) and Bloomberg (as opposed to other information systems) could do for them.

By 1987, Merrill was poised to become the world's top underwriter of stocks and bonds, something Wall Street couldn't have imagined ten years earlier. We helped Merrill get there. And, by giving Bloomberg data, Merrill made it possible for us to enter the news business years before we wrote a single word.

Overnight, and over Matt Winkler's vociferous objections, and thanks to the generosity of two giant companies—the largest daily newspaper in the United States, the *Wall Street Journal,* and the Associated Press, whose stories hundreds of other newspapers used— both Bloomberg and Merrill had achieved an importance to die for.

Within a few years, we built Bloomberg to the point that we were receiving price feeds not just from Merrill Lynch but from hundreds of other sources in the securities industry. Then any conflict issue would disappear. (And Dow Jones would eventually look elsewhere for bond prices as its competitive instincts strengthened.) Now, however, Matt was worried that the *Journal*'s integrity might be questioned. Unbeknownst to me, he argued in vain with *Journal* bigwigs to have the decision to use Bloomberg nullified. It also annoyed him that Dow Jones's product, Telerate, could have provided similar bond prices and yields and was being snubbed by the authoritative flagship publication of the same parent company.

His perspective would alter later. While eating a sandwich one day in his firm's cafeteria, Matt almost choked on his chicken salad when a colleague, Michael Miller, a technology writer, asked, "Have you ever heard of this outfit Bloomberg?"

"Have I heard of Bloomberg?" he yelped. He went on to give Miller an earful about the U.S. Treasury prices being published in the newspaper they wrote for—the legal-size sheets of prices, the runners, Merrill Lynch, Telerate, the importance of the bond market, the geriatric wire operator at the Associated Press office, the pony express . . . .

Miller stopped him. "Sounds like this guy Bloomberg is doing to financial information what American Airlines and United Airlines electronic reservations systems have done to the travel business: become influential by getting everybody hooked onto their data."

When I heard about this conversation later on, I had to chuckle. At last, somebody in the media—besides me—was thinking like a late-twentieth-century information entrepreneur. Fortunately, by the time Winkler, Miller, and my potential competitors were figuring out what we were doing, we'd already done it.

*   *   *

Although Miller didn't know much about bonds, luckily for Bloomberg, Winkler realized that he had identified a story no one had yet reported—a story that was bound to get bigger with every blink on the digital scoreboard that recorded the astronomical rise of the U.S. national debt. So the two of them agreed to write an article about a man and his machine that no one outside the securities industry had ever heard of.

When at last Matt and Michael arrived at my midtown office, I offered them the same speech that I used to convince people to take jobs with us.

"We've got the best people in the world working here. All of them think they walk on water. All of them are workaholics. Once they come, they stay for the rest of their lives because they love it. They've built the better mousetrap. They're doing something important. Giving the little guy the information he needs to fight. Having fun. Staying ahead."

Of course, like all cynical reporters, these guys weren't easily swayed by my silver tongue. So I stalked out of the room and returned carrying a two-inch-thick computer printout.

"Here," I said, dumping the paper into Matt's lap. "Here's every customer we have, by name, by firm, by phone number. Call them yourself!"

Among the first people Matt phoned was investment specialist Robert Smith, who in 1988 was managing $5.5 billion for the state of Florida's retirement system. "I'm working on a story about information technology on Wall Street and why money managers are using the Bloomberg system," Matt said to him. "I understand you have a Bloomberg terminal. What's so special about it?"

Smith told him what everyone he asked would tell him, that the Bloomberg terminal did a great job of doing what no other system did—letting him see which bonds were cheap and which bonds were expensive, without having to rely on the calculations and spiel of a bond salesperson with a vested interest in which securities he purchased. This independence gave Smith greater confidence as he traded financial instruments in the Florida portfolio, something he did a dozen times a day. Matt was stunned, he later told me, because this brief explanation from a little-known money manager in Florida potentially represented a seismic change in the investment industry. If the "buy side," the big custodians of wealth—pension funds, central banks, mutual funds, insurers—were no longer dependent on the "sell side," the underwriting and trading firms, for essential financial and commodity market information, a very fundamental power shift would occur. The securities industry would no longer dominate the investment industry. And if Bloomberg provided that indispensable information, it would become the fulcrum to the world's most important fiduciaries. Once the buyers depended on a particular system to help make decisions of relative value, then the sellers would have to use the same system too, or risk the potential disadvantage of not knowing what the customers knew.

"What did you use before you had a Bloomberg?" Winkler asked Smith.

"Telerate."

"What did you do with it?"

"I got rid of it," Smith said.

Matt had used a Telerate throughout his career at the *Journal* and considered it an essential electronic bulletin board for price quotes supplied by the three dozen or so securities firms that did business directly with the Federal Reserve Bank of New York, the agent of the U.S. Treasury. At one point, before the Bloomberg terminal, everyone needed Telerate's prices. Yet Telerate's prices weren't really Telerate's. They were prices posted by a broker, Cantor Fitzgerald & Co., who in turn acted as the middleman between securities firms. Telerate was nothing more than a vehicle of convenience for this broker and its customers. And it wasn't even unique: Depending on what was "fashionable" that month, there were three or four other equally important interdealer brokers whose prices mattered as much and who distributed their data separately.

What was worse for Dow Jones, Telerate couldn't show, the way the Bloomberg did, yield calculations based on many varied reinvestment assumptions—a function money managers coveted because it helped them do their jobs better. It couldn't show the total return of bonds: the income, price, and currency changes that determined how much money a bondholder made or lost, however long he or she held the bond. All it did was transmit an image of a page of quotes. It had no ability to *do* anything with the data being shown. Moreover, Winkler's Telerate froze too often. (Matt once told me he pleaded with a Dow Jones technician to help get his Telerate working again. The technician, a Russian immigrant, made myriad phone calls to different voice mails at the Dow Jones service department. After the last one, he slammed down his phone and screamed, "This is worse than the Soviet Union!")

The *Journal* article on Bloomberg ran September 22, 1988, right-hand column, picture "above the fold"; it was more flattering than I would have had the nerve to make it if I had written it myself. Even though Dow Jones then owned more than 60 percent of Telerate, the *Wall Street Journal* editors, in a page-one story, let Robert Smith of Florida extol the Bloomberg system and "diss" their own product with an unflattering anecdote to more than two million readers worldwide.

*   *   *

Even in its embryonic state, the Bloomberg system was already a news machine. Although it provided only numbers, graphs, and charts, it delivered the most valuable news a money manager could use: prices, relative values, and trends. And that news wasn't coming secondhand from any wire service, newspaper, magazine, or electronic broadcast: It was presented as it happened. By contrast, by the time anyone read a newspaper report on the price and yield discrepancies that create investment possibilities, it was too late. The buying or selling opportunity had probably vanished.

I had already decided, however, that Bloomberg should become something more than a niche information provider to a group of bond-market-data junkies. Our competitors provided business news, real-time stories with real text. In fact, we carried their newswires on our terminal. But if we were successful, as the Bloomberg terminal became more of an indispensable analytical tool for money managers and the securities industry, the competitive threat we posed would tempt them to stop letting us do so. Worse, for all practical purposes, there was only one real-time news organization in the United States for textual financial news—Dow Jones. There was only one news organization in Europe for following those markets in prose—Reuters. And both of them competed with us to put computer terminals on the desks of financial professionals.

We had two choices: Be nothing more than a small specialist in the information industry and always vulnerable to Dow Jones cutting us off, or challenge the giants. So, a little more than a year after I first met him in 1988, I phoned Matt Winkler—the reporter for our competition, who had impressed me with his understanding of our business and his mastery of his own.

"Hi, it's Bloomberg. I need some advice."

Matt waited several seconds before speaking. "You?" he asked, familiar enough with me to wonder why I would ask advice from anyone, let alone a reporter for the *Wall Street Journal.*

"I want to make our terminal indispensable to stock as well as bond traders. Should we get into the text news business?" His answer wasn't what I expected, although it encouraged me to keep the conversation going.

"Mike," he said, "you and the people who work with you have created a terminal that explains more about why bonds fluctuate each minute, day, and week than any collection of reporters ever could. You already provide charts and graphs that influence the major debt-trading decisions worldwide. Add text to that information and you'll have something that doesn't exist anywhere else. No one in debt or equity will be able to live without it."

He was free for lunch that day, so we met in a Japanese restaurant across the street from the Bloomberg office. Since I hadn't gotten a direct answer over the phone to my question, I asked again, as he contemplated a bowl of miso soup. "What does it really take to get into the newswire business?"

He started answering with a rhetorical question that put me on the spot but obviously, for a journalist, was a litmus-test issue to him. It would tell him whether I was serious about becoming a publisher.

"All right," he said. "You have just published a story that says the chairman—and I mean chair*man*—of your biggest customer has taken $5 million from the corporate till. He's with his secretary at a Rio de Janeiro resort, and the secretary's spurned boyfriend calls to tip you off. You get an independent verification that the story is true. Then the phone rings. The customer's public relations person says, 'Kill the story or we'll return all the terminals we currently rent from you.' What do you do?"

"Go with the story. Our lawyers will love the fees you generate."

"Good," Matt said, pleasantly surprised that I was willing to choose journalism over commerce.

"Now, what does it really take?" I persisted, because he hadn't told me the cost yet.

"Five reporters in Tokyo, five in London, and five in New York," he said, still not giving me a real budget. (Today, we have five hundred in seventy bureaus worldwide. So much for Matt's planning abilities.)

That was it for the money and operations talk that day. Until he brought up the subject, I certainly hadn't thought about the ethical conundrums we might come up against, particularly those created by the fact that we had by then let the world's largest broker/dealer (Merrill Lynch) make a 30 percent passive investment in our company. (It's now 20 percent.) In fact, our first conversation dwelt almost exclusively on that topic rather than on how to build a financial news business. Unless our news was impartial, free of any outside influence, and not tied to some hidden agenda, then no amount of money or talent would assure us success as journalists. I understood that much. Our customers at that point were loyal because they considered our data to be untainted. Customers for our news would expect no less.

History shows that any gutsy entrepreneur (Joseph Pulitzer, William Randolph Hearst, Henry Luce, B.C. Forbes, Ted Turner) can enter the news business anytime he wants. And, Bloomberg being Bloomberg, we had some advantages those guys didn't. When we started, there were lots of very competent reporters looking for jobs. In the face of the looming 1990 and 1991 recession, the news industry was cutting back exactly when we were expanding. People wanted to join us. We had a reputation as an exciting, innovative place to work. In the Bloomberg terminal, we had a distribution device par excellence. Best of all, we had revenue from terminal rentals, which meant we didn't have to worry about a news service paying for itself as a stand-alone product—one heck of an advantage.

Fundamentally, at Bloomberg we're builders, not buyers, so it never occurred to me to acquire a news organization. It's always more fun to create from scratch, and a lot less risky. And when Matt came along—someone I could connect with, particularly after our ethics discussion—I knew I had the right guy to help us start.

"We're going to do it," I told him as he chewed his last piece of sushi. "I want you to run it. When can you start?"

When he realized I was serious, he said he would call me the next day with an answer. Twenty-four hours later, he did: "Fine. Let's do it."

Basically, a handshake between Mike Bloomberg and Matt Winkler was all it took to get going in news. That kind of informal, informed decision making is something that most companies find very difficult to do. How it was going to fit in at a tactical level we'd figure out later. Strategically, it made sense. We weren't paralyzed like others who have the business school/accountant desire to quantify and predict everything before proceeding. Sure, you can count numbers and compare scenarios. But generally, projections regarding new, untried businesses are meaningless. The noise in the assumptions you have to make is so great, and the knowledge you have of strange areas so limited, that all the detailed analysis is usually irrelevant. We saw a need. We went ahead and filled it. If we had tried to come up with a detailed business plan, it never would have gotten going.

A public company would have had an even more difficult time than we did. Public companies must have specific goals and declare exactly where they'll wind up, or the securities analysts have a field day, and the investors, heart attacks. If public companies change what they're trying in midstream, everyone panics. In a private company like Bloomberg, the analysts don't ask, and as to the fact that we didn't know exactly where we're going—so what? Neither did Columbus. The truth of the matter was that we were moving forward.

*   *   *

The Bloomberg terminal, our first and greatest strength, was providing information that the other news companies weren't— even before the Bloomberg News service produced a word of text. From our first day in business, Bloomberg was making news, with numbers.

Some journalists derisively labeled those numbers "agate," even though that agate takes up more space in the daily newspaper than any reporter's column. But as I would come to realize, most media people are both ignorant and contemptuous of financial news in general. In the field of journalism, business and finance have never been the subjects of choice. None of the journalism schools taught reporters how to cover business. For a long time, none of the reporters and editors most visible to the public had any experience covering financial markets. On their way up the career ladder, no top news anchors for the networks had ever written earnings stories. No executive editor running the *New York Times,* the *Washington Post,* or the *Los Angeles Times* had ever edited financial markets stories day in and day out; the ambitious rushed to cover war, revolution, or riot. Even at the *Wall Street Journal,* it was rare to find top editors who included among their accomplishments daily stints covering stocks and bonds.

When Matt Winkler told editors and reporters at the *Journal* he was leaving, most of them shrugged, not knowing much about Bloomberg and caring less. To journalism's insiders, Bloomberg wasn't on anyone's radar screen. Even the *Journal*'s Washington

Bureau Chief, Alan Murray, asked Matt a month after he joined Bloomberg, "How does it feel to have sold out to . . . who's that firm?" That prevailing attitude became our opportunity.

Our timing was right. When the Berlin Wall came down in 1989, there was no question who had won the Cold War. Capitalism had triumphed. The forty-four-year-old battle of the superpowers had ended—and gone, too, was journalism's top tale. Money, in contrast, was emerging as the big story that needed telling at the end of the century—where money was, where it went, who made it, and who didn't. The demand for information about money was burgeoning everywhere. By the end of the 1980s, Bloomberg already had about 300 employees in New York, Princeton, London, and Tokyo, many of whom had Wall Street experience. To create a news operation, all we needed were the journalists who could translate that knowledge intelligently and communicate it as informative, concise, cogent prose.

Fortunately for us, the late 1980s were only slightly less kind to Communism than they were to newspapers and wire services. By 1990, United Press International, a once-proud wire service that had produced bylines from William Shirer and Neil Sheehan, was stumbling from bankruptcy filing to bankruptcy filing. Cities with two news dailies were becoming one-newspaper towns. McGraw-Hill, after spending three years and about $30 million, killed its nascent financial news wire just as it was about to get its first big customer. Conventional wisdom was that you couldn't compete with Dow Jones and Reuters, the two entrenched powerhouses—and if you tried, you'd end up in the poorhouse.

Until the 1980s, few newspapers even had a business section. The size of the sports staff always dwarfed the business staff. And yet, though not everyone cared about athletics, almost all people had their livelihoods at stake in the world of commerce. How people earned, saved, and spent their money helped determine prosperity, economic depression, wars, and elections. Readers might not have realized it to start with, but here was a hole. I knew Bloomberg could fill it.

*   *   *

From the beginning, we tried to be different. We built a unique product: We combined text and analytics with computer-driven tours that let readers automatically see the calculations and graphs of what we wrote about. We gave an illustration to complement what we told in words, then followed up with words to expand what the illustration showed. Our policies were not the same as at other news organizations: We made sure every company's earnings were reported as soon as we had them, instead of using the big-companies-first pecking order that was customary among wire services—and left shareholders of smaller companies in the lurch during earnings season. Thus, we had some content long before our competitors. At the end of each story, we gave our reporter's name and phone number. Unlike everyone else, we built customer access to our people rather than protection from our clients. We used customized standards. We banned the term *profit-taking* when we wrote about a market in decline. (How can everyone make money if the market lost value?) We insisted on two independent sources for important new facts. When you read our copy, it really was more accurate and better written than the competition's. Small items, but all things that we thought would differentiate us.

There are other practices that separate Bloomberg from the conventional, old news services. For some stories, we don't use human writers or editors at all. When we describe a market's value at a given instant (as opposed to why it had moved there), only speed and accuracy matter—and they are not most people's strengths. But what device did I make my career creating and managing since Salomon days? What instantly does exactly what you've asked it to do every time?

We've programmed our Bloomberg computers to "write" periodically a series of stories informing readers of the current state of the market. For example, the machine takes the predefined phrase "The Dow Jones Industrial Index is," and adds the word "up" or "down," based on calculations of all 30 stocks' moves from the previous day to that millisecond. It then adds the appropriate numbers—for example, 1 point, 2 points, 3 points, and so on. Then it prints the words "The most active stocks are" and, from continuous trading-volume monitoring, automatically translates the appropriate ticker symbols to company names (e.g., Procter & Gamble, General Electric, Walt Disney). It then adds them to the sentence. A sample result: "The Dow Jones Industrial Average was 1.09% lower at 3:01 P.M. Eastern time, down 62.14 at 5650.24. The stocks that contributed most to the average's fall were Procter & Gamble Co., which lowered the Dow by 5.55 points; General Electric Co., 5.18 points; and the Walt Disney Co., 4.07 points." A story created and "written" in microseconds—and one of many done the same way every hour.

No group of humans could as specifically and as quickly, around the clock, write these stories from markets worldwide. (There are thousands of indexes investors follow, with hundreds active enough for a textual description.) Our reporters, from the start, have been too valuable to be assigned to mechanical tasks anyway. Understanding and reinventing how news should be produced and delivered, as opposed to doing it "the way it's done," lets us beat the competition. Such new strategies are more efficient for ourselves, and they give a better allocation of resources to fulfill our customers' needs.

Were the quality and timeliness and accuracy of our stories as good then as they are now? No. Are they as good today as they're going to be? I hope not. We just forged ahead in the news business, secure in the belief that we would do the best we could and not get trapped by a set of disabling expectations or opinions.

*　　　*　　　*

When he showed up for work at 8 A.M. on February 5, 1990, Matt Winkler was already late. Bloombergers were at their desks by 7:30. That's the hour when most of our customers sit down at their desks. (Someone from a *small* software house accosted me recently at a convention, alleging that we overworked ourselves with this start time. The fact that he thinks it strange to be at work simultaneously with one's customers says he'll always be *small.*)

"Nice of you to show up," I said. He told me 8 A.M. was early in the newspaper world. I pointed out he no longer worked in that domain as I led him to his new desk in the middle of a room filled with people (he now gets to work at 6:30 A.M.). At the end of the month, Matt received his first paycheck and found out what his compensation would be. We had never discussed his pay before he joined Bloomberg.

I handed him a three-page list of what Bloomberg Business News (later shortened to Bloomberg News), as we agreed to call it, should be doing. Our purpose was to do more than just collect and relay news; it should also, ethically, advertise the analytical and computational powers of the Bloomberg terminal by highlighting its capabilities in each news story. This would make each story better and, at the same time, make it easier to rent more terminals (total rentals were then about 8,000 worldwide). With our terminal functions included, each of our news stories would be more informative than the competition's, and more people would want access to them. More retrievals meant more rentals, which meant more revenue, which in turn meant we could afford more reporters and have more news, and so on.

One most important, immediate business-development task was to prevent any Bloomberg customer from canceling a Bloomberg terminal if Dow Jones grew wary of the new kid on the block and stopped distributing its newswire over our system. That was unlikely right away since Bloomberg was a large Dow Jones customer. Bloomberg customers paid Dow Jones to receive the Dow Jones news wires on the Bloomberg terminal, and

Bloomberg itself paid a Dow Jones subsidiary millions of dollars annually to help install and service Bloomberg terminals throughout the United States.

Who knew how long this arrangement would last if Bloomberg, equipped with Dow Jones news, continued to displace the Telerate terminal equipped with Dow Jones news. Fortunately, even after Matt arrived, there wasn't anyone at Dow Jones (or any other news organization) who thought we had a realistic chance to compete with the century-old news service benchmarks. Thank God they never told me that. Ignorance is bliss.

Even so, I was asking for trouble if I didn't believe that the perception of our company could change in a second. Low-key may not have been our normal style, but for a while, we would try it. We agreed to make the relationship with Dow Jones as friendly as we could; we decided not to hire anyone else away from it. Our news formula would provide as much information as fast as possible about anything that might affect the price of a stock, bond, currency, or commodity, but without making waves. I would initiate no public relations effort to tweak the establishment's nose. With a little luck, we could build a credible news service before the inevitable confrontation with the giants, and after it was too late for them to retaliate successfully.

In August 1990, two months after the first Bloomberg Business News story crossed the Bloomberg terminal, Dow Jones said it would no longer install or service Bloomberg terminals and would no longer distribute its news via Bloomberg when its contract with our customers expired twelve months later. So much for avoiding a showdown. Dow Jones reported the announcement on its newswires and in the *Wall Street Journal*, declaring war with a competitor. Since most people still hadn't heard of our news service, a story in the nation's largest newspaper saying that Dow Jones considered Bloomberg's service a competitor, a threat—well, that was advertising we couldn't have bought. I was thrilled that the battle had been joined that way.

On the other hand, we had less than a year to convince our terminal customers that our news was good enough to offset the loss of Dow Jones news. People find all sorts of ways to become motivated and creative when they're threatened with extinction. And that's the way it was with our fledgling news organization of two dozen reporters and editors at the end of 1990. It was a similar situation with our service and installation people. When Dow Jones ended its service contract with us, it only hurt itself. It forced us into an expensive conversion to start doing ourselves what we had hired it to do, but that was good for Bloomberg in the long term. Because we installed all new equipment as we moved our communications sites in every city from its offices to ours, we improved our product vis-à-vis theirs. We came out better; it lost a revenue source and contact with all our customers.

Few analysts gave us any chance to succeed independently with our own news, so we exceeded expectations when it became clear we weren't going to lose customers if Dow Jones was no longer available on the Bloomberg system. The verdict from some of our customers was even more encouraging. In March of 1991, H. Ross Perot & Co. sent us a copy of a letter it had written to Dow Jones, explaining that it wouldn't need Dow Jones news on the Bloomberg because "We get everything we need at no extra charge from Bloomberg News." Our own news was an example of how Bloomberg could add value, save customers money, and make them more reliant on the Bloomberg system.

The big surprise came a month later. If Dow Jones news disappeared from the Bloomberg system, Bloomberg's Merrill Lynch customers might need to get their financial news some other way—which was exactly what Dow Jones hoped—and thus, the appeal of the Bloomberg terminal would be limited. So Merrill, without our knowledge, created its own set of criteria and decided to compare Bloomberg news to Dow Jones news, point by point. On four days during a three-week period, both news services were scored for accuracy and timely reporting on financial markets.

When the test was completed, we were told we scored well enough that Merrill was no longer worried. The Bloomberg without Dow Jones news was as good as the Bloomberg with!

Of course, once it became clear we wouldn't lose any customers, Dow Jones changed its mind and decided to renew our contracts. To this day, you can subscribe to Dow Jones news on the Bloomberg terminal in North America. (If this sounds strange and antithetical to the basic American idea of healthy competition, remember that big companies have lots of different divisions. You compete with parts. You buy from some, you sell to others, and you might not even notice that additional ones exist. Those kinds of conflicts and the tolerance of them are just the way the world works.)

*   *   *

But why did Bloomberg News rival Dow Jones and the British wire service Reuters so quickly? No big company thinks a little start-up company will ever become a major competitor. Invariably, by the time the big guy catches on, it's too late. The customers have grown used to having a choice. And playing catch-up isn't easy. In this case, major company complacency was furthered because Reuters and Dow Jones were growing at the time Bloomberg came on the scene; at first we were barely a distraction to either behemoth. Moreover, both of those established companies possessed a large status quo infrastructure with a vested interest in convincing management it was doing a good job, doing everything right, covering all the bases. So what management heard internally were reassuring feelings, not facts. I have always worried when our people tell me that we're doing great, that all is fine. As the "emperor" of Bloomberg, I need someone to tell me when I've left my clothes at home.

Bloomberg found niches that Dow Jones and Reuters news didn't fill. From the start, it was easier for us to add to our basic product what they provided, than for them to add what we built to theirs.

Although they were unable to replicate our analytics—the computational answers to all sorts of "what-if" scenarios in the financial and commodity markets—we started matching them story for story, interview for interview, scoop for scoop (and unfortunately sometimes, error for error). They made a dramatic mistake by not paying attention; at Bloomberg, as we keep on growing with time, we've got to be sure we don't do the same.

In fact, we would have had a much tougher time had we entered an industry that had lots of small, scrappy competitors. But we went against giants, and giants are usually easy to beat. Remember the Germans and then the Japanese versus Detroit's "Big Three" automakers? If you have to compete based on capital, the giant always wins. If you can compete based on smarts, flexibility, and willingness to give more for less, then small companies like Bloomberg clearly have an advantage. The world changes every minute, and you forget that at your peril. Ted Levitt at the Harvard Business School, in his famous *Marketing Myopia* paper, argued that the railroads failed because they should have realized they were in the transportation business rather than running trains. If they'd caught on to that idea, they'd have grown up to be General Motors, Boeing, and American Airlines, he argued. I'm not sure that's true, but I know this: Those enterprises that see new needs and react more quickly, win!

*   *   *

As an entrepreneur, I've learned to know what I don't know, get access to the people who do know, and then study hard. At the beginning, when we started Bloomberg News, I relied on professional journalists for our editorial policy and the management of our newspeople.

I always worried that, in the rush to succeed, we might confuse fact and opinion. Facts aren't always what they seem, or what you want them to be. Inaccuracy and incompleteness can make *yes* into *no* and vice versa. Errors can ruin reputations, destroy companies and their employees, even start wars and kill people. Writing news stories takes time and requires restraint. As an organization, we have to take care not to err, even if it sometimes means coming in second in the race for headlines. The balance among speed, accuracy, and aggressiveness is an issue we must grapple with continuously, keeping our demand to be first from overcoming our insistence on being right. Now, with a few years of experience, I know how hard to push, and what errors we're likely to make.

Journalists generally make lousy managers in the same way that lawyers, accountants, and consultants are sometimes better at advising than doing. Each of these professions requires great skill in gathering a bewildering array of information and providing the customer with an assessment of what it means. That's an ability different from motivating employees to produce their best, of understanding the shades of gray that are human beings. The very skills required to research and produce a discriminating, specific piece of analytical prose day in and day out are probably antithetical to the skills required to keep people working together.

Fortunately, our reporters aren't alone, our data collectors aren't alone, our programmers aren't alone. In our company, everybody's in one room and works together. The environment we've created at Bloomberg means we don't do anything independently of one another. We have been more successful in news because of that. Our reporters periodically go before our salesforce and justify their journalistic coverage to the people getting feedback from the news story readers. Are the reporters writing stories that customers need or want? Does the depth of a story's coverage matter as much as the speed with which it is disseminated? Do customers want headlines, details, opinions, or analysis? In turn, the reporters get the opportunity to press the salespeople to provide more access, get news stories better distribution and credibility, bring in more businesspeople, politicians, sports figures, and entertainers to be interviewed.

Most news organizations never connect reporters and commerce. At Bloomberg, they're as close to seamless as it can get. That's our system. We have give and take on both sides of the table. Any journalist preaching that capitalism doesn't affect him or her won't (and shouldn't) survive in this day and age. Here they don't have to be afraid of calling it the way they see it—our standards of separating editorial content from our opinions or economic pressure from our clients are as pure as anyone's—but in today's world, the economics of publishing won't permit paying journalists to write what no one wants to read. I'm proud of the balance we maintain between the dollar sign and the written word. That's news at Bloomberg.

5

"No" Is No Answer

Establishment Ignorance and Arrogance

Once we had the Bloomberg News service, it never occurred to us that our access to the events financial journalists covered, such as economic indicators briefings, would be denied by anybody. We were wrong. Journalism is no different from any other profession; it's not exempt from the lessons of George Orwell's *Animal Farm:* Some are more equal than others. And we were about to have some real barnyard battles to get fair access.

We started the news service with no plans to cover politics and policy, or Washington, DC—not, at least, at the start. We wanted to focus our resources where our needs and strengths resided: in the financial markets. Of course, every statistic about the economy—and every public policy tremor—can drive the bond, stock, commodity, and currency markets into turmoil. So, early on, we decided we needed to include coverage not only of the numbers, but also of the people who produced the numbers, and the politics behind these people. Either we had to pay someone to give us that, or we had to provide it on our own. We decided to do it ourselves, naturally. And we met more resistance in getting ourselves credentialed than the Jamaican bobsled team did in getting into the Winter Olympics.

*　　　*　　　*

One afternoon, just as we were getting started, Winkler happened to be telling Mary McCue, an official from the Securities and Exchange Commission, about Bloomberg's plans to expand coverage into Washington, DC. She interrupted him. "I'm not sure I can talk to you," she said.

"What do you mean?" Matt asked.

"I'm not sure I or anyone else who works for the government can talk to you in any official capacity."

Matt was astounded. "Mary. I've known you for twelve years now and you're saying you can't talk to me?"

"You're not accredited. We can only talk to accredited news organizations."

"What the hell does that mean, I'm not accredited? Hundreds of bylines in the largest U.S. newspaper during the past ten years isn't good enough?" By now, Matt was shouting.

"Look, Matt, the only way we can talk to journalists is if the House/Senate Standing Committee of Correspondents says they are journalists. Unless you have credentials from the Standing Committee, you can't get any of those economic numbers you were talking about, or even talk to me. No offense; but you are in luck." At this point, Mary McCue's tone changed. "The chairman of the committee is Jeffrey Birnbaum of the *Wall Street Journal.* He must know you."

"Thanks, Mary." Even if McCue was being ironic in mentioning his onetime employer, Matt didn't think for a minute that a *Journal* reporter would cross another *Journal* reporter, even a former one, over a matter as seemingly mundane and bureaucratic as obtaining a visa into Washington's duchies of access. Journalism was a club. Members took care of one another. Of course, we were wrong again.

The House/Senate Standing Committee of Correspondents consists of an annually elected group of five newspaper or wire service reporters who decide who is and who isn't a journalist. Their high and serious intention is to keep the halls of government from being littered with lobbyists, investment bankers, economists, brokers, and other "influence peddlers" posing as journalists. Elected officials, wary of interfering with the Fourth Estate, long ago decided to let journalists themselves decide who's fit and who isn't. The standing committee meets and holds hearings in government chambers. Its rulings have the effect of law among government employees in Washington, DC.

*   *   *

Matt admits now that he was hopelessly naïve about his colleagues at the competing news services. He thought the whole issue of credentials for Bloomberg News in Washington, DC, was a formality to be resolved among civilized people over lunch at the American Café across from the Capitol. He and a couple of colleagues met Birnbaum, who had started at Dow Jones & Co. about the same time Matt did, a decade earlier. Matt explained that Bloomberg was starting a news service to cover financial markets, and its two reporters in Washington needed to follow the economic indicators. These are numbers, such as the Gross Domestic Product (GDP), the Consumer Price Index (CPI), and the Producer Price Index (PPI), that are released by government officials in a quarantine-like setting so no one can trade on advance information. All serious business reporters need credentials to be in the "lock-up" where journalists get the releases before the general public. In this sealed room, they write their stories before the publishing time, and all release these news flashes at the same instant. Not being included with the other reporters would mean reporting the numbers too late in the day for traders to act, and not having a competitive news product to sell.

After the ritual greetings and introductions, Matt got to the point. "So, Jeff, how do we get these dog tags that let us report on GDP, CPI, PPI, now that we're starting this news service?"

"What are you?" Birnbaum asked, inspiring no confidence that Winkler's request was routine.

"We're an electronic newspaper," Matt said.

Birnbaum's skepticism persisted. "Who reads you?"

Matt, proud of his new professional home, replied: "Every central bank in Europe, and there are thirty of them; most of the world's biggest commercial banks, institutional investors, pension funds, and securities firms."

Birnbaum still wasn't impressed. "Where are you published?" he asked.

"On desks around the world via a dedicated computer terminal," Matt said, providing an answer that would be the zeitgeist to all journalists around the world by 1995, but was obviously obscure to all but the cognoscenti in the spring of 1990.

"What newspapers publish you?"

"Hundreds via the Associated Press, which prints our complete list of government bond prices and yields daily," Matt said. He was referring to the data we were supplying to the *Wall Street Journal* and to the AP and hundreds of its members—electronically instead of pony express style.

"Where are your stories published?" Birnbaum asked.

"On desks around the world," Matt said again.

"What newspapers publish your stories?" Now, Birnbaum was coming back to what for him was the crux of the issue. Whatever Bloomberg News was, he would require that it look like something Gutenberg produced instead of a computer derived from the Numerical Integrator and Calculator—the father of today's PC.

No problem, Matt thought. "Well, if you give us the dog tags so we can cover the numbers, we can probably get published in newspapers somewhere," he said.

"I'm sorry, Matt. We don't have criteria for you," Birnbaum replied.

Matt was stunned. That was it? "We don't have criteria for you."

"Hey. Jeff. Let me get this right. You're saying just because Bloomberg News is born in 1990, instead of 1900, and because it's on-line instead of married to a printing press, it has no right to cover GDP, CPI, PPI?"

"I'm sorry, Matt," he said. "That's right. I don't make the rules. We don't have criteria for you."

"Well, that's the biggest pile of shit I've smelled in a long time," Matt said as he excused himself to pay the check.

While he was gone, Birnbaum turned to Matt's colleagues: "Whatever you do, don't let him go before the House/Senate Standing Committee." Talk about waving a red flag in front of a bull!

*   *   *

Birnbaum's reaction was just the beginning of the stonewalling we encountered. Within a month, a new slate of journalists had been elected to the committee, including a new chairman, the defense correspondent for United Press International (UPI), Elliot Brenner. We had no luck convincing him either. "We can't give you credentials because Bloomberg is owned by Merrill Lynch," he misinformed us.

Our Washington reporter tried patiently to explain reality to him. "Merrill is a passive minority shareholder with 30 percent of Bloomberg L.P. Mike Bloomberg owns almost 70 percent."

"Right," said the chairman of the committee. "What if Merrill called in its loans to Bloomberg?"

"Merrill is a passive equity shareholder."

"Right. What if Merrill called in its loans?"

"No. You see, there are no loans. Merrill is a passive *equity* shareholder."

"Yeah. What about the loans?"

Now, here was a good reason for Bloomberg News to exist. The chairman of the committee that decides who's fit to cover the big and little stories of the day in the capital of the world had never covered a financial market in his life. He didn't know the difference between debt and equity and yet he was deciding who should cover stocks and bonds. Ignorance and arrogance are a deadly combination. They run riot in the profession of journalism, and this guy had them both.

We later learned that all sorts of folks had credentials to cover the economic numbers. They included Tass, the news agency of the old Soviet Union, and the Iraqi News Service, whose dispatches depicted Saddam Hussein as one of the world's greatest humanitarians. Reporters for the Haitian News Service, the house organ of a brutal dictatorship during much of the twentieth century, could cover Federal Reserve Chairman Alan Greenspan giving his semiannual testimony to Congress, and Bloomberg News could not.

Frustrated, we decided to accomplish by indirection what we couldn't make happen head-on. In addition to providing the Associated Press with bond prices for several years for free—a service for which AP was in turn charging its newspapers—Bloomberg was also paying AP millions of dollars a year to have AP news on the Bloomberg terminal. We figured that when you're dealing with a bully, you'd better get someone bigger on your side, and AP was the logical someone.

We asked the Associated Press, which, with three thousand reporters and editors, is the largest news-gathering organization in the United States, to ask the House/Senate Standing Committee of Correspondents why it objected to giving Bloomberg News the credentials. The AP, being a great journalistic organization of impeccable integrity, didn't have any objection at all to Bloomberg's writing about the Gross Domestic Product. When Chairman Brenner received a phone call from an AP correspondent who was wondering why the Committee was giving Bloomberg such a hard time, he said there had been a misunderstanding and Bloomberg should just "chill out"; they would get the credentials, just shortly *before* hell froze over.

So, even after AP's investigation, we were still meeting resistance. One of the journalists on the Committee told us, "All you guys up on Wall Street are corrupt anyway." We sweated through two hours of testimony in a Senate chamber in front of him and four other reporters, none of whom could define a Collateralized Mortgage Obligation (but probably wouldn't have gotten their own home mortgages if CMOs didn't exist), all demanding to know why we thought we were fit to write about housing starts. Bruce Harmon, the Washington bureau chief of Knight-Ridder Financial News, went so far as to tell the Committee, in a letter on Knight-Ridder stationery, that allowing Bloomberg News service into the Labor Department to cover employment statistics would open the possibility of insider trading. This, of course, is impossible where information is given to all journalists simultaneously in the same sealed room. Besides, if there was some way *we* could, so could his company.

*   *   *

Every problem is an opportunity, as the saying goes. Just as we were tangling with the journalists' commissar committee in Washington, Matt was asked by former Dow Jones colleagues who were now at the *New York Times* if they might be able to get a Bloomberg terminal for free. They wanted the same instant information about companies, stocks, and bonds that the money managers they were writing about now had. "We can't afford to rent your terminals. We don't have enough money for everything," said Diana Henriques, a *Times* reporter, half in jest. I believe no customers are more equal than any others, so the idea that we would give the terminal away was a nonstarter. We could, however, provide Bloomberg terminals to people who provided us with something equivalent to the monetary value of the terminals. News companies often barter, so we weren't exactly inventing a new form of remuneration. We told the *New York Times* that if we provided them with news items that they decided were fit to print, just like any other news-service stories the *Times* published, we might be able to get them a terminal.

At that time, the credibility gained from having Bloomberg News stories published in the *New York Times* was worth more to us than any cash payment. It would directly counter the argument of those who were reluctant to recognize Bloomberg because we weren't "published" in the old-fashioned way. The agreement would be simple enough to avoid any conflict of interest: The *New York Times* would decide what it published, as it always had. But when it published one of our stories, there would be the Bloomberg News byline and the Standing Committee's problem would be solved.

When Max Frankel, the *Times* executive editor, agreed to our suggestion in 1991, Bloomberg had its first newspaper customer. Within a year, every major newspaper in the United States asked for the same arrangement. By 1995, Bloomberg News was published in more American newspapers than any other news service, after the Associated Press. We provide what so many newspapers have in short supply: an army of reporters and editors who do nothing but report and explain money, markets, companies, industries, and the economy. The newspapers, in turn, provide what we need: access, distribution, credibility, and recognition for us and our products. Selling news for cash we would do, but to the ultimate users, not the intermediaries.

I am very proud of how hard we fought, what we produced, how fast we grew, and how we became a news inevitability. Yet we might never have considered newspapers as customers if the journalists in Washington hadn't created the predicament that forced us to include print media in our distribution. In 1995, the *New York Times*'s own newspaper syndicate, received by 700 newspapers around the world, asked to include Bloomberg News. It happened because someone told us, "We don't have criteria for you." Oh, and of course in the end, over a year after we first asked, we did get our dog tags.

*   *   *

In Japan, we had an even tougher time getting our reporters the access and credentials they needed. Our problem wasn't with the government. Once again, it was with a self-appointed group of journalists trying to protect their cozy fiefdom. Since we weren't Japanese reporters with a Japanese news organization, the hometown press kept us from reporting on the economy and corporate earnings in the most timely way by not allowing us into the *kisha* (reporter, in Japanese) clubs where all government and corporate press releases are distributed. Thus, we couldn't get information when it was first made public. Well, economic and corporate news was our business and we had to protect our franchise—even if it meant doing what no foreign news organization had ever done before: confronting our opponents in the Fourth Estate directly and demanding equal access for our customers, a growing number of whom were Japanese.

In 1991, Bloomberg News shouldered ahead of all the other cowed and overpolite foreign media to demand equal treatment for foreign news organizations. We made it clear we would not shut up until we got it. Our threat was dismissed with a combination of half bows and condescending giggles. Even our non-Japanese competitors were leery of rocking the boat and declined our invitation to stand together publicly on the issue.

The Japanese *kisha* clubs consist of reporters from Japan's elite news organizations. The clubs control the newsrooms at all government agencies. The *kisha* clubs decide who gets desks, who gets to ask questions at news conferences, and who gets advance copies of news releases. *Kisha* club members also are given preferential treatment when it comes to background briefings with Japan's top policymakers.

The prejudice against *gaijin* (foreign) journalists in the post-World War II era meant that no overseas news organization ever had a desk inside a Japanese government newsroom. When the almighty *kisha* clubs stooped to allow *gaijin* to attend news conferences, they did so only with the proviso that we not ask any questions.

Our loudmouthed campaign to end this system made us the most hated news company in Tokyo. Each week brought a new snub. We got a telephone call from Clay Jones, president of the Foreign Correspondents Club of Japan and correspondent for the *Christian Science Monitor*. He passed on the bad news that Bloomberg would not be invited to a dinner hosted by Japan's own Publishers and Editors Association staff. The association wanted to talk with foreign journalists about *kisha* clubs. But they didn't want us there. That marked the second time the Publishers and Editors Association had hosted a dinner at which access to the clubs was the topic and had spurned Bloomberg despite our intense involvement in the issue and an appeal from Mr. Jones that we be invited.

At stake was our ability to cover a global financial and economic story. Japan is the world's second largest economy. By denying us equal access to the figures that measured the performance of Japanese companies and the economy, Japan's news organizations were also depriving shareholders and bondholders (our customers inside and outside Japan) of news they had a right to know. It was an explicit move by one group of journalists to deprive another group of journalists of the information both needed.

At first, we tried the normal route. We applied for membership in one of the clubs. We were turned down. The official reason given was that we didn't meet the criteria for membership, though the criteria were never defined. In reality, we didn't get in because we weren't a Japanese company. To press our case, Matt Winkler and David Butts, our Tokyo bureau chief, met Osamu Asano, the secretary general of the Publishers and Editors Association, in February 1992. They were ushered into a paneled conference room and seated on one side of a twenty-foot-long table. Under the gaze of a gallery of the association's past secretaries general, the negotiations began. We said that many of our worldwide subscribers were both employees and shareholders of such companies as Nissan, Sony, Matsushita, Honda, and Toyota: We demanded equal access to the news that mattered to them. At the same time, we said we considered it appalling that Japanese journalists—who ostensibly share our freedom-of-speech views as members of the Fourth Estate—should maintain a system that blatantly discriminated against non-Japanese journalists.

Dave Butts, a native Texan, did all the talking for us. "We'd like to join the club," he said.

"You can't join because you have to speak Japanese to be a member," said Asano.

When Butts reminded him (in his fluent Japanese) that all our Tokyo correspondents speak Japanese, Asano paused. "Oh well, there aren't enough desks in the club rooms for foreigners."

To which Butts countered, "You have more than one hundred desks in most clubs, many are empty, and there are only four or five foreign organizations that would want one of them."

Then Asano smiled and said, "Right. Well, it is not really up to us to give you membership. Membership is decided by the individual clubs, not this association."

Butts persisted: "We asked the clubs to admit us and they said they can only do so if we are members of your organization first."

Asano shook his head. "Is that true?" he asked. "Well, we don't give membership to companies just because they want to join."

That response was typical of the entire discussion.

*　　　*　　　*

A year later, in March 1993, the association took the bold step of setting up a subcommittee to study the issue. Matt and Dave once again met the man in charge, Yoshio Murakami, senior editor at the *Asahi* newspaper. They didn't exactly hit it off with him. This time, the conversation was in English, and his English, after a ten-year tour of duty in the United States, was probably better than Matt's.

By now we were too familiar with disappointment to pull our punches. No self-respecting journalist ever likes to be rolled. If we could make the point that journalists restraining other journalists is shameful, maybe we could finally puncture the veneer of politeness that led us nowhere. Matt suggested that by limiting foreign press access to government agencies, Japanese journalists had become puppets of the politicians and bureaucrats. During the next fifteen minutes, Matt uttered the phrase "puppets of special interests" about a dozen times. The *Asahi* editor, a model of composure to everyone who knew him, suddenly snapped. He now told us what he really thought.

"You can go to hell!" he said, leaping from his chair and spilling his green tea.

After so many polite rebuffs, this outburst was just the kind of reaction we wanted. "Now, you know how *we* feel," Butts said.

"Will you resort to violence?" the *Asahi* editor asked in the frankness of the moment.

Butts said simply that he *hoped* it wouldn't come to that.

Two months later, we were back hammering at the stone wall once again. We asked the *kisha* club at the Tokyo Stock Exchange to let us have news releases at the same time they were delivered to club members. "No way," was the club's answer. So we decided to try a little civil disobedience.

Reporters from our Tokyo bureau stood by the club's mailboxes, outside the entrance to the club, and insisted that the public relations folks from the companies who regularly visit the club give us each release as it was distributed. To protect us, we had our lawyers there with their books defining "trespass," and even invited the TV networks to have the cameras rolling. The club members rose to protect their turf. They surrounded us, preventing the corporate crowd from getting close, and they "asked" us to leave. This is one of those confrontations that made the evening news: Journalist bites journalist. The commotion and subsequent publicity created was more than the club could bear. Under threat of repeated visits from us and the possibility that journalistic access could burgeon into a "free trade" issue at the level of Japanese automobile imports to the United States, the club promised to set up a fair system for the distribution of releases.

The Publishers and Editors Association finally followed up in a June 1993 statement: "The *kisha* clubs, as a matter of principle, should grant full membership to foreign correspondents who wish to join." The statement should put an end to foreign criticism of Japan's *kisha* club system, said the host at yet another dinner from which we were excluded. Still, to his credit, the host, Yoshio Murakami, offered to help Bloomberg; his newspaper agreed to sponsor Bloomberg for membership in the stock exchange reporting club.

But our single-minded efforts to open up one Japanese market were even now not yet successful. The *kisha* club voted to admit one of our competitors, Reuters, and keep Bloomberg out. The club's off-the-record explanation to friends who asked on our behalf was that Bloomberg might expect to get in by October 1993, if it showed more deference to the club. That meant we had to be quiet and do nothing that might be interpreted as casting an aspersion on the club. Our competitor's bureau chief, when asked by Bloomberg to wait until the doors were open to all of us, demurred.

"We used the back channel and quiet diplomacy," he said.

"Bull!" As a publisher, I was furious.

This other non-Japanese news service had done nothing. Bloomberg had done it all. Their Tokyo office had never tried to gain *kisha* club access. They never even took the trouble to report releases as soon as they were available, much less try to get them more quickly. They always published earnings and other time-sensitive stories only when they got around to it. Not being "in" had suited their customer-be-damned laziness just fine.

The Fourth Estate has a long, proud history of never letting commercial competitive interests override its integrity. Reporters *always* stand together on matters of journalistic freedom. And real journalists never stoop to using a back channel to talk to each other. They would not be journalists if they did. No reputable news service would permit it, nor would any quality journalist want to be associated with such behavior. It was a sad episode in the history of that other news organization whose journalistic standards were once legendary. Either they cared about their earnings more than their ethics, or, more charitably, perhaps their main headquarters on another island six thousand miles away had no idea what was taking place in Japan.

After a twenty-four-month battle, in October 1993, the *kisha* club finally let us in. The vote was unanimous. A year later, our reporter was rotated into the club's presidency.

*　　　*　　　*

Six years after we started our news service, the issue of credentials had become history. One of our editors, Pulitzer Prize winner Monroe (Bud) Karmin, was elected president of the National Press Club in Washington. Today, its training center proudly carries the Bloomberg name as its major sponsor. Knight-Ridder Financial News, whose Washington bureau chief went out of his way to hurt us in our infancy, was sold—a casualty of inadequate returns to its parent. In Japan, many newspapers subscribe to Bloomberg News and carry the news our reporters write. Our Japanese-language news service is used by Japanese speakers worldwide.

The New York Stock Exchange now has three "official" news organizations: Bloomberg, the 114-year-old Dow Jones, and the 147-year-old Reuters, each of whom is designated as providing sufficient distribution for exchange-listed companies to fully inform their shareholders. No other group of journalists but these three can say that, and lots have tried.

*   *   *

Was starting a newswire worth the effort? After all, in the 1960s, Marshall McLuhan, in *The Medium Is the Massage* (no, not "message") and *Understanding Media,* wrote that we were never going to read again. Books, magazines, newspapers, and other "hot" media would cease to be influential. "Cool" media, like television, which are "extensions of our senses," were the future. In the pop culture of the information age, distribution would triumph over content.

The 1990s have a similar "everybody knows." We are told all will be "on the Net." The computer is supposed to eliminate the drudgery of thinking. Research will be "touch a button" automated browser output. Contextual software, the successor to artificial intelligence (perhaps the ultimate oxymoron), replaces analysis. The mind's eye is dead. Modern simulation will show all: imagination, an antiquated concept. Disney's animators, Spielberg's wizardry, Stone's revisionism—all will make pseudoscience and politically corrected, commercialized history replace the inconvenience and unpleasantness of reality and truth. No more are we to be tortured by inconsistencies. Thinking's no longer required.

McLuhan said the medium's the message (no, this time not "massage") because the transmission device can massage its audience and mesmerize it more than the ideas it transports. The TV and PC, two devices fast becoming indistinguishable from each other, certainly do that, particularly with kids' games and entertainment shows. But are they a total replacement for the printed word? Do they represent the only educational paradigm of the future? Will they alone help society escape from poverty, illiteracy, hunger, disease, and everything else bad? We don't think so.

To us, presentation is important: Substance is paramount. It may take too much time for the world to beat a path to your door if you lack a slick format or a lot of bells and whistles, but if you have the better mousetrap when the world gets there, then you are more likely to survive and thrive. Substituting "how" for "what" is a strategy many adopt, but that's not Bloomberg's plan. Sure, we want to provide every medium, but not as a goal per se. For us, it's a means, not an end. We think timely, accurate news stories that are well researched and well written will be in demand for a long time. Technology will continuously revolutionize distribution. But our product is content. It remains consistent.

*　　　*　　　*

Media distribution is constantly changing in ways that groups like the House/Senate Standing Committee of Correspondents and the Japanese Publishers and Editors Association members won't ever be able to anticipate. The "newspaper" of tomorrow will probably be printed on artificial "cloth" rather than paper. The "ink" will be output from electronic transistors hidden in the fabric and fed over the airwaves with pictures and text, just like radio or cellular telephones receive information. It will still be a newspaper, though, with random access retrieval so you can go straight to the stories you want, bypassing what to you is irrelevant, but with simultaneous display of multiple articles alerting you to what you really need to know independently of and in addition to what you asked for. It will still be a newspaper with printed words that you can absorb much faster than is possible when listening to speech, or that you can reread, paragraph by paragraph, when you don't understand something the first time through. It will still be a newspaper with reporters to investigate, interpret, and explain; with editors to select and prioritize and preach; with photographers to speak a thousand words; and with advertising folks to bring you the great choices capitalism provides.

We'll just stop chopping down trees to make newsprint. The truck drivers and the boys and girls on bicycles will find other pursuits in the hours before most of us wake up. Electronic, convenient, and reliable delivery will eliminate the traditional paper-and-transportation expense (typically greater than the newsstand per-copy price), replacing it with the efficiency of over-the-air transmission.

With the ink no longer applied to the display medium the way Gutenberg did in the 1600s, you won't be limited to locally printed papers. Choice becomes vast. Every newspaper in every language, from every city, will be transmitted to you automatically and appearing on the same "page." You subscribe to your favorites, and they're there on your cloth "paper" whenever you want them: Even better, the stories will be displayed as soon as they're written, not hours later when the delivery truck shows up.

The more newspapers provide value, the more they'll be read, and the more news from Bloomberg they'll want to carry.

*   *   *

Newspapers will change; so will the other media we're all familiar with. The radio of tomorrow will be a derivation of the cellular or wireless phone of today. There's no reason why you should have to listen to what others are hearing, the way traditional AM/FM radio forces you to do. Your telephone is already a private, independent, interactive, electronic audio path. In the future, it will let you enjoy the songs you like, the sports stories from your old hometown, your portfolio's stock prices, the weather forecast for any destination city—all at exactly the time you want, not when some news announcer or disc jockey thinks it appropriate. As the cost of over-the-air telephones and computer-stored sound plummets, the economic viability of this transmission medium skyrockets. Digital communication for perfect fidelity and an amplifier for a big speaker are all that have to be added. Then, coupling your phone with a satellite position receiver will further tailor the programming. You'll hear programming specifically selected by you to satisfy your requests and tastes—and automatically customized for your exact present location with local news, traffic, and weather. The advertisers are salivating at this very moment, as they imagine the personalized commercials they will send your way.

With every product, the greater its utility, the easier it is to use, the cheaper it costs—the more it'll be used. Five hundred Bloomberg reporters around the world carry recorders to get "sound" for you to listen to. Technology is beginning to allow each of us to listen to whatever we want, where and whenever we want it. The more people can specifically select what to hear, the more demands there will be for our diverse group of short "wire service" reports, and the more value we'll get from our far-flung journalists generating multiple stories each day. Better radio means more Bloomberg.

And TV? The only difference between television and radio is the amount of bandwidth needed for transmission. If we can tailor radio to suit you exactly, television is close behind. It's already got a name: Video on Demand, or VOD. At reasonable cost, it's a few years away, but it's coming fast. It's the infamous "Killer Application" for the Internet: what you want, when and where, convenient and independent of others' demands.

The "data" most people desire are entertainment—the only data most will pay for. Whether via the phone companies or cable companies, whether over the air from a conventional TV tower, satellite, or microwave, how you get audio/video is only important to the employees and shareholders in each of the transmission industries. The consumer couldn't care less how and probably won't know what distribution medium's being used. The public just expects to click on a menu of titles or actors and instantly get access to their desired shows, or favorite teams, or a given kind of programming (comedy, news, and so on). Is it any wonder why those recorders Bloomberg reporters are carrying now have TV cameras and VCRs built in?

*   *   *

No matter what their medium, most firms selling information electronically have a hard time generating profits. On the expense side, creating content is costly and labor-intensive. On the revenue side, access to "data on demand" (whether sophisticated mathematical analysis or trivial entertainment television), means more fragmentation of audiences over vastly greater "program" choices. On the Internet, few receive revenue in excess of expenses. With broadcast media, increased capacity (e.g., more channels, alternative distribution methods) is starting to cause the same effect (reducing audience size and revenue per show).

What's required for success in these businesses? Why do some companies like Bloomberg, charging $1,100-plus per month for electronically delivered information, keep growing when others attempting data sales on the Internet can't keep customers even when charging only pennies, or, for TV via cable, find great subscriber price sensitivity? Simple: *supply and demand.* If you're not providing something unique, you have no ability to impose charges. Most of what's available electronically on the World Wide Web is available on many Web sites simultaneously. Most TV programs are just copies of earlier successful shows. No uniqueness: *too much supply.* Then there's the question of utility. Whether it's television sitcoms or hecklers on-line, most entertainment programming is only marginally more desirable than other alternatives or no programming at all. (The definition of entertainment is just that—nice but not necessary.) If there's no great value added, the public's smart enough to find alternatives like reading a book, watching something else, or going to bed. No great need: *low demand.* Much supply, little demand equals low prices.

But if you are selling something no one else has—say, breaking news stories or a heavyweight prize fight that's the talk of the town—buyers have little choice. Those who can't earn a living without having the information, or face their fellow sports fans without having watched, will pay whatever the provider asks.

Pay-per-view for Tyson vs. Holyfield made a fortune. Bloomberg never loses a customer to competitors that undercut our price. *Limited supply* and *great demand* equal high prices. The old economist Adam Smith did know what he was talking about.

*   *   *

As happens time and time again in this world, distribution changes rapidly. Content evolves slowly with cultural advancement. Creative people become even more valuable as their reach increases over difficult venues. The more choice the reader/listener/viewer has, the more demand there'll be for Bloomberg's product—independent, quality journalism—and the more important it is to fight the credentials battles everywhere in the world where access is denied to the people's only true representative: the free, unfiltered, intelligent, investigatory press. The message that content rather than the medium is king massages just fine.

6

Money Talks

Textbook Multimedia

Every decade has its personalities. In the 1980s, people on Wall Street started appearing on society pages. All that money from bull markets and deregulation turned both the players and the scorekeepers of yields and P/E ratios into superstars. Louis Rukeyser made stock-picking a hot Friday night television show. When hostile takeovers and junk bonds became the rage, bond traders became "Masters of the Universe." My former partner, John Gutfreund, was anointed King of Wall Street. Until then, there hadn't even been a Prince. Michael Milken graced magazine covers by uprooting corporate boardrooms for better and worse from his perch in tony Beverly Hills. T. Boone Pickens, Carl Icahn, and Ron Perelman moved from page 41 to page 1. Gossip columnists Liz, Suzy, and Cindy pounced on a new set of glitterati: the financial moguls and their wives, who, with jewels and couture, moved from middle class to aristocracy at a speed only new money and a good PR firm could deliver. Even Ivan Boesky joined celebrity status when he said a little greed was good—just before he went to jail.

* * *

I was not yet part of all that. I wasn't in the newspapers. It had been years since I'd left Salomon and was quoted as the definitive expert on stock market direction. Entrepreneurs in the booming 1980s were commonplace. My company, still using our initial catchy moniker, Innovative Market Systems, was small and virtually anonymous. Our product, the market data terminal that we were selling to Merrill Lynch and called Market Master, could have been confused with a kitchen appliance. No one knew us. No one cared about me.

But by 1984, this was about to change. Those were the days when Ronald Reagan proved how marketable ideas could be when they were peddled with charisma. You needed a spokesperson for mass appeal. Consumers and the media identified products and policies with people who pitched them: Chrysler Corporation's comeback was built around Lee Iacocca, the person. Nike didn't just make sneakers, it pushed them with a mystique that could come only from Michael Jordan. To have the best mousetrap wasn't enough; success was delivered by people promotion.

If we were going to build our business, we, too, needed a personality. The obvious choice? Me. Our competitors' founders, Messrs. Dow, Jones, Reuter, Knight, and Ridder, were all dead. I, on the other hand, was alive and out making speeches and sales calls every day in city after city around the world, turning my name and work into a great weapon that others in the financial news and market data businesses couldn't match. And since I'd spent so much time demonstrating our product, people had begun to mentally interchange me with the terminal. It was only a matter of time before traders and salespeople began referring to the black box on their desks as The Bloomberg. "Jack," some trader might say to his boss, "I'd like one of those, what do you call them? You know, the machines Mike Bloomberg sells, one of his 'Bloombergs.'"

When we had an opportunity to change company names (a potential trademark conflict arose with the Market Master name), I acquiesced to a decision the marketplace already had made. Henceforth, the product and the company itself would be "Bloomberg."

As my friend Harvey Eisen said, "An ethnic name—and all the more memorable for it."

So, just as my old partner Billy Salomon ran Salomon Brothers as *his* company, with *his* name and *his* reputation on the line, now it would be me and my name at risk. I would become the Colonel Sanders of financial information services, the target for clever barbs from acerbic columnists, but simultaneously the one whose company and product would be on everyone's lips. I'd delegated day-to-day company management to trusted lieutenants so I was free to travel. I was good at giving presentations and, from my Salomon days, already had years of practice representing a company. As the owner, by definition, I spoke with authority. And to make good copy, I gave the press a colorful personality to focus on. I was Bloomberg—Bloomberg was money—and money talked. Perfect!

Of course, no one does it alone. Telling your own story is only part of getting great press. In the quest to get Bloomberg recognition, our competitors deserve some credit too. Reuters let it be known it was developing a new system its executives haughtily dubbed the "Bloomberg Killer." Journalists love such stories and gave it maximum play. (While there are advantages to running an eponymous business, sometimes there are unintended effects on your family. My young daughter Georgina burst into tears when she saw a framed article with the headline "Bloomberg Killer!" She thought that her Daddy was the target of assassins. "No, George, not me; just the company.") Henry Becher, a Dow Jones vice president, told *Forbes*, "You tell that fella [Bloomberg] I'm gonna get him." Thanks, we needed that. Then six large banks and brokers formed a market data consortium named The Electronic Joint Venture, or EJV, for short. It was positioned by their people, and by me every chance I got, as targeting us. Another Bloomberg Killer. Spare me. The legend continues.

Journalists are just like you and me—well, sort of. They try to do their jobs and get home to the kids. If you make filling inches and minutes easier for them, they'll help you every time. What more of a layup could our competitors create? David versus Goliath! Murder threats in computerland! Ganging up on the little guy! It's hard not to feel sorry for the old giants. No wonder we became everyone's favorite.

*   *   *

The next step to notoriety was Bloomberg's expansion into broadcasting. Radio and television were the furthest things from my mind at the end of 1991, when I got a call from Jon Fram, a fast-talking executive bearing a faint resemblance to Groucho Marx. Jon was an employee of the Financial News Network (FNN), a television channel whose parent was in bankruptcy. He told me I should buy FNN in its entirety. "Mike, what you really need to do is television. It will create synergies with everything else you're doing."

"What a dumb idea," I said, cutting him off. My operating principle has always been build, don't buy. Besides, what did we have to do with television?

"Look, just give me five minutes in your office. It won't cost you a cent and I can show you a great opportunity."

I've always had sympathy for a guy with an idea or two who doesn't take no for an answer. So Fram came over for a cup of coffee. A total waste of time. We weren't going to spend $200 million or whatever it took to buy TV distribution, no matter what he said. Dow Jones and General Electric could battle each other for that privilege. After a courtesy listen, I told Fram we had nothing further to talk about and made it clear he was leaving.

Fram called back the next day as if we were now old friends. This time he suggested that instead of buying a network, we needed someone in-house to develop audio and video programming at Bloomberg. Actually, he said we needed three people: himself; one of the on-air talents at FNN, Bob Leverone; and a young producer, Janet Weinberg. Once again, I said television and radio made no sense for Bloomberg and hung up the phone.

A few days passed, then I got another call from Jon. This time he rattled off a whole bunch of reasons why Bloomberg Financial Markets was made for TV. As I listened to a longer version of the pitch he'd made a few days earlier, it occurred to me, "One of us is stupid—and it isn't him!" So I hired the three of them that day, and we took our first steps into the world of sound and pictures.

First, we bought a New York City radio station, WNEW, 1130 Kh on the AM dial. For decades, WNEW had been the closest thing to your father's radio station. I guess that's one of the reasons it was for sale. Much to the annoyance of its loyal but dwindling listeners, we had no intention of playing Frank Sinatra and Bing Crosby into the millennium. The $13.5 million we paid (an amount that constituted one-third of its market value twelve months later) provided us with the station's broadcast license and a 50,000-watt transmitter—not their studios, not their record collection, not their people, not even their call letters. Our programming would be an extension of our other news coverage: politics, diplomacy, lifestyles, science, business, markets, the economy, war, and peace. We would not do sensationalism. Our general standard would be: If I wouldn't want my children listening to it, it's not suitable for us to broadcast. Those wanting "all crime, all the time," the staple of much news radio, could go elsewhere.

We started day one by ignoring the fundamentals of conventional radio: no murder and mayhem, no prima donnas. Gone were the breathless on-the-scene reporters stumbling over the usual banalities, the self-important producers, and the separate on-air anchor talents whose only talent was reading others' copy and whose egos never quite get enough massaging.

We built technology for both efficiency and creativity: Our people had capacities and capabilities the competition could only dream of. Instead of using traditional audiotapes, we were completely digital and computer-based from the beginning. Reporters recorded their voices on a PC in a manner little different from writing text. The computer then fed the sound to the transmitter at exactly the time we wanted each story to be heard. Moreover, we could use the same prerecorded piece in multiple shows. Independent radio stations that became affiliated with us around the world could insert discrete Bloomberg-supplied stories into their lineups, or take our programming in a different order from the one we broadcast in New York. They just told the computer which story they wanted, when, and where—and out it came. Recording segments into a computer also enabled reporters to write, voice, edit, produce, and introduce pieces on their own. They could even go from radio to television and back several times during the day, using almost the same scripts for both media.

Bloomberg was breaking and remaking all the rules. For the radio industry, we were more than a little strange. We were crazy. I liked that.

*   *   *

Our first venture into television was to produce a daily thirty-minute morning show, *Bloomberg Business News,* for Maryland Public Television. Syndicated throughout the United States, it was a hit from the beginning. While Bloomberg doesn't make any money distributing over Public Broadcasting, as with our contributions to National Public Radio, we get notoriety, and the audience, which includes our clients, appreciates it.

Bloomberg produces television the same way it puts together its radio programming: Individual pieces are created at different times and "assembled" by the computer in the order needed. In fact, this particular show is really a series of consecutive shows, one recreated every half hour, each with a different financial report. Some East Coast stations broadcast *Bloomberg Business News* at 6:00 A.M. Eastern Standard Time, six whole hours before some West Coast stations that use it at 9:00 A.M. Pacific Standard Time. Our technology allows us, inexpensively and without human intervention, to keep the show up-to-date with constantly changing stock and bond markets—for whatever time the viewer tunes in. If it weren't done automatically, we couldn't afford to do it.

We even produce versions of this same show that are used on commercial TV. The computer assembles them with advertisements built in. For versions used overseas, the show's length gets automatically adjusted to fit the different time slots available there, and stories of purely American interest are automatically replaced by more internationally focused ones. Computers, when used correctly, are wonderful things. Also for Public Television, we are home to *The Charlie Rose Show* and *Adam Smith's Moneyworld.* Once again, a service for our kind of customer, with the twin rewards of helping PBS and getting us respectability.

Our next TV product became our signature production. Called *Bloomberg Information Television* (*BIT* for short), it's a twenty-four-hour, seven-days-a-week, multiscreen-format, all-news program. We do a version anchored in New York for the United States and Canada; a wholly separate version from São Paulo, Brazil, for South America; another from London for Europe and the Middle East; and a fourth version for Asia, hosted from Tokyo—all in English. Each show focuses on its own region with appropriate reports and segments from other Bloomberg news bureaus in its area. *Asia English Language BIT,* for example, has many daily reports from Wellington, Sydney, Singapore, and Hong Kong, as well as Tokyo. *European English Language BIT* has reports coming in from Paris, Frankfurt, Milan, Madrid, and so on, in addition to London.

Our audience is mainly upscale. Our niche is worldwide news from a local perspective. American content and recycled opinion out of a United States news headquarters aren't what these viewers need. They want their own programming, relevant to the part of the globe they call home, and produced by people like them. Thus, in addition to the four English language "pan-continent" versions for expatriates and tourists, we have created twenty-four-hour-a-day *French Language BIT, Japanese Language BIT, Spanish Language BIT, Portuguese Language BIT, Italian Language BIT,*

Dutch Language BIT, and *German Language BIT* for the general population in major countries around the world. Each non-English version has regional content from Bloomberg's overseas offices and from the premier indigenous independent news agencies in the countries where we air our shows (Agence France Presse in France, ANSA in Italy, Asahi in Japan, and so on). This joint production lets the viewer get the best local news *and* the best international news—from the very best specialists in each. Not American news in English; not international news translated—but local news in the local language, reported by local broadcasters, for local viewers.

Bloomberg Information Television, every place around the world, simultaneously displays on one TV screen different panels containing continuous weather, sports, news headlines, and financial market data, as well as conventional news television. It's just like Windows on your PC: No viewer focuses on all sections simultaneously, but each is there when needed—great for this fast-paced world where the viewer wants information, not entertainment. Further, with peripheral vision, the viewer's constantly assimilating what he or she needs, not just what he or she is focused on. A breaking news story flashing in one panel is sure to be noticed by a viewer concentrating on sports scores in another.

Naturally, advertisers love the format, since the audience is more likely to continue watching a commercial in one screen section while programming of interest is continuing in the others. The opposite ("no one's watching") occurs in the old full-screen presentation where there is only one thing to see at a time and viewers use the advertising message time to leave the room for a beer.

After mastering the continuous broadcast of radio and television twenty-four-hour news, we started *Bloomberg Small Business* and *Bloomberg Personal Finance* weekly TV shows. Once again, we used discrete segments assembled by technology. This strategy allows stories produced for one television program to be used in many others as well. We sometimes include a general-interest segment in our Public TV show, in four different English language

Bloomberg Information Television shows on five continents, and, revoiced into other languages, in many country-specific non-English versions of *BIT.* The economics of this multiple utility let Bloomberg do things for thousands of dollars per piece when the competition's spending millions.

People keep asking why Bloomberg ventures into radio and TV. Is there some hidden motive—for example, an executive who moves his company closer to the golf club and then declares, "The labor force is better there"; or a mogul who buys a film company for its "communications value" when his secret urge is to associate with movie stars?

Other companies make money in radio and TV—lots of it. Why shouldn't we? We have the necessary information and the technical know-how, so broadcasting's an easy extension of what we do elsewhere. Radio and television provide our company with instant visibility. The media like nothing better than writing about themselves. The more exposure Bloomberg has to the Fourth Estate, the more they'll promote us to the general public. To reach potential customers who don't yet subscribe to our print products, radio and TV are the only practical ways to get our message through. The people who lease our terminals are part of radio and television's masses. They need news while jogging, showering, driving, or sitting at home, and we've got to give them what they need. Lastly, our competitors do radio and TV. That doesn't require us to do it too, but the fact that we do shouldn't surprise anyone.

For some time, we'd been offering letters, numbers, sound, and pictures over our terminals to financial and investment professionals, selling a worldwide news service to newspapers, and publishing a magazine. Radio and television simply became other delivery mechanisms for the same content. Politicians, sports stars, celebrities, company officials, and business leaders interviewed for one Bloomberg media form get distribution via all the others as well. The more exposure the interviewees get, the happier they are to answer our questions, the more they make themselves available, the more product we have for all our ventures, and the more we can sell. Radio and TV enhance the appeal of our terminal and our publishing—and vice versa.

Bloomberg offers two kinds of media: *broad*cast communications, where many consumers get the same information simultaneously; and *narrow*cast communications, for small groups. Most people use both daily. Many watch or hear the day's key sporting event live, or view a new movie or popular sitcom the first time it's available. Many at the same time: broad consumer interest, as with traditional television or radio broadcasting. Some watch less popular programming or they view the popular content at a different time from everybody else: narrow demand, since there are very few receiving it at any one instant. Another narrowcast media form used daily is interactive electronic communications, involving only one party (you, via your computer, to and from a database) or two individuals (you, having a telephone conversation with a friend). Bloomberg, albeit with a serious focus, must deliver both kinds of "casting" or risk leaving its customers unsatisfied.

At Bloomberg, the most customized narrowcast product using the phone system is our Help Desk. Thousands of our customers call with requests for technical help each day. They all get to interact (the technical term for two people talking) with a human being after hearing the usual annoying automated answering and call-direction messages. Depending on the day and time, the helper's accent may be different, but the service isn't. Dial New York any time. In local daytime, New York answers. Call late in the evening, and Singapore or Sydney will take that same call as if they were across the street. You don't know the difference. Call Hong Kong during their nighttime hours, and Frankfurt or São Paulo may have the honor of providing assistance. That's what internationalization is really about. That's what service is all about. That's what useful technology can do.

Want to hear something our radio station broadcast hours ago? A single free phone call gets you financial markets updates

Michael Bloomberg, age 3.
The young entrepreneur
flashes his trademark smile.

Mike at Boy Scout Camp in 1955. Always industrious,
always prepared.

Outfitted in full regalia with his proud mother in the background, Michael receives the
Eagle Scout award in Boy Scouting.

Mike was Salomon's field commander for multimillion dollar mega stock trades, a role that required nerves, decisiveness, and quick thinking. (Copyright © Edward Hausner, NYT Pictures.)

Mike converses with the co-founders of his new company. Their friendship endures to this day. From left to right: Michael Bloomberg, Chuck Zegar, Tom Secunda, and Duncan MacMillan. (Copyright © Fred R. Conrad, NYT Pictures.)

Starship Bloomberg: From four founders to thousands of employees worldwide, the Bloomberg team gathers in front of the campus in Princeton, New Jersey.

The signature reception area of the Bloomberg headquarters in Manhattan is distinguished by its perpetual blur of activity. Soothing the hustle and bustle are massive tanks with rare and exotic fish. (Photo by George Diebold.)

The Bloomberg offices are a high-tech wonderland of computer consoles, clocks, wires, and feeds. (Photo by George Diebold.)

The Bloomberg terminal delivers up to the minute stock prices and in-depth reports worldwide. Users receive the latest results from Sotheby's and Yankee Stadium, *New Yorker* cartoons, restaurant listings, and movie reviews. (Photo by Duane Berger.)

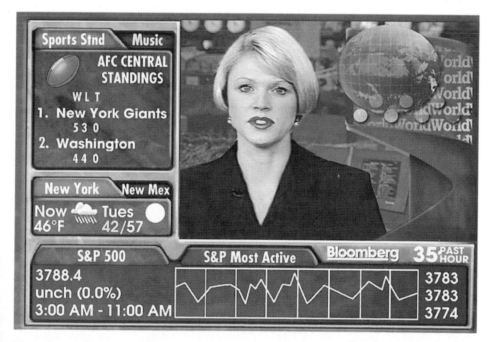

Bloomberg Information Television is a twenty-four-hours-a-day, seven-days-a-week, multi-screen format all-news program, anchored in New York, São Paulo, London, and Tokyo.

The sun never sets on Bloomberg. The Bloomberg enterprise spans the world with thousands of clients in over ninety-one countries. Here, the London office is showcased at night. (Photo by Flora Wood.)

(Right) Overlooking the Opera House in Sydney, Australia, a sailboat sporting the ubiquitous Bloomberg logo charts its course.

East meets West. "Ambassador" Bloomberg, the self-styled Colonel Sanders of his company, officiates in Korea at a Bloomberg gala in Seoul.

Flying planes is one of Mike Bloomberg's favorite activities. Here, Mike gears up to fly the Blue Angels' F/A-18 Hornet. (Photo by Mary Jane Salk.)

Apart from family and the company, Bloomberg's primary activity is his participation as chairman of the board of trustees at Johns Hopkins University where he received his undergraduate degree. (Photo by Mike Ciesielski.)

Mike is devoted to supporting educational foundations. Flanked by UNCF President William Gray (left), reporter Monica Bertran (right), and ad director Burton Waddy (seated), Bloomberg stands by one of the terminals donated to the United Negro College Fund. (Copyright © A/P Wide World.)

Bloomberg by Bloomberg. (Photo by Gregory Heisler.)

twenty-four hours a day, prerecorded and played for you on request by our computer "server," another narrowcast offering. Or, log onto our Web site. There, the audio program that your handheld phone receives is also available over the same telephone lines, direct to your computer, and with pictures. This audio on demand and interactive audio/video are new media forms that convey information: the old "sequentially accessed" broadcast media (radio and television where you can see things only in the order in which they're sent) converted by today's technology into "randomly accessed" narrowcast on-demand transmissions. Our strategy of producing many short, inexpensive "programs," assembled in real time by a computer based on individual demand, is designed for that new world.

Narrowcasting doesn't have to be as narrow as a telephone application. Our first magazine (named *Bloomberg Magazine,* of course) has a monthly circulation of 140,000. That's a lot of readers, but still it's of narrow interest. Its constituency is clients who rent our $1,100-per-month analytical terminals. When you pay that kind of money for a service, anything that helps make it more useful is welcome. Each issue of this "how to" magazine gets read cover to cover repeatedly by these professional investors. That, along with the fact that the readers' income per year is probably the highest of any such magazine, makes this a great medium for business-related and luxury product advertising.

The publication started as an even narrower idea. A number of our people suggested we publish a weekly customer newsletter. I fought the concept, arguing that our interactive terminal was a much more suitable device for customer training. Eventually, we settled on electronic teaching for specific functional instruction, with regional seminars for the more complex concept questions. Still, not all of our objectives were being met. Overcoming my stubbornness, one day I realized that those newsletter advocates had a point. But rather than publishing a limited-scope publication, why not create a highly produced, comprehensive, monthly magazine?

The articles would be broader (when and how a terminal function is going to benefit you) than the narrow training issues (how do you use it). Still, with a focus on investments, in the consumer sense, narrowcast.

Like most ideas in our company, the magazine had many parents; I was just one. The day I decided to start it, I asked one of our newswire editors, Bill Inman, if he had any ideas about how we could publish a monthly. I outlined the purpose of the magazine, what its content, size, shape, look, and feel might be. I discussed distribution and advertising policies, who would work on it, how we'd integrate it with the rest of our products, and what sort of budget we could afford. When I got to my desk at 7:00 A.M. the next morning, Bill was standing there awaiting my arrival. In his hand was a full 100-page mock-up of *Bloomberg Magazine.* He and his wife had stayed up all night cutting and pasting ads, pictures, and articles they had typed out themselves. Is there any question why he got the plum assignment to run our new project?

Most management selection in our company works that way. As a true capitalist, I've always believed in the markets' (rather than central planners') ability to make efficient selections. Here, Inman grabbed the opportunity. In most of our new ventures, a similar process takes place. We don't appoint a manager at the beginning. We simply throw everyone interested into the deep end of the pool, as it were, and stand back. It becomes obvious very quickly who the best "swimmers" are. We just watch who people go to for help and advice. And later, when we formalize a management appointment, no one's ever surprised.

*   *   *

Inman also now runs our book publishing enterprise, Bloomberg Press. It's another narrowcast media effort. Focused on business and finance, our titles will never rival the sales of famous mass-market authors like Danielle Steel or Mary Jane Salk. I know little about book publishing and take zero credit for either its initiation or success at Bloomberg—except that I did institute the system where new ideas and the best people get together. In this case, my marketing expert, Elisabeth DeMarse, and Inman's group conceived and developed the whole project from beginning to end. (While consulted before it started, I found out the name we'd chosen when my mother asked whether the Bloomberg Press she had read about had anything to do with us.)

The leverage we gain from employing creative people and letting them do their own thing is incredible. Our open physical plant encourages innovation, and our flat management structure guarantees a well-functioning meritocracy. Fortunately, for us, others do it differently. Typical company politics elsewhere stifle most free-thinking employees and discourage risk taking. The accounting oversight in most corporations prevents trying in a year the diverse creativity we institute in a month. Thank goodness. We've got enough competition as it is.

Of course, not everything we try works. One project led by Inman (but I must say, in the interest of full disclosure, pushed on him by me) was our year-and-a-half experiment publishing a monthly Sunday newspaper financial insert, *Bloomberg Personal.* The initial concept came from our salesforce, which thought large advertisers with an upscale focus would be interested. After listening to a presentation, I signed on immediately. It was a great idea, I thought.

Unfortunately, in the end, it really wasn't. We had planned on distributing through the most prestigious Sunday newspapers, but could not get many to carry us. (They thought of us as competition for ad sales rather than as a valuable supplement.) The resulting less attractive distribution meant fewer advertisers: We never sold more than one-fifth of the space we had budgeted. Then, when the cost of newsprint almost doubled, ensuring large losses every month, it was obvious we had a problem.

Inman had put together a dynamite team of writers, artists, and editors. They tinkered with the insert every issue but it was hard to improve on something that was excellent from the start. The salespeople gave it all we could ask. Try as they might, we just couldn't make ends meet.

After eighteen months of overly optimistic ad sales projections and runaway costs, I pulled the plug. It took five minutes. In a stand-up conference by the elevator, Inman and I decided to make the just-printed issue the last, and convert the concept into a subscription-based product. This would be our second magazine. We had the skills for this format in-house. We kept the title *Bloomberg Personal,* the creative people, and the salesforce from the Sunday newspaper insert. We just gave the content a different delivery form. It still meshed with our *Bloomberg Personal* Web site on the Internet ("Your subscription number on your magazine label is your password. See http://www.bloomberg.com for the latest up-to-the-instant information.") and our weekly *Bloomberg Personal* television show (TV stories relate to magazine articles relate to computer data). It still capitalized on our cross-branding policy of naming everything Bloomberg where recognition for any one product spills over onto all others. Contributions from people throughout our company were still incorporated, so we had the very best ideas. Technology we already had in place was still employed, giving us dramatic cost advantages. All vintage synergy. All vintage Bloomberg.

The new magazine was an instant success. We sold more ads for the first 100,000-circulation subscription version than we did for the last 7,000,000-circulation giveaway Sunday newspaper insert. And we went from paying others to distribute our publication to receiving subscription fees that covered our mailing and printing costs. Here a simple change of format saved the project. Generally though, deep pockets and a strong stomach help when trying new things. Few innovations are accepted right away. You must bring changes along slowly, improving them over time, building an audience with persistence and repetition. But with just as much resolve, when you find something not working, after giving it a reasonable time, you've got to take a deep breath, bite the bullet, and stop the carnage. The embarrassment of failure can't be allowed to kill the company.

The day we turned off the insert's life support, Bill and I made sure everyone worked extra late on the new venture, the subscription version of *Bloomberg Personal*. More important than any publication is our organization; we didn't want people to feel their jobs were in danger, or that they would be penalized for conceiving of or working on a "failure." At Bloomberg, all we ask is that they come up with as many new ideas as they can think of (no matter how "crazy"), and do their best on the projects we assign. If a concept is flawed, the blame and pain rest with me. The credit for whatever's right goes to them.

*   *   *

When we bought the radio station, we hired ten or so radio reporters, all with at least a few years' experience, and gave them new-world tools never seen before. For the first few months, they struggled to become accustomed to our advanced proprietary technology, which in all fairness really didn't work very well. As usual, at Bloomberg, even after installation, we were still developing. These reporters were convinced it never would work. "This just isn't the way radio is done." "It's not possible." "You don't understand broadcasting." One reporter even wanted to bring his manual typewriter to work. Today, no one questions our use of such techniques. Is it accepted? Our people act like they reported news this way all their lives. They produce more great minutes of programming per capita than any other group. And, on balance, they get paid more too. They deserve it.

With what we've developed, we routinely do things that no one else would attempt even as a demonstration—from financial reporting to weather news. Once we separately recorded every temperature, every sky condition, every form of precipitation, all possible market moves, all sports scores: the basics of what you

125

need to know in twenty seconds. Then, all day long between stories, a computer automatically checks with the National Weather Service and our Bloomberg terminal, and combines the appropriate prerecorded pieces: "At 3:12 P.M. outside, it's 50 degrees, cloudy skies with light rain, the Dow's up 3, and in baseball the Yankees lead the Orioles 6 to 5 in the 3rd." All this vital but routine information presented without a single person's involvement.

Think about having someone in front of a microphone twenty-four hours a day, seven days a week, in multiple cities where Bloomberg broadcasts, just doing routine stuff. It's mindless work—and expensive. The new economics of media don't let you stay in business if all your production is done manually. Nor will the people asked to do trivial tasks survive the boredom in this day and age. Industries other than media figured this out fifty years ago. We get more from each person by reducing the drudgery and enhancing creativity. Then we hire more people since each person now is a greater contributor. Work doesn't expand to fill capacity—opportunity does!

Some technology lets us do things just not possible manually: for example, reporting from all over the world, even when communications are poor. Digital transmission gives us perfect fidelity no matter from where we're broadcasting. Our reports from Wellington, Beijing, Johannesburg, or Prague all sound as crisp as those from New York, Washington, DC, or Los Angeles. Often, the interviewee is on one continent, the interviewer on a second, the anchor on a third, and the audience on a fourth. (Our New York writer might question, via satellite, a businessperson sitting in our Sydney office. One of our Tokyo television talents sometimes incorporates the New York interview into a segment including real-time reporting on the Nikkei Stock Index. The combined piece may then be shown on our European twenty-four-hour-a-day TV network. Does it sound strange? Happens every day.)

We try to deliver information as efficiently as possible. We prepare our broadcasts, turn our voices into data, save the data just the way print is stored, and have the computer air the programs off the hard disk while we go on to the next story. Instead of voicing our stories several times during a two-hour rotation (we must repeat them to satisfy the itinerant listener or viewer), we do it automatically. The computer, not our valuable people, wastes time doing the repetition. If we stumble over our words, we do it over again. Others, working the old "live to tape" or "live to air" way, can't. As Winkler always says, "More/better/faster."

When we first started, people challenged the notion that a computer could compete with a "live" person. But the traditional national news broadcasts on network television aren't live anymore. For most of the United States, even though Tom Brokaw, Peter Jennings, and Dan Rather are talking into a microphone as everyone watches, the stories they introduce or "wrap around" were recorded much earlier.

Today, large broadcasters are starting to do things our way, and old-line practitioners feel threatened. "There's got to be something wrong," they tell me. Why? "I don't know, that's just not the way it's always been done." Technology makes our jobs different but more productive and more interesting. Technology frees us to do more creative work. Technology is responsible for the employment of more and more people, not fewer and fewer.

Politicians and labor leaders sometimes exploit a common fear of the unknown: that technology (as represented now by PCs and the Internet) creates an underclass; that it drives a wedge through society, separating the haves and have-nots. Such fears are unfounded. We've already been through this with television. TV has been a great enabling technology, as powerful as Gutenberg's press. When television was first invented, politicians and social reformers screamed that the poor could never afford to own the "hardware" and would be denied equal access to ideas and educational opportunities. Well, everybody's got television today. In many bombed-out houses in Bosnia without sewage systems or running water, there are electric generators, TVs, and satellite dishes.

Television brought down the Berlin Wall and, in turn, the whole Soviet Union by broadcasting ideas and pictures from the West that showed a better way to live. TV opened up China. Television has unified people around the world with pop music, comedy, and drama—and the serious kind of information that Bloomberg provides. Today's new technology will do similar incredible things for society.

*　　*　　*

To most, multimedia is sound and moving pictures on a television or computer screen. To us, the meaning of "multi" is broader. Print, radio, telephones, and electronic billboards also deliver useful information and entertainment. At Bloomberg, we try to use all these. We have news-service copy in hundreds of newspapers. We print two magazines, three newsletters (for the natural-gas, asphalt, and petroleum businesses), and a whole series of books. We have real-time reports on the World Wide Web, audio financial reports available free via an 800-number telephone service, and market stories consistently updating billboards in train stations and on the sides of buildings. We have a New York City radio station and a national radio syndicate. We produce television worldwide, in multiple languages and multiple formats. And of course, we have our original product, the Bloomberg terminal, linking business, financial, and investment professionals globally.

Why use all media forms rather than focus on just one? What business are we in? Some companies declare themselves to be "in radio" or "in television" or "in newspapers," and so on. We have a greater vision. Bloomberg is in the business of giving its customers the information they need—no matter what that information is—where and when they need it, in whatever form is most appropriate. We don't shoehorn programs into less-than-optimal presentation formats, or deliver them at inappropriate times and places. With all methods at our disposal, we do better. We give our customers what they need, not just what we have. When there's a difference between the two, we create or adopt a new medium—we don't ask our customers to accept less.

Consider the range of needs. Want real-time stock prices? They are clearly best delivered over a computer terminal that can update a preselected customized monitor or satisfy requests independently of the thousands of securities others are watching. That's the Bloomberg terminal. Complex, in-depth reports? This type of information is best suited for print delivery, where you can reread paragraphs, make notes, pause to do something else, or consult another source. Books, magazines, and newspapers, depending on timeliness, cost, and location, all have their place—like *Bloomberg Press, Bloomberg Magazine, Bloomberg Personal,* and, in your local newspaper, *Bloomberg News.* The use of sound and pictures is most effective when action and human emotion are the story; reading about a gold-medal Olympic performance isn't the same as hearing it on *Bloomberg Radio* or seeing it happen on *Bloomberg TV.* Miss some vital information? Then use another medium, the telephone, to retrieve a story already aired: With or without pictures, for archived recordings, your telephone to *Bloomberg Audio* service or your PC to the *Bloomberg Online* web site lets you get things when you want them, not when someone else has decided to broadcast them. Just call our office and select a category by hitting the right buttons. Didn't understand something the first time you encountered it? That's another great use of the telephone. Call the Bloomberg Help Desk for customized personal assistance—another form of interactive media. More information on demand over the phone.

At Bloomberg, just as our content is tailored to what's best for the story, it's also made for what suits the user best. What's our customer doing when he or she needs news? Where is he or she? One can't read print or watch television when taking a shower, jogging in the park, or driving to work. One can't read a whole book when one has only two minutes to get caught up. If one's traveling, one can't receive local content easily. By having all forms of media, we can focus on utility, not just our own commercial interests.

Most companies pay lip service to multimedia, but few actually deliver. They make minority investments in each other to get "experience" in the field. But when they buy another firm, they usually run it separately from their own, with separate people, content, culture, and profit centers.

Some find external reasons for why they can't expand into new communications and technologies. Some blame the laws (prohibiting cross-ownership of TV and newspapers in the same market, or Federal Trade Commission anticompetition restrictions). Some blame the unions. (While there are exceptions, unions are not irrational. If management can make what it wants to work in the union members' interest, management will get the best possible ally.) Some cite analysts' demand for short-term results. (Investors generally aren't that stupid, and management should be worrying about its business, not its stock price. In these cases, the executives have no guts and no vision. They're afraid to take risks or accept responsibility. "Blame anyone else. I don't want to screw up before I retire" is the subtext.)

At Bloomberg, we don't resist multiple cross-product responsibility. We don't have problems blending short-term performance with long-term growth and development. And so far, we're not obsolete because the difference between those timid, failing companies and Bloomberg is people—from top to bottom.

*   *   *

That's money talking. It's what got us the publicity—made Bloomberg, if not a household name, at least a synonym for success—and ensures that some day I'll have a long obituary in the *New York Times*.

Computers
for Virgins

Technology:
Politics and Promises

My education in the 1960s and
1970s era of horse-and-buggy computer systems formed the basis of
what I did more than a decade later, when I brought the Bloomberg
terminal to financial desks worldwide. In terms of hardware and
software, we've advanced eons since those early days. What I discovered then about data management, and people management,
serves me well today. Two things haven't changed in twenty years
or twenty centuries: the need for information; and the users of
data, with their bravery, jealousy, adventurousness, and fear of the
new. No matter what systems we create in the next decades, these
two statements will be the same.

My first experience using computers came early in my Salomon
career. In the late 1960s, not too long after I was sorting slips of
paper in the Purchase & Sales department and sharpening pencils
for Connie and Ira in Utilities, I found myself staring at stacks
of *Wall Street Journals*. They were our source of historical stock
prices. Nearby, we had dozens of loose-leaf notebooks that

131

contained public stock ownership lists. Piles of papers crammed with facts about the companies behind those securities littered our desks. Each night, a clerk would painstakingly go through the day's transactions and, like Bob Cratchit, manually update all of our trade history records. This mid-twentieth-century information-gathering operation was in the tradition of the Dickensian, quill-pen nineteenth century, but it was the only way we could get the information we needed to conduct our trading business.

And we at Salomon weren't alone. Wall Street, up to its eaves in paper, was peopled by thousands of clerks who catalogued details by hand, year after year after year. Near the end of the "go-go" market of the 1960s, the paper deluge became so difficult to manage that the New York Stock Exchange shortened its workweek; for a while, it actually closed on Wednesdays. Many securities firms couldn't cope with the avalanche. In the end, Francis I. DuPont, Mc-Donnell & Co., Hayden Stone, Goodbody & Co., and Loeb, Rhoades, were among the casualties brought down by too many forms.

As a Wall Streeter in the late 1960s, I experienced firsthand the paper-driven shakeout and the frustration of not having what you needed, accurately, easily, and when it was useful—not to mention the damage done when a cup of coffee spilled over your only copy of some important document. A solution existed, however. From what I had read, computers were good at storing information. You entered your data at night when the market was closed and you had lots of time. During the day, when you needed facts and numbers quickly, you hit a button and they would come back instantly. The computer makers told us that all we had to do was buy a machine for every desk, stick in the information—and voilà, problem solved.

I approached John Gutfreund and Billy Salomon about changing an information collection and retrieval process that hadn't been altered much since the firm was founded in 1911. "We should automate this," I said to them. "I'm told it won't take long or cost very much. We'll get instant access to the data we collect manually in all those books and even to those 'inaccessible' records stored on the company's mainframe computer."

My bosses were open enough to explore the idea. I was directed to Joe Lombard, the Salomon partner who ran our Boston office and who always found time to humor young kids with crazy ideas. After much discussion, I convinced him, and in turn the administrative partner, Vince Murphy, that computer workstations for the salespeople and traders were the future for investment firms. We already had a big IBM machine to handle bookkeeping, so extending its use to the trading floor made sense. One computer or another computer—they all seemed the same. We would just wire them together and get what we wanted. It would be simple and non-controversial, and I would be doing Salomon a big favor. Or so I thought.

Murphy and Lombard went to the Executive Committee and made my case. While they probably never envisaged the producer/overseer data integration of today, they were way ahead in letting accounting information be used by those who generated it.

The answer from the Committee wasn't what I expected. "They've agreed to let you do the automation," I was told. "But you can only work on it part-time so it doesn't get in the way of your main responsibilities, selling equities."

Fair enough. I didn't want to give up my block trading power base anyway. It just meant I now had to do my regular day job with stocks and simultaneously develop a computer system in the evenings. No sweat. What I hadn't counted on, though, was the Committee's insistence that I create something for fixed income as well as equities. That directive shouldn't have surprised me actually, as bonds were Salomon's first love. Since the beginning of the century, Salomon Brothers' primary business had been making markets in government and corporate debt. During the First World War, Salomon Brothers & Hutzler was one of the biggest sellers of the Liberty Bonds that financed our military. Decades later, when there were still few firms in the fixed-income market, Salomon traders liked to say a bond wasn't worth its purchase price unless it received a bid from SB&H.

Nobody really knew how the computerization I was proposing would wind up affecting our business, nor how debt securities fit into my suggestions for automation. But Salomon traded bonds just like it traded stocks, and Salomon had bond data just as it had stock data. So why not build one simple system for everything?

*   *   *

What we eventually created at Salomon we called the "B Page" (no, B Page did not stand for Bloomberg Page, but I didn't mind if that's what people thought). When it finally worked, by coincidence, its very first message sent to all users was the announcement of my general partnership appointment after the December 1972 special partners' meeting in Billy's office.

It all began when the firm assigned me a junior computer programmer, Jessy Gerstel, who was willing to work nights in addition to his regular daytime job (for no additional pay). I bought Chinese food for the computer room operators, to get our software testing moved to the top of their queue. I bribed the data collection department with beer and pizza to gather and enter the securities information we needed. Together, in 1970, Jessy and I began building Salomon's initial on-line information system, parts of which survive to this day.

The project was not just to write some computer code. One task was to find the right display device to put in front of the traders and salespeople. (PCs didn't exist in those days.) On its equity desks, Salomon already used one that flashed stock quotes, a machine called "Ultronics," manufactured by General Telephone & Electronics, now GTE Corporation. But it was cumbersome, not suited for the bond markets, and technologically impossible to employ for the data distribution we contemplated.

These desktop terminals weren't general-purpose computers; they were just sophisticated successors to the old ticker tape. An

134

electronic screen blinked the last sale, bid, and offer prices for stocks traded on all major U.S. stock exchanges. "We should remove Ultronics and install Quotrons," I told my bosses. Quotron was another brand of terminal just becoming popular, leased by a small, private California company. "Quotrons will work better and connect with our in-house computers directly from the desks. We'll have access to our trading records, be able to retrieve all the publicly available securities indicative data (ratings, call features, P/E ratios, and so on) instantly and effortlessly, and have our own electronic messaging system for fast, reliable internal communication."

I encountered one immediate nontechnical problem in switching terminals, though. The existing vendor, GTE Corporation, was Salomon's only investment banking client of note, and John Gutfreund's personal responsibility.

"You do what's right for your project and don't worry about the rest of the relationship," John said. "Each decision has to stand on its own."

Right on! Supporting one part of your business with another is fine. But not having the independent check of the marketplace is the easiest way I know to fool yourself. "Each tub to its own bottom" is a long-term protection I've always thought as valuable as any short-term cross-subsidization gains. By all means, use skills, data, technology, branding, people, processes, and so on, from elsewhere in your company—but make sure supply/demand can kill what people really don't want.

Another contentious task in building Salomon's in-house sales/trading system was information control, exemplified by the selection of the central computer that the desktop Quotron terminals would access for pricing and security data. Until then, salespeople and traders were viewed as separate ("stand alone," in computerese) from the staff people, so no one cared what they used. Suddenly, however, these "producers" were about to interface the new desktop Quotrons to minicomputers, and, in turn, to the big old bureaucracy-controlled IBM mainframe computers.

For the first time, this path would let those generating the firm's data actually access and manipulate it themselves without the staff's oversight.

In those days, bureaucrats never let users have their "own" computers and, more importantly, access to the firm's internal information. The clerical guardians would be terminally (pardon the pun) threatened. If users could see the numbers, they might do something with them independently—thus diminishing their reliance on these gatekeepers. At Salomon, the staff went straight to Billy and John: "You can't let Bloomberg jeopardize the firm's books and records." Their real fears were that others would see how inefficient they really were, and the possibility that a new computer system could replace these mandarins. Naturally, they wanted no part of it.

Just as controversial as the issue of access was buying non-IBM equipment. This the support people considered worse than heresy, and they fought it with great tenacity. In those days, acquiring computers from small start-up technology companies was career-threatening for clerical and technical types at big organizations. The new technologies required less menial support and changed rote jobs into ones requiring thought. To protect their turf, those vulnerable pulled out all stops. Additional dissension was created by outsiders. With IBM's dominance of the data-processing business at risk, its salespeople resorted to lashing out at all involved. They went so far as to often insinuate nefarious relationships between users' purchasing agents and minicomputer manufacturers. Questioning the financial health of mongrel manufacturers was their standard operating procedure. (The possibility that others' offerings could fill the customers' needs more effectively and efficiently was never considered, which was why IBM eventually got into trouble. Not admitting your problems means you can't fix them. Changing IBM's culture to one focused on consumer need has been Lou Gerstner's great contribution to that company and the main reason for its turnaround.) And when the moneys diverted to these minicomputer manufacturers became substantial, the battle really turned nasty.

Dealings with a large, single-source supplier are always difficult to end. The seller invariably has back-door channels into its customer, which it can use to thwart change. The buyer fears the uncertainty of the new and mentally tries justifying the known devil. People feel threatened by the normal reexamination of practices that vendor-switching invariably instigates: When forced to change one thing, the boss can rationalize other changes as well. The result? Everyone potentially affected bands together and fights viciously to protect their fiefdoms and livelihoods. Given the stakes, no tactic is out of bounds.

At age twenty-eight, I was finding out an eternal truth: Making change is difficult.

*   *   *

Not only was I fighting the front office/minicomputer, back office/mainframe computer battle, but the interdepartmental computer wars as well. In every organization, each group wants its own automation needs filled independently. Not a competition for resources problem, or even an unwillingness to cooperate, but a "we need it now" issue. Separate development, being more limited, is much faster. Each department fights to go it alone, pick its own computers, write its own programs, collect its own data, hire its own consultants.

In the short history of computing, this process has played out repeatedly. Users get tired of the formal information-processing department. Those faceless bureaucrats want justification for spending money on hardware ("How dare they?" declare the users). They insist on setting priorities other than "all of the above." ("I don't have time for this detail work. Just do everything!") They ask nasty questions like, "Where will the data come from?" "Who's going to enter it?" "What happens if the needs change?" "What will we do if the computer crashes?" In other words, the experts want to make you confront all the things that have to be faced—but that you want to avoid because there are no simple, inexpensive, quick, "clean" answers.

Then, along comes the snake-oil salesperson with the PC. The key letter is "P," for "personal." Suddenly, you go to a store and buy a computer on your credit card. You sit down and write simple stand-alone programs that actually do something without all those needless contingency plans the experts want to foist on you. You dispense with backup and expandability. You don't bother using common standards to incorporate others' needs later. You go it alone. Just as you suspected: Those bureaucrats knew nothing.

But a troubling thing happens after a while. Your business gets better and now your simple programs can't handle it. No problem. Hire a few unsupervised programmers to make the software more capable (read complex). Of course fancier software means bigger PCs. Bigger PCs mean enhanced operating systems. Enhanced operating systems mean more crashes. Crashes? And we don't have backup? What were we thinking? Who *was* supervising those programmers? It's not my fault, you say. Blame the bureaucracy. They weren't part of the process? What now? And by the way, we want to merge our data with that of another department. What do you mean it's incompatible? Or that we can't borrow some parts from your computer when ours breaks? We're spending *how much*? What do I tell the CEO?

So develop the systems administrators (read information-processing bureaucrats). They start insisting on budgets and justification for hardware and software expenditures that are already eclipsing those of the old mainframe days. Unfortunately, no one has yet repealed the laws of gravity or something for nothing. You never get more than you pay for. Usually, you get less. You want more computers? More expense. Will you get more computing? Sometimes.

The new bureaucrats start forcing security and backup and commonality. With the backing of the accountants, lawyers, and consultants, the days of go-it-alone go. All of a sudden, everyone's PCs are linked together. The new fashion of the times becomes "networking." Now common standards and coordinating software development are a necessity. Each connected PC suddenly can affect all the others in the network. Viruses have to be rooted out, excess traffic banned, database access restricted, staffs supervised, allocations made, hardware acquisitions centralized. Even priorities have to be set since once again there is more to do than the resources available can handle. You've come full circle.

The differences among the three stages of computer evolution are as much human as technical. From the old big mainframes with bureaucratic administration, to limited-function, distributed, "do everything yourself" processing using PCs without any coordination or control, to centrally managed networked resources, no one's ever satisfied except the hardware manufacturers. For users, it's politics, not engineering. For the vendors, it's sales. For me at Salomon Brothers, herding all the elephants, trying to get everyone to use a common platform and computer databases, it was a nightmare.

*   *   *

By 1970 at Salomon, we had gotten the salespeople and traders, the debt and equity people, the U.S. and overseas users, the producers and support staffs, to agree on what technology the whole company needed in order to compete. It was *the* great victory needed to build the B Page (and to build any software project, for that matter). And a lot harder to achieve at Salomon than later, when we started Bloomberg in 1981. With our own company, we didn't need to get anyone's acquiescence. We just did what we thought right and that's what our salespeople sold. But this wasn't possible where we were just another group of employees. There we had to ask, convince, or beg.

In the real world, unlike the one used in business school textbook cases, corporate administration often doesn't, and sometimes can't, commit to firmwide projects across specific departments or branches. Individual units may not want a centrally selected product or service. It might conflict with something they're already doing. Or cost more. Or take longer to be delivered. In the days of profit-center accounting, some departments may just refuse to pay a share no matter how necessary the product or service is to the long-term overall corporate operation and regardless of "central's" explicit directives. Remember, the original thirteen colonies in North America started their revolt against England over the issue of taxation divorced from representation. That's relatively unimportant compared to a trader's profit and loss!

Salomon back then was no exception. The Executive Committee told us to build for everyone. But it didn't order everyone to cooperate with us, to accept the system, or even to fund it. So we had to cajole, trade, mislead, do anything short of physical violence that worked to get it done. The users on one side of the trading room demanded X to go along. The ones on the other side demanded Y. Thus, we had to deliver (or at least promise to deliver) both X *and* Y (and for someone else, Z). For some, our incentive was a carrot; for some, it was a stick. With others, we just prayed they'd "die" before we did.

The B Page gave Salomon salespeople and traders proprietary information. But with so many different people having access within Salomon worldwide, security was a big issue. Even today, people who empower others with information face a daunting, no-win task. The only perfect protection for data is to give no one anything. And that's the traditional information-processing management's instinct. Unfortunately, as more and more businesses and functions become data-dependent, those in control have no choice. They are forced to open up, albeit reluctantly.

The conflict in practice is between paying lip service to free distribution of information and actually implementing that policy. Conceptually, at least for the record, everyone agrees on the value of sharing data. But there are so many special cases where someone doesn't want disclosure, it's almost impossible for a corporate computer-system coordinator actually to implement a consistent structure. Exceptions based on who, what, where, and when, even by whim, always overwhelm any security decision. Why, I wonder, is this contentiousness never mentioned in those advertisements for computers that show users doing everything together short of holding hands?

My sympathies have always been with the information-technology managers on this issue. These people have an impossible job. If they continuously disallow or fail to provide simple, inexpensive data retrieval, they eventually get themselves fired. If they allow access and get caught in a security breach, they are thrown out instantly. Damned slowly if they don't, damned quickly if they do. No wonder they have a short life expectancy in their jobs.

Often, though, the whole data security issue is overblown at most corporations that think they have a lot to guard. Pilferage and leakage are costs of doing business. Live with them. While some restrictions make sense, many are ridiculous. Suppose someone has a copy of another firm's proprietary information. What could one do with much of it? Even insiders can't decode many reports coming from their own firm's computers, lots of which are wrong and misleading anyway. Want to know the others' secrets? Just hire a few of their disgruntled junior people. Or what if someone intercepted your commercial transactions on a phone line? Many people already have access to your credit card numbers, including all the waiters in the restaurants you frequent. In the United States, under federal laws, you as a consumer aren't responsible for unauthorized merchandise charged to your account (over $50), so, so what? What about even gaining entry to someone else's bank account? I, at least, have great trouble cashing a $100 bill, and find a $50 note unusable in a taxi. What on earth would I do with an electronic check for $10 zillion payable to cash? Besides, with today's volume and cost cutting, banks are always erroneously crediting and debiting funds to the wrong account. In the end, with a few very well publicized exceptions repeatedly brought to our attention by companies selling security, it all gets sorted out.

Nevertheless, a big part of our development job at Salomon was information limitation: deciding who had the right to the data as opposed to who had the need. This was exacerbated by our determination to give users the same capabilities overseas as domestically. In those days, letting foreign telephone access into a local office computer was truly revolutionary. Anyone wishing to sidetrack a project could always raise myriad unprovable and irrefutable potential security breaches. Today, we just close our eyes and let it happen. Utility has overwhelmed risk.

Should one office see business done by another? Should the salespeople see the eventual profit or loss from opportunities they have brought in? Or the trader see a recap of all business transacted firmwide with a specific salesperson's account? These were all policy rather than computer issues that we resolved daily while developing the B Page. And then we re-resolved them the next day when the issue was raised by someone else—invariably, in the opposite direction. And the day after, the same again. Each revision required changes to line after line of computer software. Then the users asked what took so long to deliver the system.

*   *   *

We humans are not computers; that's the main reason it takes so much time to build information-processing systems. I say, "Vive la différence," but it means we will always have trouble communicating with those devices. As human beings living in an analog world, a great part of our communications is implied; inconsistencies are dealt with by obscuration or ignorance or exception. We know what you mean, as opposed to what you say. Computers are exactly the reverse. Their great strength is that they are literal. With no shades of gray, these digital devices do very fast, and very accurately, *exactly* what you command—no more and no less. *Nothing* is left to chance, implied, or assumed. You write a program that just says, go from A to B, it goes from A to B. Period. Something unexpected in the way? Sorry. Crash! After all, you didn't tell the computer differently. Did you never mean it to go from A to B on holidays? Or when the temperature was below freezing? Or when your truck weighed more than the bridge between A and B could support? Tough. Computers take you at your word, not your thoughts. Fail to specify exactly what to do in every possible unusual situation and you have the potential for disaster. Program a ballistic missile to hit just Moscow, and it's equally likely to hit Moscow, Idaho, as Moscow, Russia.

Try to list all the things that could unexpectedly crop up in a trip from A to B. It's virtually impossible. Make it harder: Try specifying in advance which way to go in every unlikely potential conflict (e.g., normally, I'll go around a turtle crossing the road, but I'll squash it if I'm rushing to the hospital with a passenger suffering a heart attack, unless of course it's not a serious heart attack). Then, to make it truly impossible, get *all* users to agree on that course of action and stick to the agreement!

Producing even a small computer program with a reasonable number of "what-if" contingency plans is a decent-size undertaking—with costs and delays. Settling the operational issues is often even tougher. What happens if the software crashes, the hardware fails, or the input data contain errors? Does business stop? Do we close our doors? Writing the computer code isn't the problem. It's identifying possibilities and getting broad concurrence from all users as to what we want the computer to do, every time—and what is an acceptable definition of "every time"? It's convincing people to ask for a reasonable amount of functionality in a manageable set of likely circumstances, and then keeping them from changing their minds during the development process. It's deciding how the computer fits into the rest of your world. The infamous "man–machine interface": That's what's hard.

Much of my battle at Salomon was forcing acceptance of common systems for different products, for debt and equity, for government bonds and for corporate ones, in dollar-denominated areas and in foreign currency ones. Computers like consistency, and when the problem to solve is "show risk across all securities issued by a given company," something has to be used to tie them together. At Salomon, because I insisted on a common syntax (the sequence of keystrokes one enters to ask a question) that applied to all products, calculations written for one area worked everywhere. Then, by convincing the bond traders to use common identifiers, such as T for bonds of American Telephone & Telegraph Company (the same symbol used for the company's stock on the New York Stock Exchange) instead of a historical hodgepodge (TEL, ATT, AT&T, and so on), data from all parts of the company were able to be combined in new and useful ways. Sound like small accomplishments? Try getting a bunch of securities traders to agree on anything! Each always has a million reasons why something should be customized. Of course, if they all got their own way, the company would have collapsed.

Similarly with dates. In America, we write month, day, year. In Europe, it's day, month, year. Is that important? What date is 3/5? March 5th or May 3rd? With numbers, in the United States, we put commas after every three digits going to the left of the decimal point. In many parts of the world, the convention is to use commas rather than periods or "noughts," and in others, the decimal point is a comma. That's fine, but we needed one standard globally. What's domestic and what's foreign? Is it 3:00 P.M. or 1500 hours? That dollar-denominated security is in which dollars (U.S., Hong Kong, Canadian, Australian, Singaporian, New Zealand, and so on)? Once again, human issues need standardization to make technology work. Doing business around the world may sound romantic. It may even be lucrative. It's certainly complex.

*   *   *

A rule of thumb in software is that 90 percent of the costs go into building the last 10 percent of the functionality. Successful design and implementation demand the political skills and courage to reconcile the 100 percent specification needed for approval with the slightly-less-deliverables that are possible in the real world. As I found out at Salomon and again with the Bloomberg terminal, you promise users everything; then you build what you can, and what you think they need. It's the only successful strategy for a systems developer. People always say, "I can't do my job without that last little bit." But that last little bit is not only so hard to build, it's invariably so complex to use that no one ever does. Making all settle for a touch less is the job. Management has to reconcile the conflicts between stated needs and what can be delivered, and when that's not possible, to make the decision for everyone, a priori. Companies in the end need direction, not discussion.

Back then, and now, I've always insisted on building a simple "do a few things" version of software up front. Most people are terrible at understanding and enunciating what they actually do day in and day out, and on what basis they make decisions. They're even worse at defining what tools they *would* use in the future. But if you give them something they can see and touch, then both they and you can get experience as to a program's utility and applicability, or at least have a common basis for enhancements. And chances are, they'll use what you give them up front, forget about anything else that was requested earlier, and think you're a hero for delivering "what they always wanted."

Fortunately, our competitors never work this way. They study. They plan. They work toward getting consensus and approval and closure. They try to define it all up front, even specifying the end game from the beginning. Ridiculous! You can do a six-month software project in twelve months. You can probably do a twelve-month project in two years. You cannot do a two-year project, ever. Humans need to see results in time frames they can handle. A project takes too long when it consumes so much time to build that no one remembers who requested it, what specifically was ordered, what its purpose was, or even whatever happened to that since-departed person who initiated all this.

At Salomon, we promised everything and set out to build less, but something we could install before new management took over with less enthusiasm for our project. In software, you almost never deliver to the person who ordered it: Because of the time it takes to build and every organization's turnover at the top, you usually deliver to a successor. Besides, who really remembers what he or she asked for a year ago? And who is in a business that still needs what was requested twelve months earlier?

Often, to solve this political problem, managements buy outside services rather than build their own software in-house. This avoids facing the users' demands head-on and, they think, dramatically shortens the time to delivery. (Since we're in the business of providing "turnkey solutions," we obviously think this is a great idea.) But many times, since managements buy technology still under development or insist on radical customization, they're buying essentially a totally new, untried product. The risks and delays turn out to be identical no matter who employs the programmers. This outsourcing strategy often fails for two additional reasons. Traditionally, vendors get paid when they deliver, not when it works. What you order is seldom what you get, and after the check clears, you have little recourse. Then, as with building in-house, once you've already waited for delivery, projected delays always appear shorter than the time it would take to start over.

I've always thought that buyers who "outsource" should find a way to try products as they'll actually use them before they pay the bill and even, if possible, before giving a firm order. The test version, the simulation, the still-in-development scenario is not something I'm comfortable acquiring. The risks attendant with developing technology I think properly belong to the manufacturer or software writer. They get the profits if it works; they should take the grief if it doesn't. It's their business; don't make it yours. My rule is: See it work exactly the way you'll use it (same volume, environment, time of day, and so on) or don't buy it! Demand goods, not promises. If you remember one thing from this book, make it: "Buy what's deliverable, not what could be!"

Merrill did this with us. They had no obligation to take our product until it performed, and we guaranteed delivery before the time they could start developing it themselves. I wish all buyers would adopt this practice. Competitors are always contrasting our products with what they say they'll deliver later on. They will do more, better, faster, cheaper, easier, or so they promise. I love the comparison. They compare Bloomberg, an operating F18 jet fighter, with their still-being-developed "witch on a broomstick." Their plane will go faster, fly higher, turn quicker, need less maintenance, and so on, than ours—*when* they build it. Sure! Anything they say! But our system works today as compared to their laundry list of "pie-in-the-sky" impractical things for tomorrow. It's our off-the-shelf product versus their business plan, their press release. I'll never understand why we don't get 100 percent of everyone's business.

Most of our customers and competitors are not structured to write software—or even to order it intelligently from a third party. To implement data-processing systems takes compromise: Requests are often mutually exclusive. It requires flexibility: Things in practice are invariably different from the plan, and they change with time. It demands imagination: Envisaging future requirements and potential uses is hard to do, yet, because of long development times, that's what you must build for. It also calls for strength: With changing requirements and often the political problem of being a cost center without revenue, staying the course is a challenge. Lastly, it takes leadership: The great system advances are pushed on users, not demanded by them. You can't run governments or companies successfully by polling or asking for suggestions. Someone must have a vision and take others along, not the reverse.

*   *   *

While our Salomon B Page development grew, we delegated responsibilities and included more people. It really became a group effort. As with all projects, those who started it got absorbed by those who took it to the next stage. Some of the people we hired were extraordinarily talented. All worked exceptionally hard. And what we delivered was truly revolutionary. A version of the computer system we built in the early 1970s is still in use at Salomon today—and, twenty-five years after inception, is still better than most internally developed market data retrieval and analytical systems currently being installed at other securities firms. The reason was teamwork.

A manager's primary job is to get those he or she supervises to work together—particularly with technology, where many contribute to any single project. Back at Salomon, and today at Bloomberg, we do that. The resulting cooperation, more than anything, was and is responsible for our ability to deliver useful things. I once sent out an announcement to all the programmers that, henceforth, no one would have a title. I've always thought titles are disruptive at best. They separate, create class distinctions, and inhibit communications. If you don't get a title, you quit. If you do get one, you start thinking other firms may want to pay you more, now that you're officially recognized as superior to what you were previously.

The manure hit the proverbial fan as soon as I did it. The Salomon personnel department manager went ballistic. How could we manage without constantly reminding everyone who they were inferior to? He started screaming that I was out of control—to me, to Gutfreund, and particularly to my nemesis, the new Executive Committee member Dick Rosenthal. People already possessing titles complained. Those hoping to get them soon did too (but a little less strenuously). The results of the policy change? There was no increase in personnel turnover. People worked together better than before.

Another software development practice I started at Salomon (and apply at Bloomberg today) was to insist on an explanation from the programmers of what they were trying to do before I let them do it. I don't have as much technical expertise as even a junior computer whiz, but that's the programmers' problem. They've got to describe it to me in language I can understand. Again and again, if that's what it takes. Describing the "how and when" forces them to face all those things they initially glossed over when they thought about the "what"—utility, cost, maintenance, data quality, redundancy, training, cooperation. They have to satisfy me, a novice. (Do I really comprehend what they are saying? I'm a human BEWARE OF DOG sign. Programmers never know whether I really understand, just as they don't know whether there's a pit bull behind that door.)

The information retrieval system we built at Salomon in the early 1970s was rudimentary by later standards, but it made Salomon more productive versus its competitors, and more knowledgeable than its customers. It was designed for internal use only—what was needed then. The last thing Salomon wanted to do in those days was give clients enhanced capabilities and more accurate data. The end of fixed commissions in 1975 had reduced the profit margins in the industry's traditional business. Rather than acting as the customers' agent, firms were making the big money in arbitrage and trading strategies, for which buy-side clients were really competitors. Trading came to rely more on mathematical skills and less on guts. For this, Salomon needed an edge. And that's exactly what having the only useful data retrieval and analytical tool in the industry gave them in the 1970s. With the closed proprietary system we built, Salomon got for a period what no one else had. Salomon jumped way ahead, and stayed that way for a decade. In a sense, for ten years, when Salomon went to a knife fight, it carried a gun.

By the early 1980s, though, the financial world turned topsy-turvy, in part because the Wall Street broker/dealers lost exclusive control of the information and the ability to manipulate it. Services such as the Bloomberg terminal eventually became the great levelers, giving everyone access to the same facts and same capabilities. What would have happened had I been allowed to stay at Salomon after the Phibro deal? Would we have stayed ahead of the competition? Would we have given our clients a proprietary B Page to lock them in? Might internal controls have prevented Salomon's Treasury Bond trading scandal in 1991? Would it have stopped the buy-side from getting tools to even the fight with the sell-side? All useless conjecture (but fun to speculate on nevertheless).

In 1981, after I left Salomon, my successor there told his subordinates that Bloomberg had been wrong. Systems' job was not to give the organization the support it needed. Rather, Systems had to "reduce expectations." (I couldn't make this stuff up, folks!) If he could cut the demand for services, he'd have less of a problem supplying them, he argued. In turn, he'd have less maintenance to provide and lower depreciation expense to explain away, and require fewer difficult-to-manage computer programmers. All this would mean fewer headaches for management in resolving conflicting needs, making unpopular resource allocation decisions, and sometimes having to say "no" to powerful and demanding revenue producers. Of course, if he cut back expectations entirely, the firm wouldn't need him either, but he didn't plan to carry it *that* far.

While with a lower profile he did manage to survive for a number of years, Salomon almost didn't. In the late 1980s and early 1990s, tragically, Salomon went from having a distinct lead in automation support to being an also-ran. Just when its business required more computerized risk control; right when the competitive landscape for the first time required broker/dealers to provide clients with proprietary technical services or have independents like Bloomberg control the relationship with their clients; simultaneously with Salomon expanding into new markets and more sophisticated products requiring complex analytics—getting less computer support almost bankrupted the firm.

Given that the head of technology can have enormous impact on a company's success, I've always been amazed at who gets picked for this job. The lucky candidate is never considered for other jobs in the management structure. When the choice is an executive with business skills, it's invariably someone whose career elsewhere in the company is floundering (as was the case with me). Never is anyone who is destined for greater things rotated through this position to gain broader experiences. Given the function's importance, difficulty, and potential for greatness or disaster, you'd think the CEO would be smarter in his or her selections.

Systems Areas, Information-Processing Departments, Computer Support Divisions—or whatever moniker is fashionable at the time—are typically run by technicians, people whose chief skills are in understanding the internal mechanics of computer hardware. Worse, these senior people have "high-level duties" that invariably keep them from the dirty work of setting priorities, ensuring the suitability of new developments, and giving the common worker incentives. No wonder these Chief Information Officers (CIOs) have a very short life expectancy. In reality, their technical knowledge isn't valuable in supplying the function they are hired to provide. Knowing the company's products, competitive position, accounting, marketing, and personnel policies is what's critical to success for any CIO; that knowledge, along with leadership, business acumen, and hands-on management, is what's needed.

Having the ability to select, manage, and motivate people is the job. Driving the development and operations of support services is the task. Having "the vision thing" is the mission. Companies need people with imagination and energy, particularly with regard to technology. Unbridled enthusiasm and belief that anything's possible may not be the real world, but trying things with low probabilities of success and big payoffs is a lot better than the alternatives. These CIOs have to stay ahead of the curve and take the rest of the organization along. Following or doing the same old thing won't do!

*　　　*　　　*

The computerization of Wall Street hasn't always produced the results everyone predicted. Salomon got an advantage with the superior decision-support technology we built, but its earnings were no better than its competitors'. Would Salomon have been worse off without such support? Or do increased capabilities encourage more risky behavior and thus poorer performance? The same questions apply to the entire securities industry. It installed computers to handle transaction processing more efficiently and reduce risk. The volume of shares traded went up, the commission rates per share traded went down, and industry employment grew. But the industry's increases in profits came almost exclusively from new, manually processed products, not the ones the computer helped. And as trading-fraud fiasco after fiasco showed, the risk controls computers promised to bring to the Street never materialized for the poorly run firms. Technology, it turned out, was no substitute for management.

Receiving fewer benefits from computers than promised is not a phenomenon particular to Wall Street. We have invested billions in automating the workplace, and yet sales of paper to offices are up, not down. Most of us just are not ready to gamble on the general PC's reliability without hard-copy backup. Compare your desktop computer to your automobile. After a hundred years of practice (the Duryea Brothers started producing cars in Springfield, Massachusetts, in 1896), Detroit sells a product that works in a range of temperature, precipitation, road conditions, and user skills that is mind-boggling. After twenty years, the PC and Operating System manufacturers have barely started to provide that level of simplicity and "robustness," even when the computers are kept in a climate-controlled environment and used only by trained personnel. The thought of your car quitting seldom enters your head; the prospect of the PC crashing is a fear all users have each time they push "ON."

Look to our schools for more of technology's failed promises. Every parent wants his or her child to be computer literate. We all believe those without PCs in elementary school are doomed to a life of poverty and illiteracy, so we spend millions to equip classrooms with computational abilities and Internet access. The results? For all the purchases of computers in the classroom, our children don't read as well as before, have a worse sense of historical perspective, know less geography, possess fewer mathematical skills, and have reduced exposure to the great literary and cultural achievements of humankind. ("Why bother to learn that? I'll look it up if I ever need to know," a kid might say. "Forget spelling, I have a spell checker in my word processor." "Math? That's what calculators are for.") In terms of work habits/social skills, we're creating a disaster. Not only can't Johnny read, he can't speak grammatically either. Are we using technology as an excuse not to teach how to think and how to work with others? Is the money spent on hardware discouraging the best teachers and limiting the curriculum? Dollars are limited and fungible. Sending them to Silicon Valley means less for teacher compensation (worse instruction) and school construction (larger class sizes).

I vote to take the computers out of the classroom in the early grades. We should focus on teaching the basic skills of reading, writing, arithmetic, logic, concentration, cooperation, personal dress, social interaction, and hard work. With automobiles, most students will be drivers, not mechanics. They don't need internal combustion engine thermodynamics courses. Likewise with computers. They'll find the knowledge to use the latest data storage retrieval and manipulation devices when they need it. The tools are getting simpler to use and are starting to come with the instructions built in. A computer science course for kids may make parents feel good in the competitive world of the Parent–Teacher Association. ("My kid's got a faster CPU than yours!") Hooking elementary school classrooms up to the Net may make for good political theater. But a glorified video game that, at best, teaches children the marginally useful skill of better eye/hand coordination? That's hardly what today's kids need. Try the "three Rs."

Interaction with a sympathetic, understanding teacher can't be automated. For young children, it's the only way to teach the basics. It's also the only way to teach the social skills needed to survive in society. (I recently was introduced to half a dozen teenage students in a receiving line at a high school function. Not one could look me in the eye, shake hands firmly, or use their full names in introducing themselves. Time after time, I'm caught by the difference in enthusiasm and productivity of a New York City deli-counterman who is a blur of motions versus a clerk in a supermarket elsewhere who does things sequentially and slowly. Unless they're taught differently, not one of these shy slowpokes will ever get a meaningful job!)

News delivery has also not yet been transformed by computer technology's high promises. After trillions spent on television news production and delivery, serious consumers still get their basic in-depth news from a medium that existed in Shakespeare's day, the newspaper, and their real-time news from the ninety-five-year-old radio. Is a more entertaining (and arguably more informative) video presentation less important than a newspaper's direct access to what we want? Is television better than radio or is the content really in the sound? Could it be that spending money to add moving pictures to print or sound misses the point?

The "broadsheet" format of newspapers presents stories concurrently rather than sequentially. Newspapers inform by headlines we see peripherally, giving us what we need, even when we don't know we need it. From deaths, marriages, divorces, property sales, legal judgments, government actions, and religious and social events—the staples of community newspapers—to the complete coverage and in-depth analysis of the big city dailies, newspapers are sirloin steaks; radio and TV news are Big Macs. Both are great for what they do, but they are different products with different utility. Want to follow the O.J. case? Use radio or TV. Interested in science, diplomacy, politics, finance, business? Newspapers and magazines are still where it's at. For better or worse, the news agenda in every city in the world is set daily by the print media.

So isn't radio an anachronism? It's a sequential access medium where you get only what someone else has decided is in your interest. Worse still, you get it in the order in which it's sent, regardless of your preference. And if you miss or don't understand something, tough! You can't reread radio the way you can the print media, nor can you ask questions as you can with some real-time computer services.

Why then does the radio medium survive, given it hasn't had a meaningful technological improvement since inception? From the first A.M. broadcast, we still have to know a hard-to-remember set of numbers—the station's frequency—to find something. We still have no way of saying, "I want a specific type of programming"— for example, country and western music—and going directly to it. We still lose our reception in tunnels, under bridges, in steel-frame buildings. Radio survives, however, because it possesses the more important conveniences of mobility (you listen in your car or on your Walkman) and flexibility (you can listen and drive, listen and shower, listen and work). Radio may be inferior in most ways, but in the few ways that matter, it fills a valuable niche.

*   *   *

So, from Salomon in 1970 to today, where has technology taken us? Twenty years ago, pundits forecast a computer in every room of your house. Now, aggressive estimates say only one-third of U.S. homes have PCs. But almost every house possesses TVs, VCRs, telephones, thermostats, dishwashers, and microwave ovens, *all with built-in computers.* They may not look like what the forecasters and press envisaged, but they are!

Today's automobile is another great demonstration of substance over form. A driver put in a time capsule twenty years ago could return and drive a brand-new car cross-country without a single instruction. In fact, he or she needs to know less than ever to do so. The ignition key, steering wheel, brake, and accelerator haven't changed to the eye, nor has how one "interfaces" with them. But no longer does one have to shift gears—computers are all over the engine giving increased efficiency; materials and fuel are used that didn't exist two decades ago; the brakes are computer-controlled so you don't skid; the doors automatically lock when the car hits fifteen miles per hour; the radio mutes when the phone rings; the lights dim and brighten based on oncoming traffic and ambient light; and so on. The forecasters were right in the sense that matters. We've computerized our automobiles and they're simpler, safer, and more reliable than ever before, thanks to using these devices. The experts simply never envisioned what computers would look like, where they'd go, and what they'd do.

The acceptance of technological consumer products depends more on their ability to surreptitiously invade our lives than on their whiz-bang utility. Humans are loath to change and nervous about anything difficult to understand. More capabilities, better efficiency, increased reliability, fewer controls—all are benefits buyers understand and will pay for. They won't accept more complexity, change for change's sake, or so many options that no normal person could possibly remember them without the multilanguage, tiny-print, incomprehensible instruction book on hand.

The junkyards are littered with examples of technology that were introduced simply to highlight the designer's brilliance but ignored the customer's capabilities and needs. And some successful product acceptance has come in spite of its designer's great intellect. Certain well-used innovations don't get employed for the purpose they were produced. Consider the VCR: Most people use it only to play prerecorded tapes, when its original objective was to time-shift over-the-air or cable-delivered TV. Can you name anyone who knows how to set RECORD—or get rid of the flashing 12:00?

With technology and its fast-paced introduction, the key questions are more important than ever: What is the problem? How valuable is the solution? Can we provide it profitably? Where will our competition come from? When I started out with computers, I believed what the manufacturers' promotional materials promised. I grew into a skeptical, nontrusting cynic—but one who believes more than most in the potential technology has to improve our lives. What I learned on the journey was that we are all humans, and technology exists to serve us, not the reverse. The challenge is to resolve people issues, not software ones.

8

Management 101

The Bloomberg Way

When you start a company, every obstacle is a challenge. Everyone's out to get you: That's just the way it is, and you work around it. What's available to the big guys isn't available to you, like bank credit. That's an advantage; you develop a low-cost product. What if you can't find anyone to share your vision? Great. When your ship comes in, you won't have any competition. Are the bureaucrats driving you crazy? Fantastic. You'll neutralize them by playing them against one another. Is your company so small you have to do everything yourself? Wait until you're so big you can't. That's worse. I know.

At Bloomberg, we had a major obstacle to overcome after only five years in business: history. As part of our second terminal sale to Merrill Lynch, we had made an agreement that was limiting our expansion. Merrill had leased more than a thousand of our machines at $1,000 each per month. Simultaneously, they paid $30 million for 30 percent of Bloomberg's equity. We, in turn, agreed not to sell products for five years to their fourteen major competitors (Bankers Trust New York Corp.; Bear, Stearns & Co.; Citicorp; Daiwa Securities Corp.; Drexel Burnham Lambert & Co.; E.F. Hutton & Co.; First

Boston Corp.; Goldman, Sachs & Co.; J.P. Morgan & Co.; Kidder Peabody & Co.; Lehman Brothers & Co.; Morgan Stanley & Co.; Nomura & Co.; and Salomon Brothers Inc.).

This restrictive term had three more years to run in 1988 when I went to see Merrill's president, Dan Tully. Merrill was enjoying the exclusivity it had negotiated. It gave Merrill the unique conduit to the world's central banks, pension funds, insurance companies, and investment managers that increased Merrill's ability to capture institutional business. Additionally, by using our risk-management and trade-processing software, it was saving tens of millions of dollars each year in reduced trading losses and lower clerical expenses. Needless to say, the heads of each of Merrill's units (who were paid on their own department's performance) wanted this competitive advantage to continue.

Tully, on the other hand, had to take a broader view. In addition to the tactical advantages the exclusivity gave Merrill, he had to consider its investment in Bloomberg as a company. That investment would be worth a lot more if everyone could lease Bloomberg products. And it wasn't just added value arising from the extra terminals the fourteen embargoed firms would rent. A system used by all financial companies could essentially become an exchange. If everyone had access, then Merrill would have a stake in something much bigger than just a parochial supplier.

After almost a year of discussion, Dan acquiesced to our request to be released from the exclusivity clause. He thought at that point that Merrill had such a significant edge in experience with the Bloomberg terminal, it would take these other firms years to appreciate the benefits Bloomberg provided in cost reduction and improved controls, to order the terminals and have them installed, and to train their employees in their use. Meantime, as long as everyone could participate, institutional clients would come to accept Bloomberg as their preferred conduit to Wall Street. So, for years, even though Merrill wouldn't technically have exclusivity, it would have unique contacts the others could only dream of.

160

Given the way it turned out, Tully showed himself a master strategist. Three of the restricted firms went out of business (Drexel, Hutton, and Kidder). The Japanese firms (Daiwa and Nomura) imploded as their penetration of world markets failed to materialize. And the three banks (Bankers Trust, Citicorp, and J.P. Morgan) never took over the securities business the way conventional wisdom of the mid-1980s had predicted they would. In the meantime, Merrill kept growing and dominating in every area where it entrusted its processing to Bloomberg, particularly compared to the remaining six formerly embargoed brokerage firms.

*   *   *

By the late 1980s, Bloomberg had established offices in New York, London, Sydney, and Tokyo, with more than five thousand customers spread over forty countries. We were growing 25 to 30 percent annually and adding staff almost as fast as our business enlarged. This presented new challenges in running our organization.

Companies expanding at that rate are particularly vulnerable to supervisory gridlock and loss of control. Often, the original managers' abilities fall short, as administrative and leadership skills, compared to product knowledge, become key. Letting go and delegating sometimes proves impossible, often with disastrous consequences.

I was, of course, there in the beginning; I too think I can do everything better than anyone else. I believe my design instinct, sales savvy, and management skills are the best around. Still, my ego does allow for the remote possibility that someone might be as good at one or two little things. I've admitted there's a slim chance that ideas coming from others could be valuable as well. In other words, I'm the same as every other entrepreneur. But at least I know what I don't know.

Over the years, as Bloomberg has grown, I've managed to delegate the running of the established parts of Bloomberg and focus on our new projects. No longer do I make decisions day to day.

Susan Friedlander, our chief of all administration, has one-third of the worldwide company reporting directly to her; and Matt Winkler (news), Stuart Bell (Princeton data collection), and Lou Eccleston (North American sales) have much of the remainder. My function now is to encourage others. I'm there to solicit new ideas from everyone ("Let's develop a real estate product"). I make sure we allocate resources to new, innovative, and risky development projects ("We need to do something in insurance"). My job is to ensure that new products come alive at Bloomberg and to integrate them with the rest of our system ("Let's go after the energy market"). I direct customer feedback to the appropriate parties and see that it gets listened to ("What about a corporate-loan database?"). And once a new project is going—once I've added my ten cents—I make sure that we put people in charge who can take it to the next level—and that the rest of us (including me) leave them alone for a while to do their own thing.

At the beginning, I sat with the programmers and watched, learned, and oversaw. Later, I did the same with the salesforce. Then service people got much of my time. At one point, I made myriad phone calls each day to the data-collection group. But as each area developed its own experienced and talented supervisors (almost all our management is "homegrown"), my involvement with that group diminished. Partly, it was a conscious effort to avoid diluting their authority. To some extent, it was just the lack of time that prevented me from micromanaging. Mostly though, it was that the people we put in charge didn't need me anymore. They were the new guys, and as *Forbes* magazine claims I said, "The new guy can do it better."

One growth impediment I still wrestle with personally, however, is our chronic office space problem. Every time we've leased real estate, it's proven to be too small for our needs. Our crowding shows my inability to plan for our rate of growth, but it's also a safety valve: Space available puts a limit on how many people we can hire, and, God forbid, should sales slow, keeps the overhead in check. One time, though, we were so out of space in our New York sales office, a carpenter came in on a Friday night after everyone had gone and cut eighteen inches in width from each desk. We then added new ones of the same type in the reclaimed space. It was hours into Monday morning before anyone figured out why suddenly everyone had a seat. As I always maintain, if you really want to do it, there's a way.

We always have our offices in the best and most expensive parts of town while our competitors look for bargain space in the low-rent districts. It gets back to who you think is more important: your people or outsiders. I believe our people matter. The best for *us.* This is true not only at "headquarters," but everyplace. Our offices around the globe all work and look the same. The best locations and decor money can buy. Lots of warm wood gives a feeling of luxury and comfort for every employee. Big saltwater fish tanks provide light, white noise, and some relaxation. Glass-walled conference rooms improve interaction. No one has a private office, including me. The waiting area for guests is in the middle of our employees' snack bar: It shows off our people and the normal excitement at our company. If being invisible from your colleagues is what you crave, we're not the right place for you.

I've always believed that management's ability to influence work habits through edict is limited. Ordering something gets it done, perhaps. When you turn your back, though, employees tend to regress to the same old ways. Physical plant, however, has a much more lasting impact. Ours is an open plan layout. People must develop the ability to concentrate, despite myriad distractions. But the good part is, they absorb information peripherally while focusing elsewhere. Openness also constantly puts them in front of their peers, preventing childish fantasies that coworkers are out to get them. As is true with markets, transparency produces fairness. I issue proclamations telling everyone to work together, but it's the lack of walls that really makes them do it. (Of course, this will last only until the next management team brings in the construction company to build barriers, something they inevitably will do the day after my funeral.)

Openness also shows off our most important asset, our people. They *are* the company. You can replace our technology, data, reputation, and clients, but you cannot duplicate the group we've put together and the culture they've developed. We are a team. Every year, to increase intracompany and interfamily communication, we have both a company summer picnic and a Christmas party with spouses, children, and significant others. These events are the talk of the town. (Our kids learn where Mommy and Daddy go during the day and whom they work with.) We constantly encourage one another. (We play sports together, work on charities as a group, teach one another new skills.) Our young people socialize with one another. (We've probably introduced more people to their future spouses than most dating agencies.) We work together. (A number of people have told me that every employee they've seen at Bloomberg has had a smile on his or her face, and that wasn't true elsewhere. I hope they're right.)

Compare us to our competitors. Typically, they have reception areas with deeper carpeting and more wood paneling than elsewhere in their organizations. Their receptionists are chosen for physical attractiveness rather than interpersonal skills. The average employee there is relegated to non-VIP elevators. Clients see only representatives who are sanitized, less human than presentable. What are those companies ashamed of? The fact that your average computer programmer dresses differently from the typical salesperson, or has longer hair, or is shy? That's what programmers are. So what? This is who we are.

*   *   *

I've been criticized for refusing to attend "going away" parties or to wish departing employees good luck when they leave (our turnover is minuscule, but occasionally someone does quit). Why should I? I don't wish them ill, but I can't exactly wish them well either. I wouldn't mean it. We're dependent on one another—and when someone departs, those of us who stay are hurt. We needed that person's contribution or he or she wouldn't have been here to begin with. We're trying to feed our families, and his or her leaving makes that task more difficult. Him or her, or my kids? That's an easy choice! And God forbid one of our people go to work for a competitor; then we all heartily and cordially really do hope they fail. In their new job, they have an avowed purpose to hurt their old coworkers. They've become bad people. Period. We have a loyalty to *us.* Leave, and you're *them.*

I long ago declared that we would never rehire anyone who quit for other than family reasons. What choice in the matter do we really have? Two people work side by side; one leaves for greener pastures, and the other hunkers down and does the work of both. Later, the one who left us in the lurch realizes the grass wasn't greener after all and wants all forgiven. How could we ever again look in the eye the one who stayed if we let the "traitor" come back? My reaction is the same to someone who has received an offer elsewhere but will stay at Bloomberg in return for an immediate raise. "Goodbye!" What would we say to those who aren't threatening us if we bought someone's loyalty?

We handle perks differently, too. At Bloomberg, as you move up the organizational ladder and your compensation increases, you aren't expected to work less and take more vacations. Quite the contrary. You're more valuable, you get paid more, and your coworkers should get more out of you. The increase in your compensation is for current and future services, not rewards for past performance. Don't want to commit to that? Then don't accept the promotion and raise. We'll have no hard feelings—and someone else would love the chance.

We have no reserved parking spaces for senior executives. If you want to leave your car right by the door, just come in earlier. Creating class distinctions isn't constructive. That's why I don't believe in executive dining rooms either. The issue isn't fairness. If we constantly remind those people at the bottom that they are not at the top, do you really expect them to be "gung ho" about the company? Remember, shoot the bottom 50 percent and half of everyone remaining joins that lower group instantly.

If we expect dedication, cooperation, and performance, we've got to protect, assist, develop, and pay. The social contracts work two ways. The Bible says you reap what you sow. Yes, we expect you to put in long hours. You absolutely must show up for work even on those days when a lay-about seems more attractive. Sure, you sometimes have to work alongside people who aren't your favorites. Of course, you've got to produce rather than lollygag around the water cooler. How else can we pay all employees more each year?

Our company has to do its part. That ranges from physical security to disease and injury prevention programs, and to the most expensive health care plan money can buy. Our company builds employees: Constant training, retraining, coaching, and instruction from on-staff, full-time experts increase everyone's worth. Our company creates opportunities: Management that's promoted from within, transfers to other offices around the world, and chances to move to new areas make us different. Our company shares its financial success: High salaries, significant revenue sharing, and generous expense reimbursement are part of everyone's package.

Do our employment policies work? Compare us to our competitors or even to any similar-size organization. We have phenomenally low turnover for a company employing many young programmers, salespeople, and reporters, and we attract a pretty diverse labor force. Women's groups always cite us as a model place to be employed. Our assistance to young graduating students beginning careers is legendary. Almost everyone wants to join us—and only a handful elect to leave. Employee satisfaction and loyalty have let us expand and have made everyone's compensation increase an average of 15 percent per year—every year. Where else could they work and be able to enjoy that?

Loyalty is everything. Our people expect me to have it to them, and vice versa. Be honest, work hard, treat each other fairly and openly. Add a dash of competency, and we'll be together for a long time.

*　　　*　　　*

In business, growth is a necessity: You grow or you get out. No company can stay anchored to the status quo, no matter how successful it is. Customers come and go; their needs change with time, and the services that help them do their jobs are always in flux. Woe to the supplier without the best offering. If you're depending on longtime personal relationships, and not the quality of what you provide, start working on your golf game: You have a friendship with the buyer—your competitor already has one with his or her successor!

Nor can a company depend on just the best offerings to carry the day either. They're always transitory or eventually the patent just runs out. Remember Wang's word processor, Prime Computer's mini, Sony's Beta, or IBM's PC? Consumers have an insatiable appetite for improving their lives—and zero loyalty to past products or brand names. Time may be kind to great literature, art, music, dance, design, or philosophy, but in the commercial world, it's out with the old, in with the new, overnight.

Every day at Bloomberg, we face challenges that jeopardize our comfortable life. We constantly have to fight established competitors trying to take food out of our children's mouths. And then there are the start-ups that want to destroy everything we've built. Stand still and their products will overtake ours. If we're not careful, one day it'll be easier for them to add our features to their products than for us to add theirs to ours. Growth makes us a moving target. No growth makes us a sitting duck.

What makes the challenge even tougher is the threat of being swallowed by industrial giants who covet our business after we establish a market. These interlopers buy their way in and wreck the

167

economics we have built. They hire away our people with pre-emptory starting salaries, not realizing that few employees of any company are that valuable when stripped of the team doing the blocking and tackling.

And there's another insidious source of competition waiting to get us, one that's particularly galling. Our customers get blasé about our service. If we provide it competently and consistently, they think other companies must be able to do so as well. All of a sudden, these customers start calling in others to make proposals and pressing us to reduce prices. Then they start thinking they can provide the same product or service more cheaply themselves. Perhaps they can even build it and sell it to others as well. So, to survive, we must grow and improve. Any supplier who offers today what it sold yesterday will be out of business tomorrow.

Companies must grow for internal reasons, too. Without the challenge of the new, employees' minds and spirits atrophy. Work devolves from fun to drudgery. Without growth, no new opportunities are created, and employees who work hard to get a promotion have no place to go. If we tried to promote them anyway, we'd push the most productive people into meaningless senior slots. That would neutralize our greatest contributors. So we must grow to create new valuable positions, or watch our best and brightest quit for management jobs elsewhere and dissipate everything we've built over the years.

*　　　*　　　*

Bloomberg grows primarily in the traditional way: We expand our basic product. After all, that's what we do best. As the old western song goes, "Dance with the woman that brung ya!"

We make our products global. As our clients, opportunities, and suppliers move to new cities, new countries, even new continents, so do we. Of course, other physical locations require that Bloomberg employees master different languages, understand unconventional conventions in bond calculations, handle unfamiliar customs in client service. We must deal with employment laws inconsistent with those at home, build new relationships with strange sources, and cope with unknown regulators in everything. We must adapt our product to other markets, other types of securities, other formats, and other terminologies.

We increase our product's functionality. Customers' needs evolve and we provide what they want or lose their business. For example, Bloomberg disseminates information on companies, including earnings statements, balance sheets, press releases, news stories, and government filings. Bloomberg also provides myriad details of the securities these companies sell, such as terms, conditions, restrictions, holders, and transaction prices. But today our clients demand more. Lately, they've wanted to know who runs these companies, who analyzes their prospects, who trades their securities, and who invests in their future. They want lists of these people, accessible by name, address, affiliation, or function, complete with personal pictures, backgrounds, schools attended, past employers, titles, salaries, honors received, publications, speeches given, board and club memberships—everything except shoe sizes. There's no limit to the information available on each and every one of us—all in the public domain, all just waiting for collection, scrubbing, and intelligent indexing. Collect it we must.

Fifty people working at Bloomberg are devoted to the "People Project" I've just described. It's a good representation of how we work. We started collecting data on senior managers just as we did with myriad other overwhelming tasks. First, we entered facts about the CEOs of the major U.S. companies where we already had the information elsewhere in our files. While we were putting that into a useful database, we collected the same type of information in Europe and Asia-Pacific. Then, in turn, we went back and started to add the lesser corporate officers. Next came board members and more junior decision makers and contact people. Then, we reduced the minimum size of the firms we'd put in the file, and started the process again.

We worked step by manageable step, each one valuable in its own right, each instantly upon completion providing a service to our customers and producing revenue to fund the continuing collection process. Most important, we had the opportunity to see how customers used the data we were still in the process of collecting. There's nothing like a sample to help in development.

When you add a new product to your company lineup, existing ones usually need modification too. Products are interrelated. Concepts developed by one group of clients are envied by others, particularly fashionable terminology and technology. Your average customer may use only the conventional, but if you lose your reputation as the expert—the guru, the one who's pushing the envelope—you'll lose the loyalty of all those who live by association. Constant "modernization" is just part of the game.

Just growing a product isn't enough to make it succeed, though. Infrastructure must expand too. Backup, contingency planning, reliability—all become even more important than new offerings. The longer you have clients, the more they depend on you. The more clients you have, the more you have to lose. The more you're viewed as the establishment, the more the old reliable reputation is worth.

Keeping serviceable what you've built is a never-ending process. Every day, something you never thought could go wrong, does. So every day plus one, you fix a problem you previously didn't know you had. Of course you're locking the barn door after the horse got out—but now the next horse can't escape. Each day, there's one fewer animal potentially running amok. With time, you grow your service record. It gets better and better—never perfect, but more and more acceptable.

*   *   *

Our company standards also grow and evolve. No company's accounting systems adequately accommodate growth without constant enhancement, nor do any company's stated ethics and behavioral practices survive long without modification, particularly as you go worldwide. People on the other side of the world are *not* just like us but with funny accents. Practices acceptable here are often taboo there, and vice versa. Disclosure, drug testing, "considerations" (bribes, to an American), harassment, fraternization—all have very different meanings in different cultures. What is normal or correct in one place may be blasphemous in another. What is in the public domain here may be a state secret there, with disclosure being a capital offense.

Employment practices—hiring, firing, vacation, maternity, disability, and compensation laws—vary greatly worldwide. Using constant standards can cause no end of confusion and illegality. For any company doing business in two or more countries, it's perfectly possible that a single policy complies with rules in one place and violates the law in another. As a company expands, growth, flexibility, and fresh expertise in the human resources department must occur.

Similarly with security. We fret about losing our intellectual property rights and our wealth, but if we're not vigilant, we could lose things equally as important, our physical well-being and freedom of speech. Not all parts of the world are safe or open. Identification badges around our necks at work are becoming commonplace, another case of how leadership by example is key. Does the CEO in your company wear his or her identification badge? You should remind your boss that security's not a game. X-ray incoming packages? Report strange phone calls to the police? Look for unusual behavior in visitors or whoever's standing outside? Particularly after you write something controversial. It's your life that's at stake.

Many companies go overseas with the help of a partner. We've never done it that way and that's slowed our entry in some countries by years. (It took us eight years to get business permits in Korea, something we probably could have accomplished in months jointly with a local company.) Still, I believe we're right in going it alone. Since we don't have separate profit centers, we'd never know how to share the spoils. Since nothing in our company stands alone, anything pushing one product or area at the expense of another is untenable for us. Our standards, business practices, and ethics are different from those of other organizations—not necessarily better, just different. Do something together? It's hard enough to run our company. How could we run theirs as well?

When we decided to open an office in Japan, the two pieces of advice I got from everyone were: Get a Japanese partner (satisfying government regulations would be impossible without an insider's help, I was told), and don't send women (Japanese businesswomen in those days wore uniforms and served tea). Bloomberg being Bloomberg, we opened without a local partner (and had no governmental problems) and sent two women to run the place (who were accepted and able to hire men to work under them). So much for convention.

Maintaining gender equality as one grows in the international workplace is a real challenge. I'd like the company to be 50 percent male and 50 percent female at every level, in every function, in every one of our offices. (Remember, I have two daughters—and I want them to have the same opportunities as your two sons!) But many of our customers don't have the same policy. They don't care that the world's population is roughly half women and half men. Frequently, we go to high-level meetings where everyone not serving tea is male. Often, our clients will ignore our female manager and address all conversation to our male representative sitting in the meeting right next to her. (Even in our company, we have a manager in Asia whose wife walks a step behind her husband when they go out together. She considers it her rightful place. You can imagine the indignation when a young western woman visits them.)

We do what we think right—and let others discriminate or not as they wish. Personally, from a selfish point of view, I hope our competitors always use some employment criteria other than competency. We need all the help we can get!

*   *   *

The other basic way to grow is by product diversification—entering new businesses that are at best only tangential to a company's existing offerings. Companies diversify with a variety of motives. New products look appealing, and management thinks its traditional endeavors have little earnings potential left. The marketplace predicts a period of slow growth (read low price/earnings ratio, thus a low price for the company's stock, thus possible criticism of management). Or maybe the CEO is bored and wants the glamour of being in more trendy industries. Others make the old classic synergy argument that one plus one is worth more than two, like when Scientific Data Systems was bought. (Xerox paid $1 billion in 1969 for this "strategic fit" company—and wrote it down to *zero* only seven years later. A billion dollars was a lot of money in those days.)

Occasionally, product diversification actually benefits the company's employees, stockholders, and customers. Mostly, though, the history of corporate growth through new directions is disappointing. Could it be that, often, no growth in a company's traditional business is caused by poor management, and that lousy supervision and erratic decision making are the real consistent parts of these companies?

When is diversification appropriate? Only when it fits with what you already do. Companies have ethics, talents, and structures suited to specific businesses. Those who think their skills and management abilities are easily transferable aren't being realistic: Generally, they're not. Synergies are seldom more than constructs for consultants' reports. (Apples and oranges are both fruits from trees, but are grown in totally different environments by farmers with differing skills, tools, time frames, and economics. Buying an apple orchard when one already owns an orange grove probably just adds rotting apples and eliminates time to care for the oranges.)

Well-run organizations, whether commercial, political, educational, military, or philanthropic, have conceptual goals stated long in advance. New possibilities are always tested for fit against these predefined objectives. This insistence on a prior specific mission statement against which all proposed actions must be judged tempers the emotions to follow the "fad of the day." Smart managements plan strategically beforehand, and don't do anything tactical that's not consistent with the plan—particularly in the heat of some once-in-a-lifetime, do-it-now-or-lose-it-forever opportunity brought to you by a breathless investment banker. If it's not your business, it probably shouldn't be.

The same applies to Bloomberg. We've grown dramatically over the years, and our diversification has stayed consistent with our mission statement. Our goal is to provide the information and analytical capabilities serious professionals need to be well-rounded and do their jobs. The focus of our computer terminal product is clearly for the high-end, sophisticated user. Our radio and television, with our serious-news, no-crime policy, seems to rule out all but the most upscale listener and viewer. The publishing parts of our business target investment professionals or consumers interested in personal finance. (With book titles like *Option Adjusted Spreads,* who else would we attract?) And our telephonic media products complement the other offerings (help desks for the terminal, Web site for the magazine and TV shows, and financial market radio stories accessible via phone). So far, what we've done, fits.

After we look for relevancy versus our strategic objectives, we at Bloomberg look for overlaps with existing products. Will it help what we already do? Can we use the same people? Is the technology required consistent with what we know how to produce? What can we do that our competitors can't? (There's no reason to do a "me too" product. You can't make any money with a "commodity.") Do we have limitations that would disadvantage us? (As a news organization, we have great access, but we can't be seen as a promotional device for our sources.) Are we suitably structured? (We have a corporate culture that works only with a certain business model: well-paid employees enjoying great job security and expensive benefits—luxuries possible only with a high-margin, low-volume product.) Last, we insist on doing profitable things. (I've never believed Bloomberg should be a charitable institution—nor would my kids if they thought about it.)

*   *   *

We're frequently presented with opportunities to grow or diversify by acquisition. I almost never let a seller's representative send us offering memoranda. If we're not seriously interested in making a bid, it's disingenuous to look; and I really don't care anyway. If the company being shopped was good enough for us to consider buying, it wouldn't be for sale. It may be interesting to know what others have done, but the only thing that matters is what our customers need. Looking would just get us worried and have our practices influenced by managers we'd never hire.

At Bloomberg, we're builders, not buyers. I'd make a terrible venture capitalist; every company I look at seems overpriced. I always think we can create it more cheaply ourselves. Whenever I think goodwill (the accounting treatment for paying too much) is justified, I rush to take a cold shower. What's for sale may be worth it, but why? All these companies appear to me to have problems I'd find difficult to fix, something I'd have to do since, if I ever did buy anything, I'd want to make it my baby and grow it forever. I'm not a seller either.

The real problem with acquisitions is that neither corporate cultures nor technologies mix. The momentary advantage to the buyer adding an existing operation often gets dissipated quickly, and then one's stuck with the reasons it was for sale in the first place. More times than not, when two good companies combine, they stay as separate functional organizations, having contact only through common ownership. When poorly run companies get together, they tend to do it at the operating level, where the worst of both can do the most damage to each other. It's probably inscribed someplace (or should be): Two negatives *always* produce something worse!

In our company's history, we've made only two purchases: a three-person company and, later, a twelve-employee one. Both worked out, but I had too many sleepless nights each time to make acquisitions a habit. Growth by acquisition is a bet-the-store, high-risk gamble. It's true that a few (very few) work. But it's the kind of "all in up front" risk that leaves me uncomfortable. Maybe I'm just not that smart. When I'm looking to expand, I prefer starting with a little capital that we can afford to lose, and a few people we can always reassign to other projects. This way, we never feel we're committed to stay with our mistakes, nor are we so overextended we can't handle other additional experimental ventures simultaneously. (Out of deference to our professional service providers, I won't mention the savings in accounting bills, legal charges, and investment banking fees we also get with this build-versus-buy strategy.)

Just as important is the people issue. Growth by building gives us the chance to reward our best employees with newly created management jobs. Growth by buying would just force us to fire a bunch of people I've never met who haven't done anything bad to me. I'm not sure how I'd explain that to my kids, or why at my age I need to give myself that task.

There will be an exception or two that will present themselves in the future—companies with brand identification we'd never replicate, or distribution channels we can't buy, or the opportunity to end a dependency on a supplier we're uncomfortable with. What will we do? You'll see when it happens. (Unfortunately, if we ever seriously looked at acquiring something, our major competitors would probably rush in and outbid us just to stop the process.) All I can guarantee is that if we ever buy another company, it will fit our mission statement and sell at a price I think is lower than the cost of replicating that company's products.

*　　　*　　　*

Whether by building or buying, there are dangers in growth you ignore at great peril. We insist on management depth at every position. Lack of it would leave us vulnerable when someone quits or gets hit by a truck. (I want the loss of anyone in the company to hurt us, but not fatally, including the likes of me.) Every job performance review I give my direct-reporting managers includes the question, "Who's your replacement? If you don't have one now, I can't consider you for bigger things. If you don't have one the next time I ask, you may no longer be a direct report."

What happens if I die, become incapacitated, or retire? What will keep the company going, protect my estate, ensure the jobs of our employees and the service to our customers? The rules apply to me as well. I've got to ensure succession the same way our other managers have to. Otherwise I'm not fulfilling my obligation—and can't consider doing something else myself either. What have I put in place for Bloomberg *without* Bloomberg?

Our clients have long-term contracts with our company. Thus, the company's revenue base is very stable, and my successor will have time to grab a comfortable hold on the wheel before anyone could think of taking their business elsewhere. Our employees have a long-term compensation participation in the firm's success. The person replacing me will have to win their confidence and respect, but at least he or she will have some time to do so. Our financing is all long-term borrowings that mature in small, gradual tranches, something that should be manageable in virtually any financial scenario. Our company carries an extremely large amount of key-man life insurance on me, payable to the firm upon my death. Any cash flow problems when I die will be mitigated by that windfall. Since I'm leaving the bulk of my estate to a foundation, inheritance taxes won't be an issue.

Who will succeed me? Our board of directors has my views, which I continuously update. I've said what I would do. But remember, when they pick, I'll be dead—and I can't run the company from the grave. They'll have to choose the person they think right at the time, but not necessarily the one I'd select today. Meantime, with no publicly designated No. 2, everyone at Bloomberg still has a chance to move up to my desk. Everyone still has the incentive to expand his or her skills and experiences. Everyone still has to be a team player—which is the right incentive for the company while I'm around.

As we face the issue of growth, we need the best managers we can train—and the best people to build our internal accounting, measurement, and control functions. The most important programmers we have at Bloomberg write software for our use, not for our customers'. If we don't stay in control, nothing else matters. We've got to be able to service our clients, pay the bills, collect the revenue, file our tax returns, detect fraud, spot trends, and so on. If there are no controls, there's eventually no company.

Due to their size, our competitors have limited ability to respond to threats. We can't become inhibited in the same way as we grow. Big companies allocate expenses, thereby causing divisiveness in their organizations. We don't run our company with "profit centers." With their focus on cash flow versus earnings (they never consider depreciation a real cost, a stupid assumption given today's pace of obsolescence), they never have the funds available to give the customer the latest and greatest service and technology. We're aggressive with depreciation and assume it's real. They have equipment in the field that, if quickly upgraded to a better product, would cause accounting writedowns and kill their credibility with lenders and Wall Street analysts. We provide new equipment and services to clients when they are available, not when they fit our P&L statement. As a private company, we report to only a few who understand and have a long-term perspective.

Without knocking the value of the accounting profession, it is true that "numbers lie—and liars use numbers." Only with superhuman effort can a company keep accounting from being misused as it gets bigger. I can't count the number of times I've watched people incorrectly make decisions that confuse incremental costs with fully allocated ones, or misuse present value calculations.

These concepts can be useful tools, but slavish adherence to them can produce cockeyed results. Had the person who invented the wheel used "net present value," we would still be walking!

Size also limits growth by inhibiting (or at least making more difficult) communications, which make sensible controls, not constricting policies, all the more necessary. In big companies, meeting after meeting is required to include and inform all concerned before anything happens. Is greater knowledge worth the extra time? I tend to just do my thing and apologize for not posting others after. Secretly, no matter what our rules and procedures, I wish all our people would. Once, I got frustrated at a get-together where each participant read a summary of his or her department's progress for the week, right from the printed notes handed out to all at the meeting's start. The next week I had the chairs removed from the conference room before we started. It's amazing how much quicker and more focused stand-up conferences are. Size also leads to a cover-your-rear mentality that slows down development. Each manager protects his or her own turf, which is particularly true when they can't see what the others are doing. Size hides.

Size's economics of scale are seldom realized. Take the great misconception in our business about software: that maintaining a program is cheaper than developing it. It isn't. The fact is, software needs to be updated constantly to retain value. The inputs to it change. The hardware and communications change. People always need new formats, sorts, fields, and calculations. That's why we constantly hire more programmers. Or what about the belief that hardware is a one-time "capital expense"? People always say something costs N to buy (a cost they "capitalize") and then assume that's the whole cost. I always figure on 40 percent of N *every* year, forever (a cost you expense versus earnings)—10 percent interest, 10 percent maintenance, 20 percent depreciation. That adds up to 40 percent in my book. Don't quibble with details. Use 40 percent. Trust me. Whom do you want to kid? Yourself?

Our greatest challenge today? Fighting the stultifying effects of success, the paralyzing results of growth, the debilitating cancer of entrenchment.

*   *   *

Management must promote growth, while staying within the mission statement's guidelines. Unfortunately, managers are human beings, too, with personal interests, egos, and insecurities similar to those of real people (the people they supervise). There are many examples of an acquisition and/or new initiative begun for noncommercial reasons and justified ex post facto. Fortunately, a more open and competitive world has reduced these abuses. And in all fairness, most managers really do try. The success of American business is ample testimony to their high ethics, hard work, and superior talents. Still, people are people—and managers are human beings first and foremost. What does it take to succeed as a manager?

The primary function of those at the top is the care and feeding of the company's most valuable asset, its employees, including designing and administering a compensation system that encourages cooperation, rewards risk taking, and gives inducements to work hard—Job One for the CEO.

The leverage a great team provides makes management a fantastic investment for a company's stockholders, but phenomenally overpriced when the executives can't get the organization to perform. All the magazine surveys of CEOs' compensation based on earnings growth or stock price performance miss the point. It may be a standard of success harder to measure, but rather than raising stock prices and even generating earnings, building, leading, and motivating the staff a company needs for the future is what managers should be paid for.

Being the spokesperson for the company is an important part of running any organization, and perhaps the hardest to delegate. Everyone wants to hear the top person's views (even if someone else wrote the speech). Guests want to shake the boss's hand (even though no one remembers who was who after the meeting). If you want to exchange business cards or have a picture taken jointly, no one else but the top boss will do. So, while the senior manager may have other pressing duties, he or she has to set a high priority on accessibility to the press, the stockholders, the employees, and the customers. At Bloomberg, I handle all our firm's internal and external public relations. It's just too important to give to anyone else.

(It's always fascinated me when I, as the head of my company, say something and people listen politely, categorizing my statements as opinion. But if I say it to a reporter, and he or she then prints it, the same thoughts, with less accuracy and no substantiation, have a vastly greater validity. Why? What is it about a journalist's blind repetition of our self-serving promotional meanderings that implies truth, when the version that comes straight from the horse's mouth does not? And why do people take what's said so literally?)

Then there's old-fashioned leadership. It's the top person's policies, personal and professional deportment, and working hours that the organization tries to emulate. While the only difference between stubbornness and having the courage of one's convictions may be the results, it's a natural reaction to attribute superior strength, knowledge, and consistency to those we follow. (But the slightest sign of vacillation can kill that image forever.)

Say something as CEO and the organization responds. It may only be by analyzing, criticizing, ridiculing, or specifically deciding to ignore the pronouncement, but notice it they will. You go to the other side of the world and find a nonsensical business policy instituted by your most remote office—perhaps everyone wearing hats indoors. Why? "Well, years ago you said in a memo to keep your head covered." Yes, perhaps you did as a throwaway line, without much thought, outside on a very cold day, applied to a totally unrelated situation you've long since forgotten. But the CEO's the parent, teacher, clergyman, politician. Everyone's watching all the time. Wanting to believe, aching to follow. Are you not comfortable with leading the company twenty-four hours a day, seven days a week? Then step down.

The CEO is also the company's morale officer. He or she must promote an atmosphere in which ordinary people who try new things that fail are encouraged to try again. Projects that succeed always get support and provide their proponents sufficient adulation. It's the failures the timid watch. A belief that trying new things could jeopardize one's career stifles creativity. Lose the contribution of the average employee, and you lose the war.

Last, there's the "who's in charge" function. THE BUCK STOPS HERE was a sign President Harry Truman had on his White House desk. He didn't make most decisions, but he did bear responsibility for his staff's actions. (Something modern politicians disgracefully walk away from. "A mistake was made" has become a euphemism for no one takes responsibility.) It's the same with the corporate CEO. He or she can get help, delegate, farm out, get advice, and so on. But in the end—it's one person's decision, one person's responsibility. A major part of the CEO's responsibilities is to be the ultimate risk taker and decision maker. Truman had it right.

*   *   *

Companies that do things correctly for long periods still seem to get in trouble eventually, however. Is it always the CEO's fault? When it's because of the CEO's new game plan every month, you bet. Consistency and predictability are important requirements if an organization is to function well. But the opposite is also true: Let the hierarchy remain static, and you get disaster. The good quit for lack of opportunity or out of boredom; the bad entrench themselves. Stirring up the chain of command is another part of the CEO's job. Not easy. Not pleasant. Not even always explainable. Too late to do in bad times, and never thought of in good times. But don't do it—and you'll get killed from within.

In academia, the publish-or-perish ethic with peer review gives a scholar constant feedback. If a professor's losing the edge, the school finds out and can react. (Unfortunately, tenure may prevent the school from doing very much about it. But at least it knows it's in trouble.) Lack of competition is the equivalent of no peer review process. When the inevitable competitor arrives with a better way, the organization previously without a need to improve has grown so lazy it has trouble reacting.

When I look at a company, I pay little attention to its accounting statements. A good accountant with a creative mind can make numbers paint any desired picture. No one understates revenues and profits when they're trying to show off. Presumably, the financial situation is always equal to or worse than stated. A better way to evaluate a company is to talk to the experts. No, I don't mean journalists or analysts. I mean those who *really* know what's going on and what the potential is. First, I call those most knowledgeable, the customers. "Do you plan to buy more or less of this company's product?" I ask. "Are there competitors coming along with better offerings?" Then, I call the other insiders, the headhunters. "Do people want to go to work at this company, or are they trying to leave in droves?" Management, accountants, and other outsiders can say anything they want. Clients and employees never lie.

*   *   *

Competition's great—obviously for the consumer, but even for the providers. Every morning when we get up, we relish the day's upcoming battles. They keep us alive, and they keep Bloomberg's corporate family thriving. We can't wait for tomorrow. Who says we can't do that? What do you mean they'll beat us? Have them put on their boxing gloves, and send them into the ring. We're ready!

9

Coming Up Next

America's a Wonderful Country

Periodically, while surrounded by the fruits of our success—the profits, power, notoriety—I get frustrated and dream of starting again. But something stops me. Perhaps I'm too old. Perhaps I'm afraid it was all luck. Or maybe, deep down inside, I really do like the trappings I've accumulated. Nevertheless, when I find we just "cleared it with legal" or had a meeting to "keep others in the loop," or are "justifying" staff versus producers, I want to scream. We used to have the Nike sneaker company attitude: We just did it! Now, there's a "why we can't" lurking in the background. Keeping it from coming out while we grow is our number one management focus today; human resource development is our second.

In our company, what started simple, with time has become complex. Existing contracts have to be honored, so change is difficult. A single straightforward policy has picked up exception after exception over time. Products have grown to overlap. Some have become both redundant and inconsistent, simultaneously. Development, marketing, sales, and support are always in different

185

stages. No one's got an excuse—but everyone's got a reason. Maddening!

Why not just quit then? Chuck it all? Sell the business? Take the money and run? Certainly at a particular size, it's the prudent thing to do. After all, there is a limit to how much you can spend—or prudently leave to your kids. And on the downside, even a reasonably sure double-your-money bet isn't worth a small risk of losing it all, once you've got it. It's one thing to bet the store when the store is worthless, and quite another when you're older and tired, and have gotten used to the good life. Cash in, take some money off the table, play it conservatively, relax a little?

Real entrepreneurs never do, though. And I probably won't either. Is it greed? Is "enough" never "enough"? Is it insecurity? What will people say, that when the going got tough, Mike didn't have the right stuff? Or curiosity? Can I get us over the next big plateau? How big can we get? Or lack of alternatives? What would I do if I sold it? Go into politics? Retire?

Generally, real builders are so focused (a.k.a. one-dimensional) and dedicated, they'd have a nervous breakdown after two weeks of sitting around. Their challenge—even their reason for living—would be gone. (Would Steve Jobs [Apple Computer] or Ross Perot [Electronic Data Systems] have sold out if he'd known? Why swap fun, influence, challenge, and more money than you could ever spend—for only a multiple of more money than you can ever spend?)

In my case, I can't think of anything better than my current situation. It's hard to see how else I could have so much fun and satisfaction. Where else could I create so much? Or help as many young people start careers? Or produce a product our customers actually can't live without? Or have people say, "You're the greatest. You've changed my child's life, helped our family survive, given me a second chance," and mean it? What other situation would provide as great a forum to express my views or permit my level of philanthropy or give me such notoriety (or guarantee prestigious table reservations at top restaurants)?

Sell? I dread the unsolicited call from someone with a "concept" wanting to buy us out at ten times what we're worth. (I'll say no— I think! There's always hope for you buyers, however. My estate will have an auction, you'll pay a lot, and I won't be around to see it.)

Go public? And have to answer to more partners, stockholders, and securities analysts? At my age? I know why the investment bankers all want us to issue stock—but why would we want to do it? We're going in the other direction. We've already bought back one-third of Merrill's investment in our company for $200 million (twenty times what they paid for it). They've been the best part-ner anyone could ever have (and I hope they feel the same way about us). Why swap them for an unknown? No, thanks. For the moment, answering to essentially no one is the ultimate situation. Forever? Call back in a few years.

So back on the treadmill. Ratchet up the risk. Enter a new medium. Start another software or hardware project. Improve. Develop. Expand. Go for it!

*   *   *

The future holds great promise for Bloomberg the company, and for all of us as individuals. Thanks to agricultural improvements, a smaller percentage of the world's population now goes to bed hun-gry than ever before in history. If that doesn't qualify as progress, I don't know what does. In turn, fewer people are illiterate today than in yesteryear. Once folks can feed themselves, they take that critical next step to self-sufficiency, learning to read and write. This in turn facilitates the dissemination of ideas, and invariably leads to more responsive and open governments. Thus the resur-gence of democracy in these countries. Sure, there's still war and famine and totalitarianism—but every day, less than before.

Better electronic communications technology exposes alterna-tive political and economic systems to public scrutiny. When you see others doing better, day in and day out, eventually you want the same for your family and yourself. No government, no matter how harsh and repressive, exists without the will of the majority of its citizens. Show the people something better—they'll get it!

From the time civil engineers separated the sewage system from the water supply (causing the single biggest jump in life expectancy ever), technology has been a boon to humankind. Smallpox has been eradicated worldwide at a cost less than what we used to spend vaccinating kids in the United States alone. Now we cure childhood leukemia routinely where before there was no hope. Polio, with its "iron lungs," is something for the history books. Most encouragingly, public health programs increasingly prevent disease from attacking the vulnerable. Fluoride in the drinking water literally put half the dental schools out of business in America. Adding a single drop of bleach to drinking water in the world's poorer countries saves millions of lives annually. Giving minute doses of vitamin A to children there keeps 500,000 kids from going blind and two million from having fatal diarrhea each year. The great tragedy is that the political will has not kept pace with scientific and technological advances. So much could be done if we cared just a touch more.

In addition to increased longevity, the quality of life is constantly being improved by technology. I remember my mother describing how as a girl she traveled by horse-drawn carriage. Today, we fly from New York to London or Paris by Concorde in three hours. Growing up, she had gas lamps for illumination. Now, Monday Night Football is played outdoors in what's essentially daylight. She hand-delivered messages to her friends as a child. Her grandchildren carry alphanumeric beepers. When she was a teenager, the telephone at the corner store was used only for emergencies. Today, we can call someone in a moving auto on another continent from our cellular phone as we walk down the street. Think these "improvements" are trivial? Increasing commerce, comfort, and communication are strong inducement for everyone to avoid World War III.

Tomorrow, things will be even better. Medicine is closing in on cures for cancer, AIDS, strokes. Public health organizations are working to prevent much of the world's famine and pestilence. Small-battery technology is adding mobility to every conceivable kind of electronic device. Global Positioning Systems (GPSs) that use satellite receivers to calculate location and altitude anyplace are changing our world. Moving maps for automobiles are becoming standard in rental cars. Soldiers, hikers, flyers, sailors, even cargo containers might never be lost again: GPSs are starting to tell them where they are; cellular phones are reporting that information to others automatically. Computational ability to create "virtual reality," data retrieval from anywhere in the world, commerce conducted electronically are all coming soon—virtually "free," by today's standards. Audio/video on demand is just around the corner. Whenever you want, watching any program or movie or listening to any kind of news or music will be "Haven't we always?" before you know it. Home picture telephones are unavoidable.

Amazingly, these advances will be used in the poorer parts of the world only slightly later than in the "rich" areas. The potential for health improvements there is obvious. And one of the great barriers to the deployment of technology is the existence of infrastructure and the financial impact of scrapping it, a problem obviously not felt in places that start with nothing. New, high-quality wireless phone systems routinely get installed where previously there were no phones at all, while the large "copper-wire telcos" fight to keep such systems out of their often poorly serviced "developed" areas. Much to the politicians' annoyance (read *ability to regulate and tax*), satellite and GPSs work anywhere.

*   *   *

Technology is clearly improving our lives, but not all effects prognosticated will prove accurate. Take the prediction that we'll all work from home, for example. The tools needed are portable enough. Homes across the country have multiple phone lines, faxes, scanners, PCs, high bandwidth communications, copiers, and so on. With the dramatic increase in two-income and single-parent households, there's a need for flexibility to accommodate work and family simultaneously. What's more, the growing service industries (as opposed to the declining manufacturing ones) better allow independent "tasking."

Nevertheless, for the immediate future, I think this concept isn't about to revolutionize the workplace. While working from home is a central tenet of the professional futurist's mantra, there is no current meaningful increase in office-in-the-home lifestyles (away from those forced out of their prior jobs and not yet placed in new ones). In fact, the trend is in the opposite direction. Unions are violently against home offices. The image of the home office is poor for those who run their own businesses. It's not even clear it fits with real family life. "No commute" sounds fine, but traveling separates and distance delineates—and sometimes that's good for both marriages and children. As the competition for employment heats up, people have more need than ever to be where the action is and where the politics are played out, at the office or factory. Tougher, more competitive times are not suited to reduced interaction with fellow workers or more lax supervision. Those arguing that e-mail is a replacement for gathering around the water cooler must be academicians. For a handful of professions (writing, philosophizing, and so on), the home is a fine workplace. But for most other occupations, serious businesspeople and real managers find the entire concept of independent work out of your home ludicrous.

Some think computer expertise is required for future success. I don't. Thinking and interpersonal communications skills have been, are, and will be keys to survival. Technology's not going to change that. To prosper, work on your people-to-people relations more than your typing speed. Take a psychology course and one on how to use the Scientific Method rather than (or in addition to) a computer science course. We exchange ideas more than information, and we do most of that orally. Having text and visuals to add to understanding is nice. But we're men and women, not machines. Face to face, or over electronic media, we need to transmit and receive sound. (When Samuel Morse invented the telegraph, he gave us electronic interactive digital text communication. Nevertheless, we flocked to Alexander Graham Bell's analog voice telephone instead, because it better mirrored the way we live. We talk rather than write to each other.) Now, technology is adding to Bell's system the ability to send letters, numbers, and pictures over a medium formerly used exclusively for voice. This is new functionality, but ancillary to the phone system's basic two-people-talking service. It's not really a new medium, but just an additional incidental way to use the existing physical connections and efficient switching/billing systems already in place. Your job will remain to create the what and disseminate it; technology is monkeying around with the how. It's what you have to say, and your ability to present it in cogent, believable terms to yourself, your family, your coworkers, and your community that are important.

While technology is creating broader distribution of information, with enhanced "targeting," it is also causing the size of each audience to become smaller and more knowledgeable. You'll have to be even better prepared in the future to get ahead; the people you'll interact with will be too. Alternative delivery systems for news and entertainment, and increased "channel capacity," mean more choices. This fragmentation has shifted network-dominated television toward cable-carried specialty services in sports, history, cartoons, news. Solve a few technical distribution problems and the number of newspapers will skyrocket as well. But the circulation of each, just as with the audiences for specific radio or TV shows, will decline as consumers' choices expand. In turn, this produces much more homogeneity as to age, sex, economics, education, and so on, in those reading, listening, or watching a single specific story or program. Smaller groups, but much more focused ones.

The cost of communicating ideas is declining rapidly, and it's an odds-on bet that this will continue for the foreseeable future. The stock market predicts daily which technology will triumph as the carrier of choice. But all transmission media are solving whatever limitations they have vis-à-vis their competitors. Many are providing essentially the same service, and advances in capacity already prevent any distributor from maintaining charges at a very profitable level, a problem for them and their employees (and an advantage for the consumer) that will be exacerbated with time. The outlook for companies and workers providing transmission service is problematic at best. Lots of ups and downs lie ahead, no matter what the equity markets say. For the average person, however, access to data quickly and affordably, and the ability to compare your ideas to those of others, will surpass all predictions.

All communications systems in today's world are, or soon will be, digital. Then all text, sound, still pictures, and full-motion video (which is just thirty still pictures shown to the eye every second) will be the same. When sending any of these digitally, technology converts all these media into numbers by turning a series of switches off or on (represented by 0 for off or 1 for on). Fast computers using fancy mathematics take these 0s and 1s and reduce the number of them actually needed to adequately represent the text, sound, or picture. The better this reduction or "compression," and at the other end, expansion or "decompression," works, the fewer 0s and 1s need to be sent, the less capacity needs to be rented from the carrier (e.g., the phone company), and in turn, the cheaper it is to get the message across (particularly important with video, which requires many more 0s and 1s than does voice or text). At the receiving end, technology changes these 0s and 1s back into sound, pictures, numbers, and letters for the ear and eye. Important, though, is the fact that until that "reconversion," digital sound, text, and pictures are all *exactly the same.*

This commonality (all forms of media in the digital world represented the same way) lets us send telephone calls over cable-TV systems, television programs over telephone lines, and both over the air, via satellite or by microwave. For better economics, we can even combine different kinds of data (text, charts, graphs, talk, music, pictures, video) at one end and sort it out at the other. And since it's all identical regardless of which delivery system was used (the beauty of the concept is that, after all, 0s and 1s are 0s and 1s), the consumer benefits from the price competition that the lack of product differentiation invariably brings. More information available, faster and cheaper. Understanding what's important for your job will be paramount.

The electronic retrieval and manipulation of data in your home will increase. Instead of getting the data delivered by automobile (e.g., renting a film on VHS tape from a store you drove to) or by post (e.g., a mailman-delivered CD-ROM encyclopedia), on-line, on-demand delivery will vastly expand the diversity of alternatives, be far cheaper, and certainly offer simplicity in selection. Those investing in tape or CD-ROM technologies are buying dead-end technologies. Whether via the Internet or the other bandwidth leasing plans (e.g., Intranets, of which there will be many), whether distributed over phone lines, cable, microwave, satellite, or cellular, there are enormous benefits in delivery directly "to the door." TV listings, catalogs, and sports scores rather than Shakespeare, serious news, and financial data may be your data fare. That's your choice. How they will be delivered to you in the next several years—that battle's already over except for the shouting.

I think schools are generally headed in the wrong direction with their course curriculum. There will be a smaller premium placed on specialized skills versus general knowledge. You'll need courses in logic, not Word Processing 101. The great advance in product technology is coming from a new internal complexity that will give greater external simplicity and utility. The trend in medicine toward all-around primary care physicians is but another example of technology becoming so smart, the understanding of context and appropriateness is the value added, not the details of any individual test or procedure. In the office or on the production line, tool selection and use is the key, not how each aid is constructed. Being well-rounded, inquisitive, perceptive, logical, and communicative is more valuable than knowing a given sequence of buttons to push. In the future, technical details will matter less—big picture, more.

The competition for advertisement awareness will skyrocket. The innovation of the marketers seems boundless, and technology will create placement opportunities never dreamed of before. People are bombarded constantly with ever-more-targeted messages. The mixing of commercial information with the editorial or entertainment content in most media will grow to be complete. Improved ability to screen out unwanted intrusions on TV (e.g., channel jumping, fast forwarding, running to the fridge for a beer) require that sponsors counter either with combination tactics (the brand name on the shirts of the athletes, the star holding a can of cola with the label showing, all of which could even be added by computer electronically for different parts of the country) or with Bloomberg's solution: a multiscreen format that tries to keep the viewer watching through commercials.

America is as well-positioned for these trends as any large country could be. Its citizens speak English, the closest thing ever to a universal language. (There are more than 250 million people in China today who speak some English. That's equivalent to the entire population of the United States.) It has free internal borders with one currency, so manufacturers in the United States have a single large market for their products, something the European Community is still trying to create. Its securities markets, thanks to strict Securities and Exchange Commission regulations and enforcement, are viewed as open and fair. America's capital availability for industry and start-ups is unmatched anywhere.

Those countries previously enjoying double-digit growth through low labor costs are in for a rude awakening. When your raison d'être is "cheap," no one makes much and anyone more desperate can undercut you anytime. Low wages, low profits, and low taxes where there are high social service demands eventually lead to serious unrest. It is the same in some wealthy countries with a tradition of confrontational and inflexible management/labor relations. Much strife lies ahead.

By comparison, America's labor force is mobile and willing, even anxious, to learn new skills. American workers have aspirations to advance and improve their situation. Over time, and sometimes with great pain to individuals, the United States has refocused away from the old smokestack, rust belt, agricultural industries and toward the future's service, technology, and entertainment economies. America's concentration on value-added industries (as opposed to commodities businesses that compete based on price) puts it in a position to maintain margins and salaries, and generate the capital to reinvest in even greater labor-saving technology.

America's competitive position couldn't be better.

*   *   *

Much of the data, radio, and television access you'll have soon will come from the Internet or its many successors. This "revolutionary" system is often confused with its transmission medium. Technically, the Net isn't another way of sending data. There are no cables under the road marked Internet. It's probably fairer to think of it as simply another way of renting transmission capacity (called bandwidth) from the telephone companies and other carriers to use for information transmission along with an on-line, worldwide telephone book.

On any phone line on your street, there are interspersed blocks of 0s and 1s representing Internet traffic, stock and bond prices from market data companies such as Bloomberg, national television networks sending programs to local TV stations, regular phone calls like Aunt Agatha arguing with Uncle Charles, and even messages from the Defense Department checking on the health of its nuclear deterrent. Each item is inserted onto the same physical phone line by a different "provider" who rents and uses, or rents and resells, the service its customers need and then bills its clients in the manner appropriate for its particular business. The great magic of technology is that, at the other end, everyone's messages get sorted out and routed to the proper user.

For many years, individuals have rented "carriage" directly from those owning wires into everyone's home and office. When we make regular phone calls that appear on our monthly bill, we rent this transmission capacity and pay per minute used. Many of us also sublease capacity on a per-minute basis from wholesalers, companies who lease in bulk from the big telephone companies and, in turn, rent it in pieces to individuals.

The Internet is another leasing variation, another economic model designed to fit people who want to use PCs to communicate for long time periods with multiple, unpredictable destinations. A nonprofit cooperative organization, The National Rural Telecommunications Cooperative, supervises the rental of large quantities of bandwidth from all the telephone companies worldwide and the subletting of unlimited use to individuals at a flat rate per month. This is no different from Bloomberg, which for twelve years has bought and resold transmission capacity for its private Intranet, another type of Internet with access restricted to a certain group (e.g., one's clients, one's branches, all sports fans, a group of universities, and so on). As do private individuals and the Internet, we've been buying from the telephone companies and passing on the cost to our clients monthly.

The Internet focuses on giving low price. It sells as much capacity as people want to buy, whether it's available or not (thus the occasional delay in getting on-line at busy times), and uses many switches to give one-to-multipoint capability (a cause of general slow response) so one can "visit" Web sites around the world.

Compare this to the typical voice telephone call. This leasing plan has unlimited switching capabilities to call anyone in the world, along with guarantees of capacity, so that every word spoken always gets through instantly. That's required where pauses in the transmission of your voice are unacceptable, unlike on a computer screen where they're merely an annoyance. And although the costs are high on a per-minute basis, this system works, given the typical short duration of the average voice telephone call.

In a further variation of providing bandwidth, market data providers like Bloomberg typically communicate from one point (the user's desk) to another point (the vendor's central computer), so they don't use many switches (and thus have fewer delays). And in order to ensure throughput even at busy times, they resell no more bandwidth than they have available. This is a costly proposition given the need for twenty-four-hour-a-day service and instantaneous response, but one important enough for these professionals to pay for.

Not all of the multitude of "messages" we send go over the phone companies' twisted copper wires. Sometimes, we communicate via microwave, satellite, fiber-optic glass, or coaxial cable. When you think about making contact, you think in terms of logical paths from point to point and a single transmission supplier. The path from me to you could be one straight line provided by a single phone company. But in fact, we are more likely to connect via many different lines and media and suppliers, and often not directly. Connecting me in New York to you in New Jersey may at various times of the day take us via California, at other times via Texas, and sometimes, "as the crow flies." You don't know the difference, and you don't care. Circumlocutory multicarrier connections are masked by the technology that provides great economies of scale, enormous capacities only dreamed of a few years ago, and phenomenal reliability. All of it happens faster than your ear can hear or your eye can see.

There will be many ways to rent communications capacity from the phone and cable companies. Depending on how much you're willing to pay, you'll receive different degrees of reliability, speed, security, and backup. Intranets within individual companies are already commonplace. New ones serving individual industries are appearing. Expect networks tailored to specific causes, just as we have single-focus Web sites.

Likewise for one-purpose use networks. The future of radio and television is digital delivery on demand via a unique electronic path derived directly from today's Internet data retrieval model. Those whose jobs are at stake don't want to hear it, but the days of "broadcast" as opposed to "request-retrieval" delivery are numbered. Radio and television will come over high-speed digital modems attached to either the cable or telephone lines or by microwave or satellite systems. The old days of sending the same thing to many are going fast!

*   *   *

Of course, I may be wrong. In predicting the future, we all unconsciously slant our prognostications toward a brighter world for ourselves. It's really too terrible to contemplate a scenario that terminates our ability to earn a living or predicts the destruction of our assets. No one has enough intellectual honesty to do so anyway. We always assume that "it will all work out." Some trends, however, are so certain, they're coming no matter what, and we'll just have to learn to live with them and adjust our behavior accordingly.

Positioning ourselves to respond is what competition is all about. Since Bloomberg is up against companies many times our size, we have to enter each commercial fight with an advantage. I don't believe that business battles should be even. If that were the case, the odds wouldn't be good for a company our size. Remember the math: The chance of coming out ahead in a fair contest is one in two. In consecutive tests, that chance becomes one in four, one in eight, one in sixteen, and so on. In other words, the likelihood that we will prevail five times in a row in a fair fight is only about 3 percent. That's not a risk a small company like ours can afford to take. We don't want fair fights. We want to go into contests with an advantage.

Working harder and being smarter give us a head start. So does thinking clearly about what we want, what the other guy wants, and which compromises are acceptable—before we make business decisions. Quicker decision making, less self-delusion about our capabilities and limitations, and the discipline of sticking to what we do well all give us a leg-up advantage over our rivals.

Doing what's right will let us compete. Like working for the stockholders and receiving reasonable compensation. I'm always amazed when I read of employees having two commercial jobs. Occasionally, they'll even start a second business to exploit a new idea while working for the old company. Why is the second idea they come up with not the property of the firm paying them to work full time? Or, they invest personally outside their companies. Our shareholders and employees have every right to expect a share in 100 percent of my activities, whether generated by my sweat or capital. Bloomberg's *Code of Ethics* states this clearly. You have one job. Period.

Compensating top management appropriately, particularly vis-à-vis the rest of the employees, also influences how hard everyone works together and how well a company does. How much to pay the CEO? Try roughly the amount other competent managers make in other fields. Management skills generally are fungible across industries. The argument that someone is worth tens of millions of dollars in compensation per year because his or her company's market value went up many times is so ludicrous that I've always been amazed anyone can espouse it as fair with a straight face. No one suggests the CEO reimburse the owners when the stock goes down. Nor does anyone actually believe that a major company would collapse if the CEO got hit by a truck (whether driven by a stranger or a representative of the board), or that he or she could have done it without the stockholders' money.

My salary is equal to the lowest-paid full-time employee we have (currently, $19,000 per year). Everything else I get is from my share of the firm's earnings (and income tax regulations encourage me to reinvest most of that in research and development). I have the incentive the other stockholders and employees want me to have: to maximize the company's long-term value. It also encourages me to delegate and let others run parts of our organization so we can go into new areas and products. I don't want any manager here to do the same thing for too long, and I shouldn't either. If everything works, I get paid; if it doesn't, I shouldn't, and with our structure, I won't.

Most companies, most of the time, grow and contract with the market they're in. Management often makes the difference only at the margin. Changing executives periodically almost always improves results: No matter how entrenched the CEO is. Mythology to the contrary, no one's irreplaceable and there are few revelations in business. The corporate change that works is *evolutionary* change, not *revolutionary* change: The quick fix, like buying a competitor or growth through acquisition, usually boosts earnings only for a short while. Corporate fixes through public relations and industry analyst "stroking" aren't worth much either: Stock P/E ratios go with the group, which is why they call it the herd instinct.

As a private company, we don't have a stock price to worry about. But we do have to give employees the incentive to go in the same direction as the owners. I have a firmwide, long-term interest in the company's success; everyone else must be rewarded in a similar manner. All our staff get a salary commensurate with what the local market pays for their specialty and experience. Additionally though, they all share in the worldwide overall revenues of the company. The system works well and fairly. We have a complex product; people buy it for a variety of reasons. Sometimes, it's the salesperson's demonstration skills and ability to meet objections. Sometimes, it's because of our service people's help, or a useful news story written by our journalists, or the data and the ability to analyze them as categorized and interpreted by our collection and research and development people. Often, it's because of those who are our first line of offense and defense—

the people who answer the phone when you call, or greet you when you walk into our offices.

Since everyone here can and does contribute, we share in a common pool. Some areas grow fast, some slowly. Next year, it could be reversed. That's why, at Bloomberg, not just the salespeople are on an incentive plan. Everyone participates in our firmwide (as opposed to branch or product or department) success. For senior people, this revenue sharing can be 50 to 75 percent of their total yearly compensation. If we have a bad year, the most junior employees get hurt, and those who are running the company do too. In good times, both groups have smiles on their faces.

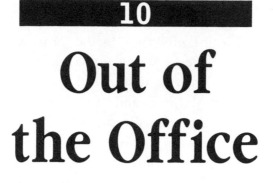

Out of the Office

Character and Consistency

There are defining moments in one's life, discrete events we all remember as turning points: graduation, marriage, births, deaths, career changes. But even more lasting impact comes from experiences that stretch over long time periods. Like one's home life. From my years growing up to my family life today, I've been shaped by the people around me. And I've tried to live that life with a sense of adventure—not just in my work life but in my private life as well.

I was born in Medford, Massachusetts, on Valentine's Day in 1942. My father, William, was a bookkeeper for a local dairy company and worked six or seven days a week all his life. My mother, Charlotte, stayed home as a housewife until he died. Then she went out and became the breadwinner. She taught me you've got to do what you've got to do, and to do it without complaining. I remember her making us wait every night for my father's return from the office to have dinner together as a family. We ate in the dining room with a linen tablecloth, linen napkins, and the family silverware. The food didn't come out in pots; only serving dishes came to the table. She insisted the best should be for the most important people, our family, and she did for us what my friends' mothers did only for guests. We've got to take care of each other was her message. No one else will.

My younger sister, Marjorie, and I would sit across from each other, with my parents at opposite ends of the table. My father described what he did at work that day. (One of his jobs was to buy actual tank cars full of milk for the dairy to make into cheese and, once in a while, he'd even resell them when they had too much inventory. I think he thought of himself as a great commodities trader. Perhaps that's the source of my interest in Wall Street.) And each of us around the table in turn did likewise. It wasn't a formal thing; we just all were interested in each other's activities and, as a family, shared them.

I didn't play baseball with my father or do crossword puzzles with my mother (I'm a so-so athlete and a terrible speller), but we did other things together: driving to New Jersey for a family vacation, sightseeing, going to a movie, dining at a local inexpensive family restaurant. Never did my parents argue (at least not in front of my sister and me). Never did anyone say "mine" as opposed to "ours." It really was a cohesive, happy, sharing unit. If I screw up my life, I can't blame my mother, father, or sister.

Our family always got together for the traditional annual events of Passover in the spring and Thanksgiving in the fall, along with the occasional birth, bar mitzvah, wedding, or funeral. School vacations seemed to split the family rather than the reverse. Some went skiing. Others went to the sun. Still, we always kept in touch. To this day, I call my mother first thing every morning when I get to work.

Taking care of your family when I was a kid was a given, something I hope my own children have learned. Similarly, I preach again and again at work that everyone in our company is family, that we must take care of one another. We really are related in both an emotional and a fiscal sense. Anyone who goes through life successfully receives the help of others. And no organization succeeds without most of its members contributing.

Having outsiders you can depend on in a time of crisis is help-ful as well—as when my niece, Rachel, was arrested in Egypt. (As I remind her now, we have a "criminal" in the family.) While Sue and I were in England attending my father-in-law's funeral in 1996, Rachel went sightseeing across the Israeli border into Egypt. When she came out of the ladies' room at a bus stop, the police arrested her, claiming they had found a gun in the bathroom. The protocol of this standard shakedown was to "confess" instantly and pay a bribe on the spot. Rachel, being Rachel, refused. We had to get Bloomberg's Jerusalem reporter, our London bureau chief, the Cairo bureau of another news organization, and a family friend in the State Department to prod the United States embassy for help. Such scams happen all the time. After she was released, an Amer-ican diplomat warned my sister, "Now, don't tell anybody about this. It would hurt our relationship with Egypt." Of all the dumb things. Who on earth is our guy protecting? How will other par-ents know to warn their kids? Talk about misplaced priorities. That diplomat never learned my mother's lesson of taking care of "us" before "them."

*   *   *

The day my acceptance to Harvard Business School arrived, I called my mother, knowing she'd be pleased.

"Don't let it go to your head," she said. That's how she reacts to everything.

The person who would have been really thrilled was my father, who had died a year earlier. For Dad, an average working-class guy from Chelsea, Massachusetts, Harvard was a rarefied and almost unattainable waypoint on the trail to the great American dream. The B School, the Salomon partnership, and our notoriety today, all would have meant even more to him than to me. My mother, while she's certainly proud of her son, puts it more into perspective. Sometimes, when people say to her, "Are you related to *the* Bloomberg," she'll say "No," just to avoid the conversation. My father would have said, "Absolutely! That's my boy. Let me tell you what else he's done."

They were always two different kinds of people. His was a less wealthy upbringing than hers. Dad's immediate family immigrated from Eastern Europe as children and never had much money. My mother's parents were born here and had done better financially. Perhaps that economic disparity, combined with the fact that one was first-generation and one second-, explains their different personalities. I remember my grandmother on my mother's side as very American, but my grandfather on my father's side was more old-world.

I'm proud of both families. Remembering your roots is important. Still, if you were to ask me who I am, I would say "American." I wouldn't think of saying Russian American, white American, or male American. For me, no modifier is necessary. Is it that I am assimilated? It just never occurs to me to think I need to be. I am part of this country—no more and no less. Where my parents came from, my lineage, just doesn't matter. As far as I'm concerned, I came from Saint Elizabeth's Hospital in Brighton, Massachusetts, where I was born.

Today, it has become fashionable to describe the United States as a mosaic rather than a melting pot. I hope that's just current politically correct rhetoric, soon to pass. The separatism it creates is not good for our society. The derogatory stereotypes used by some, the voluntary segregation allowed (compared to what used to be imposed) in school dormitories and clubs, the misguided teaching in "native" languages to immigrant children (as opposed to forcing them to learn the language they'll need for success)—all go toward dividing our society rather than melding it. Remembering and being proud of where you came from is fine. But here we're all part of a great big family, the American one. And as in the traditional smaller families, we have to live together, communicate among ourselves, and help one another to survive.

My father's death came as a surprise to me, even though it shouldn't have. He'd had rheumatic fever as a child. In those days, that disease severely damaged your heart and dramatically shortened your life span. I once remember playing with his white metal World War II air-raid warden's helmet and asking, "Why didn't you join the Army?" "Too old," he said. But I never bothered to do the math myself. Had I thought about it, I would have realized he wasn't too old; his bad heart kept him out of the military. So until I was a junior in college in the spring of 1963 and got a call from my mother, due to my intellectual laziness I didn't know the true state of my father's health. She told me about his problem, that he was in the hospital and not doing well, and that I should get on the next train from Baltimore. He was unconscious when I got to Boston. The doctor told me he wasn't going to live. Today, he could have survived; medicine wasn't as capable then as it is now. They didn't know how many days he had left, so my mother and I agreed I'd go back to school. Forty-eight hours later, my uncle called to tell me to come back. I returned that night for the funeral. Thirty years later, I still miss him.

My sister was then a student at Antioch College and about to enter one of the on-the-job training phases of its work-study program. She selected a job in Boston to be closer to home. "You can come back to Boston if you want, but you're not going to live at home. A young college girl should be living outside and building a life of her own," my mother said. And that's what Marjorie did. She worked the next six months in Boston but lived in a rented apartment. Forcing your children and protégés to go solo—and leaving them alone while they struggle as adolescents with relatively simple problems—is something parents and mentors must do. It's not easy, but it's necessary if they're to survive later on their own.

My mother is a very practical person. When my father went into the hospital, she read the instruction manual on how to operate the gear shift in the new family car. Until then, she'd only driven an automobile with an automatic transmission. After practicing by herself on the local streets, she started chauffeuring the visiting family back and forth to the hospital.

She doesn't get upset when things are beyond her control. She never complains. I think I've inherited that "just do what you can do and go on to the next thing" approach. Still, I'm a bit of a screwup who does much spontaneously. By contrast, my sister is focused and deliberate. My father was direct and to the point as well. Had you asked him, "How are you?" he would have told you. Ask my sister, she does the same. Ask my mother how she is and she'll always say "fine." Ask me, a little of both, depending on my mood, I suppose.

*　　　*　　　*

I had close friends in high school, but after graduating in 1960, we all went our separate ways, and I never saw any of them again. In college, I had two real pals. One took exactly the same courses as I did for years. We'd sit on the steps of his or my fraternity house each night and talk until 3:00 in the morning. We argued sports and politics and civics, and so on. When I went to Harvard Business School, he went to work for the government as an engineer.

Years later, I went to visit him for a weekend. It was a depressing episode. He had been one of my best friends, but after a decade apart, we had little in common. He'd been working for the military, and I'd been in graduate school and then gone to Wall Street. He was married with young children and lived in a small house. I'd been dating, partying, and traveling around the globe. We'd moved into very different worlds. I never saw him again until our thirty-year college reunion. We said, "We must get together," and of course, never have. A great guy, but a lot of friendship is built on common experience. End the commonality—and you tend to drift apart.

My friendship with the other guy, Jack Galotto, who was a year ahead of me in school, has withstood the test of time. He's a physician and I'm a "mogul." He's in Washington and I'm in Manhattan. What was the difference in the two friendships? Why did one last while the other didn't? Perhaps because I was also friendly with Jack's wife, Mary Kay? Or that Jack traveled and socialized with people not very dissimilar to me? Or that both Galotto children worked summers for Bloomberg? Or that he and I had actually lived together in our fraternity house while in school? Fraternities at Hopkins weren't much different from those in the classic John Belushi movie, *Animal House*. Though Hopkins was a serious place, and very competitive scholastically, we did drink and party a lot together. Maybe all that enjoyable "wasted" time had long-term benefits after all.

I was the first Jew to be admitted to the Phi Kappa Psi fraternity. After I graduated, the same local chapter admitted the first African American in its history. In those days, all fraternities were either predominantly Jewish or Christian. I joined one of the latter just because I liked Jack and wanted to be in his. (He was assigned to "rush" me as a prospective brother and stayed with me morning, noon, and night during the four weeks of rush. I don't think I ever had a chance to see another fraternity for comparison. It certainly wasn't a mistake, though. For four years, I loved it.) I always seem to be going a little against the mainstream.

Today, I've come to believe schools shouldn't tolerate campus organizations or living/eating arrangements that favor one religion or race. Education's purpose is to give students the broadest experience practical. Adults can associate with whomever they want after graduation—that's what freedom is all about. Still, teachers should require young people to try the unfamiliar so their future choices are intelligent, well-reasoned, and based on knowledge, not hearsay. Our bill of rights may apply to all, but it doesn't prevent us from forcing our youth to learn.

After school was finished, my first ten years working in New York were "play hard/work hard" times. As a bachelor who traveled with a big expense account, I had a girlfriend in every city, skied in every resort, ate in every four-star restaurant, and never missed a Broadway play. Nor did I ever pass up a chance to have one more business dinner with a visiting client, tour one more customer's office, or make that next overseas call in the middle of the night. With bachelor friends like Hugh Lowenstein and Michael Charles, I set new records in "burning the candle at both ends." There was never enough time in the day to do it all—but I always did.

Even now, decades later and a bit wiser, I still think the perfect day is one where I'm hopelessly overscheduled. Jog early in the morning and get to work by 7:00 A.M.; a series of rushed meetings; phone call after phone call; fifty or more voice messages and the same number of e-mails demanding a reply; a hurried business lunch between myriad stand-up conferences to solve firm personnel, financial, and policy problems; perhaps give an interview to some foreign newspaper where we get needed publicity; often make an image-building speech at some local conference in person or by satellite video-conferencing to the other side of the world; constantly welcome visiting clients; an early dinner with customers or a group of employees, followed by a second one with friends (where I actually get a chance to stop talking and eat); fall into bed, exhausted but satisfied with the day's accomplishments. That's the best weekday one could ever have!

*   *   *

In 1973, I started dating Susan Brown, a loyal subject of the British Crown who'd just moved to New York. As she's said, over the next three years our dates progressed from Monday night inexpensive Mexican food to Saturday night fancy French cuisine— and there was nothing else to do but fall in love and get married. We had two daughters, Emma in 1979, and Georgina (George to everyone) in 1983. At first, Sue was uncomfortable traveling with me on business or entertaining clients. She grew to enjoy it just at the time I got pushed out of Equities at Salomon Brothers and into

Systems Development, where there was much less nighttime or out-of-town activities. With two children to raise by that time, it was just as well.

While Sue certainly knew a lot about what I did at work on a conceptual level, other than on the most general terms we never talked business. ("How was your day?" "Fine.") I never brought the company's politics home. No matter how absorbing and consuming professional life can be, I've always felt it important not to make my business dominate the family conversation. To do so wouldn't be fair to my family—or to those at work expecting me to treat their problems in confidence. The company's business is the company's business, and I tried to keep the worlds separate; leave work problems at work, and home problems at home.

The concept of "corporate wife" or "first spouse" really turns me off. No one actually needs to know the inner workings of their spouse's place of employment, nor should he or she have a ceremonial role representing the company, or even our government. This remnant of feudalism is a fiction perpetuated by sycophants. Nepotism of any kind has no place in business or politics. Jobs should be available to all, and allocated on merit, not given as a reward to someone because of whom they are sleeping with. If the spouse wants a job, he or she should apply for it. (Or run in the next election!)

When leaving Salomon Brothers, I said to Sue, "I'd like to start a business. It'll mean I'll have to work a lot harder than I've ever worked before." (Which was difficult to do, given I was working six days a week.) "Are you okay with that?" And she responded "Yes." Years later, she would say, "You're working so much, you're never with the family," and I replied, "I told you it would require a commitment. This is what we agreed." Of course, that's *my* version of the conversation.

Having a business career and raising a family create inherent conflicts. Investment of time is the primary controllable determinant of success in both. The one constant in life, however, is the clock. You can only do so much. So Sue and I always worked it out. Generally speaking, I always tried to be home for family dinner on weekdays. Every weekend and vacation I spent with our daughters on the competitive horse show circuit or at our country house.

When it comes to managing my time, there are things I do to mitigate the everything-at-once conflict. I sleep less, combine my social life with business entertaining, and make my commute to work short. Rather than succumbing to the temptation to nap, I use my cellular phone to make business calls and read reports and newspapers while traveling. An understanding former spouse and kids help. I create an agenda of what I want to accomplish each day, and I stick to it. And a thousand other time-saving strategies. In other words, I focus more, combine activities, and attempt to become more efficient.

Still, as you balance work and family, the inevitable either/or will invariably arise: the hockey game or the board meeting, the horse show or the sales call. Raising the family *and* earning an income to support it. Professional child psychologists (and most of the ones I know either have no normal children or are bizarre themselves) won't understand the conflict, or the resolution: Sometimes you go to one and sometimes to the other. Nothing and nobody's perfect! Doing this has resulted in raising two children who've grown into your normal American teenagers, with your typical craziness. You always love them—even when as a parent you do everything you can to keep from exploding at the outrageous behavior that comes with the territory.

Of course, mine are different from yours. I know exactly how to raise your kids. Their problems are easy to solve. Sibling or parent/child conflict resolution can be easily accomplished with one of my flip comments. I'll just tell them to do what I say, and I'm sure they'll comply. Unfortunately, with my offspring, it's been a bit more difficult. My children are the only ones in the world with serious and clearly unresolvable troubles. Rivalries, insecurities, and complexes (and what I can only describe as simply irrational adolescent behavior) never happen with Emma and George. They are never wrong. As to their parents' responses, Sue and I are the only parents who say "No," the only ones to insist on a curfew, the only ones who are unreasonable. We have our daughters' word on it!

We had a great marriage for a long period of time, but in 1993, Sue and I decided to divorce. Over the years, we had gradually drifted apart. We developed different interests, and as our daughters became more independent, the differences became more apparent. I like skiing; she doesn't. She likes the movies; I don't. She likes to stay at home at night; I like to go out and party. I like to travel to certain places while she likes to travel to others. Business is a very important part of my life; she almost never came to visit my office. Nothing went wrong per se. We just developed separate lives doing different things. One day, we looked back and found things had changed. It was a slow evolution, but it happened.

As was true with my parents, Sue and I never argued or fought. When we disagreed, we worked it out, or one of us simply stepped back and went along in the interest of harmony; it's been the same since we split. We didn't battle then, and we're certainly not going to do so now. People think our relationship is strange. "Your divorce is so civilized," we're told. When you have children to raise, and you care about each other, how can you let it be otherwise? Sue's a wonderful person, perhaps my closest friend and confidante, and to this day, we still do things with the kids as a unit, like weekend horse shows and holiday dinners together.

*   *   *

I've always thought much of my early career success wouldn't have been possible if I had been married at the time. Without the family responsibilities, I was able to channel my efforts toward business. Today, I've got a similar situation. The kids spend more time off by themselves, and since I'm divorced, the choice of playing or working is often strictly up to me. Right now, while I'm writing this page, for example, the sun is shining and my friends are out playing tennis, golfing, flying, lying on a beach. I could join them, or do this. Obviously, I've made my selection—the same one I did long ago, when I was starting to work at Salomon Brothers. Life's a compromise. Will the satisfaction derived outweigh the sacrifices required? Of course. I never look back.

*   *   *

Ever since college, I've been engaged with independent projects and adventure, on my own terms. I've never been a spectator. I've always preferred doing things myself to watching other people do them, which is why I'm not much of a sports or movie fan. I'll never throw a football like Johnny Unitas, hit like Ted Williams, skate like Bobby Hull, or shoot like Larry Bird. I don't look like Harrison Ford or Kevin Costner either. But I'd rather try than just watch and daydream. Even with the young people's sports, when I see the kids snowboard or rollerblade by, I've got to give it a whirl.

The same with skiing and flying. Almost as soon as I joined Salomon, I learned to fly—airplanes, helicopters, you name it. It's been fun, it's been a challenge, and it has taught me a lot.

One Monday, in January 1976, a Salomon partner came into work waving a story from a small local newspaper. "You crashed your helicopter this weekend, huh?" he said loudly in the partners' dining room—calling attention to a newsflash I had conveniently "forgotten" to mention that morning.

I'd been flying a rented helicopter all by myself off the coastline of Connecticut, that Saturday when suddenly, "BANG." As I found out later, a defective piston rod had broken and smashed through the engine casing. The crankcase oil then spilled out onto the hot manifold cover and caught fire. All I knew then, however, was that I'd lost power and thick black smoke was starting to billow into the cockpit. I've always had a habit, when going over water, of staying

214

high enough to make land in an emergency. I also always monitor an active airport radio tower. With the noise of the explosion, I wasn't sure what was going on in the engine compartment behind me, but I certainly knew I was falling and couldn't breathe. I was going down. The only question was whether I'd walk away once I got there.

Fortunately, all helicopter pilots practice something called autorotation, where you can land softly without an engine. Without thinking about it—because you don't have time in the ten seconds left aloft to reason or panic—I hit the "push to talk" button and said to the local tower, "Helicopter 9272 going down, small island off Norwalk." And I heard the controller say, "Understand, Helicopter 9272 . . . ." By then I was below the horizon and I couldn't receive the signal. But I knew they'd heard me and would send help.

I was falling fast. I disconnected the engine from the transmission to let the overhead rotor spin free and build up kinetic energy. Then, a few feet above ground, I changed the pitch of the blades to generate lift. This stopped the fall just before the helicopter contacted the surface. I'd practiced autorotation again and again, and it worked. When I gently touched land, I had the helicopter skids firmly on the island and the tail over the water. The blades were just skimming the tree in front of me. Grabbing the fire extinguisher, I opened the engine compartment and extinguished the flames. It smoked for a while, but I was safe.

There were ice floes all around and some duck hunters in boats nearby. One rowed close and asked if I was injured. I would have been more than "injured" if I had gone into the frozen water. But I hadn't, so off they rowed. Was I scared? Well, there'd been no time for any emotion when I was in the air, and on the ground I was safe. So the answer is *no*—unless of course you count the internal shaking I couldn't stop for the rest of the day.

Fifteen minutes later, an Army Reserve helicopter showed up. They landed and offered me a ride back to Westchester. I asked for transportation to Teterboro Airport in New Jersey, where I'd rented the chopper and left my car. They didn't have time as they had to get back to their base in Albany, but they told me a rescue helicopter was on the way and would take me anyplace. So like the duck hunters, off they went, too.

Shortly thereafter, the Coast Guard arrived. Looking up at the giant white machine hovering overhead, I knew it was much too big to land on the small island. They opened the door and held out a blackboard with the words, "Do you need assistance?"

There I am, standing by a smoking aircraft in the middle of winter on a postage-stamp-size island with nothing but ice floes for miles around—and they're asking me if I need help? They lowered the rescue basket with instructions taped to the ends. I got in, hooked my feet under one restraint and grabbed a handhold on the other. They winched me fifty feet up in the air, banging me against the bottom of the helicopter for effect while they aligned the basket with the door, right in the fierce rotor downdraft with the deafening engine noise. But finally, I was up and in.

"What happened?" they asked.

"Engine quit."

"Where do you want to go?"

At Teterboro, my instructor was standing on the tarmac waiting for me, furious, because I was now two hours late. Somebody else had the helicopter rented after me and was screaming about his reservation. Then, instead of coming back in the little rented Enstrom F-28 helicopter, I showed up in an enormous Coast Guard rescue craft from Sikorsky. Surprise!

I've always valued practice. There are occasions when there just isn't time to figure out survival procedures, no matter how smart you are. Repetition builds instinct. I'm living proof. And preparation. I subscribe to the expression, "Stay ahead of the plane." It basically means, "Do things now while you have the time, so you don't have to later when you're rushed." I try that, not just in the air, but on the ground as well. You never know when an unexpected demand will prevent you from addressing something important you could have seen to earlier but didn't. If I'd not kept altitude or monitored an active airport tower, history might have been different.

*　　　*　　　*

I was tested in a similar way in 1995. I had a propeller fail while I was flying my nephew, Benjamin, on a tour around Manhattan. We had taken off from Westchester Airport, and since it was bumpy, I had asked Departure Control for clearance to a high, hopefully calm altitude. We were climbing through fifteen hundred feet above the ground when all of a sudden, "POP." The engine was going around fine, but I had no thrust! Instantly, we went from a very powerful airplane to a very heavy glider.

High-performance propeller-driven airplanes run the engine at a constant speed no matter how much thrust is needed. To get more or less "push" (really "pull"), you change the pitch of the propeller blades. In my case, the governor in the propeller failed, and the oil pressure it controls suddenly couldn't keep the prop at an angle. Instead, the blades flattened, which gave us no forward drive whatsoever, no matter how fast they were going around.

My instrument gauges went crazy. The engine was running, but it might as well have been dead. (At least with a dead engine, it's quieter.) I had no time to play amateur mechanic. We were going down. Instantly, I started a 180-degree turn and called Air Traffic Control (ATC): "Departure, November five zero four Mike Bravo." That was my plane's call sign. "Emergency. Engine problem. Going back to Westchester."

"Contact tower, one nineteen seven. Will advise." The response from ATC was instantaneous.

Switching frequencies to 119.7 MHz with one hand while flying with the other, I said to the controller, "Westchester, four Mike Bravo back with you." Departure had already briefed the tower controller over their land line.

"Clearing all runways. Your choice. I've scrambled the equipment." That meant he had called out the fire engines.

"I'll take three four," I said as I carefully and methodically went through my prelanding checklist.

Turning to a heading of 340 degrees magnetic, I had just enough height to glide down, lower the landing gear, land on Runway 34, and roll off onto a taxiway to a dead, and I mean dead, stop. If I had been at a lower altitude, I wouldn't have made it back. Who knows where I could've put the plane down. The Hudson River? Landing in the water wasn't on my "to do" list. But I was lucky. Or, you could say my safety habit of always gaining altitude as fast as practicable had paid off. It's always the little things that buy you a slight extra margin, that in turn saves your rear (or your life). And if you never need it, that's even better.

My private, unprovable theory is: Nothing's going to happen to me in an airplane or helicopter from now on because, while the likelihood of one accident is small and the likelihood of two minuscule, there are no measurable odds on the likelihood of three happening to a single person. (Unfortunately, this isn't true in reality. Each is an independent event, so I'd better continue to take care. Still, it's somewhat comforting.)

I don't think Ben quite understood what was going on at the time. As I went into the turn, I said, "Ben, there's something that needs adjusting. We're just going back for a quick check." The engine was running, so as far as he knew the plane was fine. After I made the turn, he could see the airport ahead. And when the controller in the tower said he had "scrambled the equipment," Ben didn't know what that meant. As we landed, fire engines converged on us from all sides, at which point Ben figured out what was happening, but from a nicely safe vantage point on the ground. The lesson I suppose is: Don't panic. Do what you were trained to do. No more. No less.

My sister wasn't thrilled when she heard what had happened. But as I told her later, any landing you walk away from is a good one. Of less importance, there was no damage to the plane except that I overboosted the engine when I lost power and had to get it overhauled. That made the day an expensive tour of Manhattan that Ben never had.

Why fly? I like it when you have to do what you say you're going to do. You must "walk the walk," not just "talk the talk." Instrument pilots make a formal agreement with Air Traffic Control as to what they'll do under all circumstances. Everyone else in the clouds has done the same. You take off, go into a storm that's just three hundred feet above the ground, fly for two hours, and come out of the clouds just above the treetops, perfectly lined up for a runway hundreds of miles from where you started. This works even when you lose all your radios on the way. There's something about arriving safely that's very satisfying. You must do exactly what you agree to do or you might die. You apply all those rules and concepts you learned. You use those numbers, techniques, gizmos, and gadgets on the instrument panel; they really mean something.

There's no hypocrisy, no "fudging." What you say is what you do! All pilots learn to make a commitment and stick to it, follow the book, and depend on others to do the same. Those who don't, don't survive. Consistency in thought and conduct in the aviation world is required to live. In our everyday life, it's important for success as well.

*   *   *

My lessons and adventures also happen on the ground. Once I was skiing from a helicopter with some friends in British Columbia, Canada. The snow was unstable and our guide told us to stay far apart in case of an avalanche. He went down the hill first, followed by an old friend from California, Bob Brandt. Then my friend Eric Borgen fell. Another friend, Tom Weisel, and I stopped to give him a hand. Everybody else got stuck behind us. As we were ready to start again, somebody screamed, "Look, it's moving!" The snow right in front of where we were standing was moving downhill at an ever-increasing rate. The guide saw the avalanche coming, and skied up onto an outcropping. Brandt, unfortunately, looked over his shoulder, then tripped and fell—and the snow just covered him.

Suddenly, as the slide stopped moving, there was deathly silence. We realized that a human being who was there a second ago wasn't there now.

When you ski in back country like the uninhabited Bugaboo mountains, everyone wears transmitters under their clothing. If you need to, you can turn these transmitters into receivers. Then, as you go near somebody who's buried, their transmissions from under the snow will get louder and louder. As you get farther away, quieter and quieter. So you go back and forth in one direction until you figure out where the person is on that line. Then you go up and down 90 degrees in the other direction until you pinpoint your fellow skier, who should lie beneath the point where the lines cross.

We all skied down next to the avalanche and took off our skis. Everybody stopped above a large ice formation. But Bob couldn't have been above it. I didn't know how avalanches work, but I was sure they didn't carry you up the glacier, and I remembered Bob falling after he had passed that point. So I stopped a little farther down, took off my skis, and walked onto the hard snow with my beeper turned to "receive." Instantly, I picked up his signal. "He's down here!" I shouted.

"No, no. He's up here. We have him." They were clustering around each other digging like mad with their hands.

I knew right away what had happened: In the general panic, somebody up the hill had not turned his or her "transmit" to "receive." Their receivers were listening to a signal from someone in their own group instead of from somebody buried. Except for me. I was a hundred yards down the hill and there was only me above the snow. And I was hearing something. I didn't have any question whatsoever that I was right.

The guide had panicked along with everyone else. He should have stopped and checked, particularly when I was down there insisting they were wrong. His behavior was an example of believing what you want to, irrespective of possibilities raised by inconsistent facts.

He did do one thing right, however. He called the helicopter that had been ferrying us to the mountaintops. This helicopter was servicing multiple groups of skiers. It dropped one off, and while they skied down, it took the others up. When the helicopter brought in the second group to help with the search, their guide had time to make sure everybody was on "receive." While they were flying, he gave them shovels and calmly explained to them what they should do when they got on the mountain. They tried to land where I was, on a flat area that made a great helipad. But I wouldn't budge. I just kept signaling them to back off. The pilot kept gesturing wildly and trying to push me away. I refused to move, so the helicopter had no choice but to land below me and balance on a precipice during unloading. Everybody jumped out, furious with me for being stubborn and slowing them down. But as they came up the hill, I yelled, "I have the guy here. They must be doing something wrong above. Listen carefully as you come by."

Sure enough, as they came up the hill in a line with their receivers on, there was no question that I was standing right on top of Bob Brandt. They could detect him, too. When we dug him out, he said he could hear me the whole time, but I couldn't hear him screaming for his life. Maybe it was the wind, or maybe the snow muffled the sound. He wasn't harmed, just panicked. Later that year, he came down with colon cancer, had an operation, and was 100 percent cured. So, twice in twelve months, he cheated death. He's still alive and well today. And he certainly doesn't mind that I was a bit stubborn.

People accept things as gospel even when they don't understand them. They don't sit back and say, "Explain that to me." "Say it again." "Does that make sense?" I find it annoying when people talk freely about the XYZ—some acronym representing something or other—and when I ask, "What does XYZ stand for?" they don't have a clue. Too often, people do things automatically, thoughtlessly. It has nothing to do with their inherent intelligence. It has everything to do with their inquisitiveness. Our schools too often fail to teach logic and skepticism. We are taught facts and techniques, not concepts and thoughts; we learn to accept, not question. This terrible failing in our educational system penalizes students for the rest of their lives.

Lack of consistency is another common failing that hurts us. People say, "We'll always go in this direction," but when they are faced with a real-life situation, they often act independently of their previous plans. Either their original resolution wasn't well thought out, or they just don't have the intellectual honesty to do what they said they'd do. Picture an airline pilot. When there's a fire in engine No. 3, do you really want him or her playing amateur aeronautical engineer? No! He or she should follow the instructions arrived at much earlier in a controlled environment by aviation and safety experts: Take out the book marked "Fire in Engine No. 3," and follow the checklist, slowly, deliberately, and carefully. That's what will save the plane and its passengers. We should all do the same in our daily pursuits when relationships and careers are at stake. Think. Prepare. Plan in advance when there's no time pressure. Then, in real life, do what you said.

*   *   *

There are many reasons why some succeed and others don't, why some just continue to grow and others spurt up and, as quickly, collapse. Three things usually separate the winners from the losers over the long term: time invested, interpersonal skills, and plain old-fashioned luck.

You are born with a certain genetic intelligence level. Given the current state of medical science, you're probably stuck with whatever God gave you. Nor can you change much of your environment in any practical sense. But does that mean you should give up? Sit back and just accept the hand you've been dealt? No, of course not. Someone once surveyed both English and American "men on the street" as to their self-perception. The English generally described themselves as being blue-collar. The Americans virtually all said "middle-class." Some people, no matter what their nationality, see themselves as upwardly ambitious; some settle for what others expect of them. Some feel destiny is in their own hands, while others see fate as something they can't ever master. (Fortunately for Great Britain, habits do change and necessity eventually forces people to "get off their rears" and do something about their lot.)

Most fortunes are built by entrepreneurs who started with nothing and generally got fired once or twice in their careers. And throughout history, the vast majority of great writers, artists, musicians, dancers, jurists, and athletes have come from the less financially secure families. The CEOs of most Fortune 500 companies went to State U rather than Ivy League schools (or had no college at all). Could it be that good "prenatal intelligence" (the ability to pick the right parents) is possessed by those born into poor families as opposed to those who are children of the rich? Or that the traditional prerequisites of success are not terribly important today?

The rewards almost always go to those who outwork the others. You've got to come in early, stay late, lunch at your desk, take projects home nights and weekends. The time you put in is the single most important controllable variable determining your future. You can try to beat the system by winning the lottery, but the odds are terrible. You can hope the government tries to equalize with Robin Hood tax policies and throws some money your way. Unfortunately, every time it's been tried in the past, all went down to the lowest level—not up to the highest one. You can hope that "anti-exploitation" labor laws protecting workers with mandated coffee breaks, two-year maternity and paternity leaves, six-week minimum vacations, and a cap on hours you're allowed to work will keep your competitors down. The Communists tried to eliminate any form of meritocracy for seventy years and, in addition to wrecking their economies, they literally starved fifty million people to death in the process.

If you put in the time, you aren't guaranteed success. But if you don't, I'm reasonably sure of the results.

Still, the Socialists had at least one thing right. No one does it alone. We can't each have our own army to protect our freedoms. Insurance only works if we spread the risks. It's in everyone's interest to educate all the children who will run our society when we're in our dotage. Only pooled resources can cure diseases we haven't gotten ourselves (yet!). Society is a collection of individuals: Our ability to act alone at a microlevel is provided by sharing certain responsibilities at the macrolevel. Even animals band together for companionship, protection, and food. We're better positioned to control our own lives than ever before in history, and simultaneously, in a nuclear world, we're less able to go it alone.

*　　　*　　　*

I've worked hard. You bet! But time after time, even sometimes when I didn't know it was happening, my destiny has been determined by others. Among those influencing my fate were my parents, sister, wife, kids, teachers, friends, and coworkers. Those who counseled me, those who comforted me, those who lent and shared and stood aside so that I could advance—all of them contributed to my well-being. There are other ways to say thanks to them (the best being by my conduct in life rather than my words on this page), but no other context is as good as this book to publicly state their importance. Plain and simple, my success is theirs, too.

The selfish loner who phrases everything as "I" or "me" will never go the limit. Not one of the businessmen and businesswomen at the top really deep down inside thinks that he or she did it alone. Every one of them credits others. The press may write about Dede in art auctions, The Donald in real estate, Martha in homemaking, Bill in software, Estée in cosmetics, George in investments, Katherine in newspapers, Rupert in media, Beverly in opera, or Ted in TV news, but Colonel Sanders doesn't cook every piece of chicken you buy at a Kentucky Fried Chicken store (in fact, he's been dead for years). The more successful you are, the more likely it is that "you" is a group. To win big, you must have an ability to leverage your work by identifying, including, convincing, and inspiring others to follow your vision. Then share the praise, or they won't be there for very long to help, and soon there'll be little for you to talk about.

If you work hard and cooperate with others, are you guaranteed to be a billionaire, win a Nobel Prize, raise great kids, and become a household name? Not always. There's that other component: luck. I know people who have done all the right things and still don't come out on top. Some who by chance have been part of organizations where some idiot has wrecked everything they've built. Some who went into a business where unforecastable changes in technology, war, disease, or taste obsoleted, eliminated, or made unfashionable their product. Some whose health gave out at much too early an age, and others whose family needs kept them from trying something new. Any of a thousand other unfortunate, unforeseeable, and probably unpreventable obstacles can arise.

If I had not gotten thrown out of Salomon Brothers, I'd never have founded our company. If I'd been thrown out later, the opportunity to compete against those distracted growing giants would have been less, and our success would probably have been diminished. Suppose I hadn't been accepted at Johns Hopkins or Harvard Business School, or met Sue, or found just the right people to work at Bloomberg, or had the same college friends, or safely landed that helicopter or that plane. My life would be very different.

Work hard. Share. Be lucky. Then couple that with absolute honesty. (People are much more inclined to accept and support someone they think is "on the level." We all will forgive if we don't question the intent.) And never forget the biblical admonition, "Do unto others as . . . ."

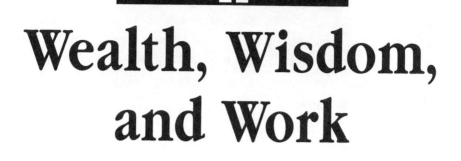

Wealth, Wisdom, and Work

Philanthropy and Public Service

On October 1, 1981, I began the entrepreneurial phase of my life. That Thursday, my prospects for future success were uncertain (unless you count the $10 million I was receiving for my stake in Salomon Brothers). I'd just been fired, and no one was offering me gainful employment. I was starting a new company to compete with corporate giants that had decades of history, hundreds of offices, thousands of workers, millions of customers, and billions of dollars of assets. I wasn't broke, but I was going against the odds.

Fifteen years later, on October 1, 1996, I sent a multimillion-dollar check to the Johns Hopkins University and Hospital as part of a $55-million contribution I'd made to this great institution's capital fund-raising campaign (which I was chairing). In the previous twelve months, I had made two other seven-figure gifts to cultural and educational organizations. The years between had been good to me—and now I was going to give some of it back.

Philanthropy and public service are my two great loves after my daughters and my company. There are few people as lucky as I have been. Depending on your perspective, I deserve it or I don't. No matter which, I have it. And now, rather than complain about this world, rather than watch the less fortunate suffer, rather than miss the opportunity to leave my kids a better world, I'm using my time and wealth to improve it.

* * *

My first exposure to public service was as a Cub Scout when I was seven or eight years old. Each year, on Election Day, we volunteered to escort the elderly from their buses or cars to the voting booths. Wearing our uniforms, with every badge and medal we'd earned, and (of course) the American flag sewn on our shirts, we beamed with self-importance as we played what we were told was a "critical part" in the democratic process. Allowed the freedom to cross the police crowd-control barriers at will, we felt power and privilege. With banners flying, police standing about, poll workers handing out campaign literature, we were overcome with pride and excitement, just like in a Norman Rockwell painting.

Twice, I had the privilege of escorting the town's most renowned citizen, the mother of the lost aviator Amelia Earhart. She must have been in her eighties then, and needed to hold tightly to my arm as we walked. Everyone cleared the way and showed great deference to her as we moved slowly, step by step, to the polls. Being the center of attention (or at least next to the star) was heady stuff. I was impressed with myself, even if no one else was.

Around the Korean War period, Americans expressed their patriotism openly. On Patriot's Day, every April 18, hundreds of adults would gather in the town center for the reading of the Henry Wadsworth Longfellow poem, "Paul Revere's Ride," celebrating the start of the American Revolution. A mounted rider in period attire would retrace the famous rebel messenger's historic route from Boston to Lexington and on to Concord. To the delight of the children lining the sidewalks, he'd scream, "The British are coming, the British are coming," as he galloped by.

228

Perhaps the proudest moment of my early life was being chosen one year to read this famous rhyme on the raised platform overlooking the assembled revelers. With "Paul" on his prancing horse in front of me, the high school band playing John Philip Sousa marches, and newspaper photographers snapping away, I read aloud into a real live microphone the famous poem: "Listen, my children, and you shall hear/Of the midnight ride of Paul Revere,/On the eighteenth of April, in Seventy-five;/Hardly a man is now alive/Who remembers that famous day and year . . . /One, if by land, and two, if by sea;/And I on the opposite shore will be . . . /And yet, through the gloom and the light,/the fate of a nation was riding that night . . ." I can remember it still.

Memorial Day, honoring those fallen in defense of our country, was another big celebration in Medford. Back then, all towns (as opposed to a very few today) had parades and wreath-laying ceremonies at the local cemetery. The police on motorcycles, the fire department in their trucks, the fraternal organizations, churches, and veterans' groups with flags and bands, and the regional branch of the National Guard, with rifles at the ready, all marched. From school, we filed two by two in orderly rows to the parade finish at the town's war memorial. There we would stand at attention very solemnly pledging allegiance "to the flag of the United States of America and to the Republic for which it stands, one nation under God, indivisible, with liberty and justice for all." Then the lone bugler played "Taps" and the jolting firing of the Honor Guards' guns in salute closed the proceedings.

I was friendly with a girl whose father had been killed in World War II; his name was engraved on a bronze plaque at a nearby traffic circle. She was the first person of my generation I knew who had lost a parent. Once, we were chosen together to carry the school's Memorial Day wreath to the monument as everybody looked on. It was quite a responsibility for children. Our classmates, the parade participants, the elected officials, all watched as we moved slowly in step to the drummers' cadence. Heaven forbid we would trip, cough, sneeze, or otherwise break the solemnity of the occasion. It was an honor to participate and it made those carefully listed rights and privileges we studied in civics class somehow more real and important.

*   *   *

My support for a strong, well-disciplined, and fully civilian-accountable police and firefighter force arises from what I learned as a child. We played on the fire trucks when visiting the fire station to pet the traditional firehouse dalmatian. We talked and joked with the police officers handling traffic at the corner school crossing each morning. While civil servants' uniforms create fear in many parts of the world, the familiarity born of constant interaction always left me feeling the wearers were employees of "we the citizens," and there to protect and serve. (A favorite philanthropic cause to which I have been long dedicated is the New York City Police and Fire Widows' and Children's Benefit Fund. The unhappy purpose of this mostly Wall Street charity is to provide funds to the widows of the newly fallen officers and firefighters who died protecting us. Unfortunately, the list of beneficiaries grows longer each year.)

It's unfortunate that we don't always have the same feeling of service when thinking of politicians, another group whose salaries we pay. It's true that other than at election time, the concept of who's working for whom does get a little foggy. It's true politicians often divert the police from protecting us to give visiting officials from whom they're currying favor extra security. (Sure, he or she is at greater risk. But nobody forces anyone to run for office! Why should we be less protected in order to ensure the safety of those choosing an acknowledged risky career?) Sure, elected officials sometimes pull rank and travel by motorcade. (Why should we have our streets closed so they, our employees, don't have to wait in traffic while we endure insufferable delays?) Yes, these servants receive a greater standard of airline safety than the Federal Aviation

Authority tells us we, the average citizens, need. (Could someone explain that to me someday?) Doesn't somebody have the roles reversed, you ask? Shouldn't they be running risks and inconveniences *for us?*

Poll after poll shows that most people rank elected and appointed officials at the bottom of the "most respected" list—right down with us journalists (where maybe I can understand the general contempt). I am certainly not above taking cheap shots at politicians' hypocrisy and their "reelection at all costs" mentality, but no one in public service deserves that much vilification!

Politics, no matter what the cynical say, is a noble profession. What a shame that some who hear the call to run for office ruin what's so good in America. It's a disgrace that a few in office are selfish, corrupt, lazy, incompetent, and shameless. Holders of high office who philander, obfuscate, and act duplicitously cheapen our society. We should insist that officials deliver after the election what they promised during the campaign, and conduct their personal lives in an appropriate manner. It's a sin that some of our highest elected officials or their families come up so short.

In a democracy, we need good, smart, hardworking people to run for office. We need choice from which to select able souls to provide governmental functions. Society is too complex for us to run things ourselves. Somebody has to bring us to a centralist consensus acceptable to most, with the minimal imposition on those at the fringes. That's what politics is all about. It's hard to think of a tougher challenge or a more needed service (or a more satisfying occupation for those who do it well).

I've never run for political office myself. I have no interest in being a legislator. The pace, the focus, and the compromises don't appeal to me. The legislative process is so boring that I'd last for all of five minutes as a senator or a congressman. If I ever ran, it would be for a job in the executive branch of government—mayor, governor, or president. I think I'd be great in any of these three executive jobs that mirror my experience. (Those wanting competent government needn't worry. I have no current plans to enter the public arena.)

It annoys me how many people presenting themselves as candidates for high office have an interest in running for any position they can get elected to, with no thought of what their skills are, or whether they'd be better at administration or strategic thought. When considering candidates for an executive job, we shouldn't think that serving in a legislative position prepares that person for the totally different responsibilities of the other. Or vice versa. In the real (commercial) world, where performance is the only thing that counts, these people would never be considered for promotion to positions requiring totally different talents. Only in government does anyone have the hubris to argue that serving in a lesser office and doing one thing poorly prepares you for higher responsibilities doing another.

That doesn't mean I'm not involved in elective public service. Quite the contrary. As a wealthy Democrat who has given consistently to my party, I am called repeatedly by every Democratic candidate, from those running for dog catcher on up. All want my "insightful views," all want "to tap my vast array of experiences," all feel I've got a "great deal to contribute"—and oh, by the way, all will gladly accept a significant financial contribution to their campaign fund. (And don't worry about any mandated campaign spending limits. With typical political hypocrisy of telling the voters they seek campaign reform while not cutting themselves off from the mother's milk of contributors, the politicians looking for donations can always find a vehicle that permits the transfer of your money to some entity that gets them elected.)

Do I give? Of course. Democracy only works if we support it. The alternatives are untenable, and I certainly want to leave a free, healthy country for my kids. I send checks to individual candidates I believe in. I send checks to candidates running under my party's banner, even sometimes when I don't really believe they are the best on the ballot. And I send checks to most (but not all) of the candidates my friends ask me to help.

Some find these concepts of party loyalty and "You scratch my back, I'll scratch yours" dishonest and distasteful. Why should you give to someone you think is second-rate? Why contribute to someone who's running against a candidate you're already supporting? They're wrong! Party allegiance and who's asking are both as important as the individual who's running. Having someone (even if the individual candidate's not the best) who will help your side win a majority enables the laws you support to be enacted. Helping a friend get someone elected whom you're not thrilled with may be a small price to pay when that friend will reciprocate and support your urgent favorite.

If we ask others for help, how can we not respond when they call in turn? The same is true in philanthropic fund-raising. We've got to support one another's causes. I find it infuriating when my former wife asks our old friends for help with her fund-raising and they ignore her. How dare they, considering all those years both she and I together supported their charities and political candidates? People need to understand that life, like it or not, has to be quid pro quo.

*　　　*　　　*

In addition to giving me a sense of public service, my family taught me about private philanthropy when I was very young. Every year, my father received a publication listing contributors to his favorite charity. During dinner, he would look down each page of the book for familiar names and remark on the size gift made by people he knew, or the complete absence of other names from the list.

What his acquaintances gave certainly influenced my father in deciding on contributions for the following year. Peer pressure: Its impact in the philanthropic world is hard to overstate. People are very conscious of their place in any pecking order. Contributor lists, grouped by amount donated, very often get donors to stretch to the next highest level. When soliciting for donations, always ask for more than you think you'll receive. You may be wrong and get it. The potential contributors will be flattered that you thought they could give that much. And they certainly will give more than they previously planned, when confronted with the bigger target. We are all followers. I gave one large gift to Harvard—and a few months later, someone else donated three times that amount for a similar purpose, citing my gift as the impetus for their generosity.

When asked for a major contribution, if I'm interested in the cause, my first question to the solicitor is, "What did the organization's board members and you personally give?" If you and they don't support the cause, maybe it doesn't deserve my help. Not everyone can give large amounts, but a gift significant to the trustees' and requester's personal circumstances is a prerequisite to getting me interested. Conversely, when I ask others for donations, I always start the conversation by describing my company's support. Those I'm asking have a right to know, and I'm proud of what we do.

Asking other folks for money is difficult and distasteful. But unpleasant as it is, you have two choices: Don't ask and don't help as much as you can, or ask and maximize assistance to your favorite causes. Do you care enough to swallow your pride, summon up your courage, commit your resources, and take the time to pick up the phone? Those who do follow through don't necessarily find it easier than those who can't bear to make the call—they just care more about helping.

Many people of average means give generously, but it is from the rich, in fact, that philanthropic organizations get a disproportionate percentage of their funding. Those decrying the disparity between the haves and have-nots, and those in government desirous of redistributing wealth, should take note. The Carnegie, Mellon, Rockefeller, and Duke fortunes were largely given back to society by their makers and heirs, creating institutions that have had much more lasting impact than the politicians would ever have delivered by taking that same money through income and inheritance taxes and spending it on "public works." The original fortune builder, and one or two of their successor generations, may have lived well, but unlike their envious critics, most contributed more than they took. The world (and America) is much better off because of them.

Are today's wealthy as generous? The Forbes 400 list (better to be on it than not) has both stupid misers and brilliant generous benefactors scattered throughout its numbers. So does any catalog of Americans. In 1989, there were 1.3 million American millionaires; today, there are probably three times that number. I'd rather bring my kids up here in the United States than anywhere else; America really is the land of opportunity and of helping each other privately. Whether through IPOs, promotions, or new substantive businesses, whether as a result of investing in stocks, commodities, or real estate, the amount of value we've created in our country is truly extraordinary, and the willingness to share success is unique. Think other places are fairer, more egalitarian, more generous, offering a better life to average persons (particularly for those traditionally discriminated against)? Get serious. When people vote with their feet, they *always* come in this direction.

And Americans give wealth away in record amounts to help others. Every philanthropic organization I know has record receipts. The number of such institutions is also skyrocketing. We may have more than others—but we give more help to those who have less. Where else are there as many privately funded universities, museums, symphonies, hospitals, churches, and so on?

*   *   *

Consider any very lucky individual here in the United States. Once they make a fortune, the real question is, what's it for? That sounds ridiculous to the average "working stiff" daydreaming about the lottery, but after you've accumulated a certain amount of wealth, you've got a serious problem. You can only eat so many meals, have so much domestic help, travel to so many places, and live in so many rooms. You can only sleep in one bed at a time.

The reality of great wealth is that you can't spend it and you can't take it with you. All you can do is give it to other individuals (with large gift or inheritance taxes to pay), or give it to philanthropic organizations (usually with large income tax credits to receive). The issues left to your discretion are only to whom, how much, and when to give.

So, after you've gotten used to living like a king, what do you do? First, forget worrying over taxes. More people do more stupid things trying to avoid the inevitable than they can count. Our country gave you the opportunity—now pay back your share and get on with it. Second, don't spoil your family. After you've worked for a lifetime, your legacy shouldn't be strife, anguish, and heartbreak, particularly for those you love. Leave them enough to have a crutch in hard times, a boost in good ones, and fond remembrances for the rest of their lives. Third, be selfish! Buy yourself enormous pleasure. Give most of your wealth to charity!

How much should you carve out first for your loved ones? Do you really want to eliminate the need for them to work as hard as you did? Do you really want your children to be like those who thought themselves your betters while you struggled? Letting them have too much money is really a lot worse than letting them have too little. I've watched family after family destroyed by excessive distributions to descendants, and by family patriarchs' and matriarchs' attempts to be able to control others' behavior from the grave. With wealth comes power. With power comes the ability to damage. Gifts and inheritances influence those you love most. Inheriting too much money at one time destroys initiative, distorts reality, and breeds arrogance. When the money runs out—as it always does—those left bereft of cash can't cope. And having money with "strings attached" often creates unintended and perverse distortions in behavior. No one can visualize the future and what will be needed.

If you want to help those you love in an intelligent fashion, pass on some of your money to them while you're alive and can still teach your values and actually see the money's effect. After you're gone, have your bequests parceled out in small amounts so your heirs' lifestyles are improved gradually, at different stages of their growth, perhaps even giving them a second chance following a few mistakes.

And treat all your heirs the same. Time after time, families are ripped apart by unequal bequests to siblings. There's always an excuse for excess and favoritism (different skills, maturity levels, ages, sexes, interests, etc.). Better to burn your cash. Children have no God-given right to an inheritance (although inheritance laws often do guarantee something to spouses), and if a fortune pits sister against brother, or causes self-destructive behavior, having given your hard-earned wealth to them turns out to have been the worst thing you could have done.

As to giving to grandchildren, few realize just how far removed two generations really are from each other. To memorialize one's name or minimize taxes, people in their wills include relatives who are little more than strangers and who will never remember their benefactors anyway. How stupid! Many of the recipients even eventually change their names to better fit the new society their inheritance buys. So much for immortality.

My solution is to create trusts for my children and a foundation for philanthropy. The trusts will ensure my offspring a helping hand to start their own lives, and a crutch should they run into problems. They'll have to work to support themselves and their families, but I'll be providing the best education and a grubstake to start them off. Later in life, should they need assistance, I, my executors, or the trusts' administrators will always be there to help in an emergency.

The real financial legacy I'm leaving my kids is much more powerful. They will be the key trustees of our family's foundation and, as such, will possess great influence. For the rest of their lives, along with their mother and a handful of my closest friends, they'll distribute large grants to worthy institutions and creative individuals needing support. In their hands will be the ability to channel cultural development, further scientific and medical research, shape the political process, mold our youth, and support their religious organizations.

Every so often, they'll get together and approve grants, set investment policy, and administer the foundation. Both sisters will have to work together and with their mother, something that will keep the family from splintering. Perhaps the conversation will go, "What would Daddy have done?" or "Daddy would have gotten a kick out of such and such." They might choose to sustain some charity I supported when I was alive. But within a few broad guidelines I've set in creating the foundation, they'll spend their time picking the worthy causes they think best. (An occasional remembrance of their father wouldn't be so bad either.)

And they'll work on the foundation's board with my friends, to whom I'm not bequeathing any money. Most have done well in their own careers and don't need it; all would be embarrassed to accept it. They are already philanthropically minded (if they weren't, they probably wouldn't be my friends) and will know how to counsel my daughters in selecting among hundreds of worthy requests. And they'll get the satisfaction and recognition they deserve, along with a periodic reminder of our friendship.

*   *   *

You and I today (and my foundation later) can pick from an endless list of philanthropic causes to support. We can further our religious beliefs; educate our youth; help prevent early death, blindness, and misery around the world. We can participate in finding a cure for diseases that might later strike our descendants;

enhance and enrich our culture by supporting artists, musicians, and museums; beautify our environment; or give opportunity to those needing a break.

In every case, our influence and memory will continue long after our physical presence is removed. And if we make the gifts (or at least the commitments) when we're still around, we can get the greatest satisfaction available for cash today, watching the process of helping others unfold. Having our names on a plaque, on a scholarship, on a research grant, or on a list of generous donors who make possible the furtherance of a philanthropic organization's goals rewards us as long as we live. It puts everyone else—our entire community, our country, and even the whole world—in our debt. What greater satisfaction could we possibly get than watching ourselves do great things for humanity? Not only great things, but things we, not someone else, think should be done.

Both Johns Hopkins University and Yale University had benefactors who experienced this firsthand. Zanvyl Krieger, a Baltimore lawyer with a great feeling for humanity, had planned to leave the magnificent sum of $50 million to Hopkins after his death. Then, in 1992, he asked himself, on second thought, "Why wait?" Why let another generation go without an education? Why let some cure for a disease be discovered after more have died? So he gave the money then, rather than leave it in his will. Were the adulation, recognition, respect, and pleasure he's been receiving over the past few years worth it? He'd say it was the smartest thing he ever did. "Should have done it even earlier."

Lee Bass had a different experience, a less pleasant one, but another reason to make gifts when you are alive rather than as a bequest. He gave $20 million to Yale for a particular program. For a variety of reasons, they could never get it going. So he took his money back (and will, no doubt, give it away to some other equally worthwhile cause, but one where his wishes are satisfied). Had he done it by bequest, he'd have had no second chance.

Even if you don't have great wealth, you can make a difference. Small gifts add up and do great things collectively. Also, from a less altruistic point of view, one's success in business and society is often influenced by the contacts, respect, and satisfaction one's largesse generates. Giving something away often leads to receiving back much more later. Perhaps tax avoidance, deciding how much to leave the kids, and similar high-income problems aren't your concerns. Maybe they will be later. But you can still become part of the future with your generosity, and remain a positive catalyst in others' lives long after your own is concluded.

Private philanthropy is really an American tradition—one of our unique contributions to humanity, and one of the reasons for our country's great success. It is here in the United States that basic research is funded by those willing to expand the realm of human knowledge without a commercial return. It is here that the diversity of charitable programs initiated without governmental central planning produces the unexpected breakthroughs. It is here that funding for the unusual, the unlikely, the "cutting edge," is available so that there's something for everyone.

America's generosity is like that of no other place in the world. For all the cynics' carping, helping others is valued in the United States as much as success in the arts, in the home, or in commerce. From the great "robber barons" before World War I to today's philanthropic giants (Annenberg, Bass, Getty, Hunt, Huntsman, Lauder, Packard, Tisch, and so on), those who achieve much for themselves are generally those who give the rest of us the most.

Philanthropy dominates the social lives of the wealthy in big U.S. cities. Rather than purely selfish entertainment, much of the evening get-together functions (dinners, dances, and boat trips) these people attend are fund-raising events. Even sporting activities are used to benefit worthwhile causes rather than just be selfish pleasures. The style section of our city newspapers chronicles which celebrities attend which philanthropic dinners each night; the most celebrated are honorees there, partially for their past achievements, but also for their current fund-raising abilities. Executives and socialites solicit each other for their favorite organizations. They attend events where they bestow small tokens of appreciation on one another after suitably flattering speeches. Fun evenings for fine causes.

Unfortunately, philanthropic circles are a more limited group in every city than they should be. The same names are on the donor lists each time. Where are the others? Where are the athletes who benefited from scholarships and then made great fortunes without helping their alma maters? Or the entertainment community that, with a few notable exceptions, responds only to the media crisis of the moment in the environment, social welfare, and health fields? With a donated evening of their time, they could help so many on an ongoing basis. Athletes and entertainers make great livings off the public. They owe something back. There are too few Bill Cosbys, Paul Newmans, Larry Johnsons, and Andrea Jaegers who do great things for others. We must get others involved. There's so much still to do, so many we could help.

I've always respected those who try to change the world for the better rather than just complain about it. Some devote their time, some their money. Some focus on philanthropy, some on government. Take the politically active millionaires like Steve Forbes, for example. While many are at the opposite end of the political spectrum from me, I greatly admire those who put their own money, time, and reputations where their hearts and mouths are. Against all advice, Steve has spent a portion of his to run for office, subjecting himself and his family to the scrutiny of the voters through the press, running the physical risks of being in the public eye, and trying to help with no motive other than to change the world (presumably he doesn't need the political job for income). That takes guts and generosity and dedication. We need more like him: people who don't just complain, people who do something about it!

The same in philanthropy. In New York, those like Peter Grauer, Henry Kravis, Morris Offit, Jack and Lewis Rudin, Dan Tully, and

Dave Komansky, who do so much for local philanthropic causes, donating their money, getting others to give, contributing their wisdom, doing the work (all while devoting themselves to their families and running their own businesses). In every other American city, there's a similar list. Those of us who don't participate are lazy and selfish by comparison—and shortsighted. We're depriving ourselves of the greatest pleasure life offers, the chance to make a better world.

*　　*　　*

Today, much philanthropy is corporate. Helping others is good for business. Companies give to improve their community, change the economic environment, influence public opinion, reciprocate favors, accommodate clients, curry political favors, and gain access. They donate money to charities and cultural organizations directly, or by matching employees' gifts. Businesses give merchandise to groups that redistribute it to the needy. They contribute second-hand equipment for charities to use. They lend their people or encourage their employees to donate their own time.

I'm on the board of directors of the Central Park Conservancy. CPC raises private funds to renovate and maintain the wonderful famous green space two blocks from our New York office and close to the homes of hundreds of our employees. The city doesn't have the resources to maintain the park, but our company's ability to attract good people depends on maintaining a positive and inviting environment. Not only do I use it, but Central Park is where many of our other employees exercise, relax, and congregate. Bloomberg (along with the most generous Dick Gilder, who donated $17 million toward the park's restoration) donates moneys and hosts fund-raising events for CPC. Because CPC renovates the park, the city's better off, we get better workers, and our company prospers. All companies should do the same. We should support similar local causes in every city where we have a branch. It's good for business because it's good for people.

Good business is also providing summer jobs to students. Bloomberg employs close to two hundred summer interns each year. They all get paid the same amount, ten dollars an hour—a lot for them, and, in all fairness, not a lot for us. We try hard to make their experience for the few months they work with us as meaningful as possible. Young people get to see what our company and the business world are like. In a few years, we'll be in competition with other firms for these same kids or their friends. Hopefully, based on their familiarity with Bloomberg, they'll choose us.

We give some of these summer job openings to philanthropic organizations to auction off as a fund-raiser ("What am I bid for an internship at Bloomberg for your child?"). We hire the sons and daughters of employees, customers, and suppliers for a few months. We do them a favor that is repaid in loyalty or enhanced relationships with our company. And many of our summer jobs go to kids from less wealthy families where the parents have no "contacts" to exploit. With these, we expand our identification and awareness in communities where we normally wouldn't attract full-time applicants. The kids spread the good word that helps us later in recruiting. And we've had a chance to identify students we want for permanent employment after they graduate.

One of our difficulties in getting the most productive workforce is attracting the broad spectrum of candidates we need across gender, religious, and racial lines. Having a diverse workforce is required by law in the United States. Having a diverse workforce is also required by capitalism in the marketplace. It increases the likelihood that the next great idea will be born here, not at some other company.

Getting the best and brightest of each group to apply for jobs at Bloomberg sometimes is a challenge. Often, they don't know who we are or what we do, don't think they could get the job with us, or don't even consider business as a career. So we have our own customized, self-serving affirmative-action recruitment program. We advertise in newspapers and magazines likely to be read by our target groups. We interview at the schools they attend. We go to trade and job fairs where they network.

Some of our target groups are in great demand by our competitors as well. We've got to find a reason for them to choose us. To attract them, we lease our terminals to college libraries for student use at half price. (We used to charge nothing, until we had over one thousand free terminals at schools. Now, by charging a little, we can help more schools and still not create a great burden on any one of them or on us.) The kids use our product for research, and when we come to interview, they are more likely to be interested in signing up to see our representative. We even have a program in which we provide free terminals at forty-one schools participating in the United Negro College Fund. Those schools tend to be small, have minuscule budgets, and lack a group of wealthy alumni to defray even our reduced college-rate charges. Their students generally haven't had exposure to commerce, to Bloomberg, or to the functions we perform. Nor do most companies stop by these schools' placement offices. Nevertheless, the next geniuses may be matriculated there—and we want them!

We support a number of other local, cultural, and educational organizations for similar reasons. Lincoln Center for the Performing Arts and The Jewish Museum, on both of whose boards I serve, enrich our city. Another organization, Prep for Prep, sends the brightest minority kids to private schools they could not otherwise afford to attend. It's a great cause helping our society. Along with New York philanthropists Leon Black, Marty Lipton, and John Vogelstein, we get a chance to change the lives of so many deserving kids. Letting them in on the American dream is one of the most satisfying things I can do—and one of the best for our company. Once again, I give my time on their boards, and donate my own and the company's funds to further their objectives. We get paid back by having a better society to live in, better employees, and great satisfaction. (My participation on the U.S. Ski Team Educational Foundation Board is strictly for personal reasons. It's a kick, given how much I like to ski. Philanthropy can be fun, too.)

*   *   *

My greatest love, however, is helping educational organizations. My work with the Academy of Finance helps prepare high school students across the country to thrive in the commercial world after graduation. I give money and serve on the board of my daughters' prep school. It's a great school and tuition never covers the real costs, particularly for scholarship students whose parents can't pay the full charge. I'm also on the board of the Institute for Advanced Study, at Princeton, New Jersey, a think tank for postdoctoral students working on the more theoretical problems in the social and natural sciences. Who knows what great advances will come from its members? (Albert Einstein was the Institute's first faculty member.)

My primary activity, apart from my family and the company, though, is at The Johns Hopkins University. I serve as chairman of its board of trustees (attempting to follow Morris Offit, who single-handedly changed the history of this great institution), an activity that takes me to its Baltimore headquarters, on average, one day a week. It is hard to imagine anything else I could do that would be as challenging, as rewarding, and as much fun.

Hopkins has three primary missions: educating our young people, those who will lead us in the future; researching to discover, invent, and create that which will shape our lives and prevent, eradicate, and cure diseases and infirmities that cause such misery around the world; and lastly, helping the military defend the liberties that we so often take for granted in America.

Johns Hopkins helps the places where it has campuses: Maryland; Washington, DC; China; and Italy. More than that, Hopkins helps the world; education, knowledge, and culture go worldwide. So when I donate my money (Johns Hopkins is the primary beneficiary of my philanthropic gifts), when I donate my time, when I give the little insight I have, I make a global contribution to society. When the next Johns Hopkins researcher, diplomat, or writer wins a Nobel Prize, I'll share in it in spirit. He or she couldn't have done it without my participation. It'll be my prize, too. Just as much, it will also be the prize of every one of the hundreds of thousands of donors of cash and time to the various Johns Hopkins institutions.

As a citizen of the world (and a lucky one at that), I have a responsibility to improve other lives. I do it with my money, expertise, and time (wealth, wisdom, and work—the three contributions one can make). And I have tried to do it in the way I think does the most good. Years ago, in honor of my mother's seventy-fifth birthday, I endowed a professorship in the study of art history at Hopkins. It's something she's interested in and the school needed. To this day, she gets great pleasure knowing the Charlotte Bloomberg Professor is teaching, researching, and enhancing our culture. Currently, my mother, my sister, and I annually award four grants to people contributing to Jewish causes, another of my mother's great loves. The Charlotte Bloomberg Awards and the yearly awards ceremony are something she looks forward to each winter. You can see it in her eyes as she helps to select the winners and bestows the honorarium.

I've endowed a professorship/fellowship at Harvard University to study and research philanthropic and volunteer policies and practices. It's named in honor of my late father, and while he's not around to see it work, his wife, children, and grandchildren all are. Every two years, this "chair" passes from one school at Harvard to another (Divinity, Law, Government, the College, and of course, my alma mater, Business). And so, every twenty-four months, a new person will study, teach, research, and write from a new perspective about my interest, philanthropy. Will they make great contributions to society? You bet. Will there be great leverage to continue the work I love by teaching many? For sure.

Will my family and I get enjoyment, satisfaction, admiration? Absolutely.

*   *   *

The role of individuals in philanthropy and public service in America is clear: We must help or our successors will suffer—and they could be the descendants we care so much about. Those opposed to private contributions, who argue that they eliminate the rightful role of government, miss two points. First, the government can't do everything. Second, the government doesn't do everything well. People should support personally what they think society needs.

The role of companies in philanthropic endeavors and public service is somewhat different. Management generally has a legal responsibility to maximize the assets of the stockholders. Nowhere is there relief from that objective (nor, given the potential for abuse, should there be). Activities not furthering that cause are generally prohibited. Just because management thinks something's worthwhile from society's point of view, they can't (or shouldn't) give away the stockholders' assets. Companies have an obligation to distribute dividends and let the individual shareholders do what they see fit. Likewise in the conduct of their affairs. If it doesn't further the corporate purpose, it's outlawed.

Still, when helping others helps the company, it couldn't be more in the stockholders' interests or more appropriate as a corporate activity. In our organization, I'm repeatedly solicited by every worthwhile cause. When it's for my school, my religion, my personal enjoyment, the donation is from Michael R. Bloomberg. However, when the solicitor's a client, or the company's employees get direct benefit, or when a contribution specifically helps our business, Bloomberg L.P. makes the gift. Personal interests, I take care of; business ones, all the investors in the company contribute.

Private companies, like individuals, enjoy greater freedom than public corporations to do what they think is right. We refused to enter the South African market during apartheid. We adopted this policy before many U.S. municipalities required it for their suppliers. Later, when F.W. de Klerk started dismantling the racist practices in South Africa, we led again by opening our business there to encourage continued progress along those lines, even though U.S. policies still requested restraint at the time. Sometimes, you just have to do what you think is best for society, even when it's not popular or profitable.

Still, even what private companies can do is limited. Resources, both time and money, are never adequate to do everything. Like many other companies with a feeling of community service, we employ a full-time person, Patti Harris, whose sole job is to decide which philanthropic activities are appropriate for our company and to ensure we get our money's worth when we donate time, money, and jobs. One of Patti's questions is, When does helping others help us? Another is, How much can we afford to do, given a never-ending call for assistance? A third is based on compassion—sometimes we've just got to do it anyway.

We give to charities our clients support as a way of saying thank you for their patronage. We make donations to organizations that improve our brand recognition and image. We assist worthwhile causes that improve the environment our employees enjoy. We join with others where the relationship, the contacts, and the mutual experiences will be useful to our company later in our commercial activities.

Not only does Patti commit our dollars, she also follows, influences, and directs how our gifts are used, ensuring our objectives are met. And often, smaller charities without large professional staffs need our help and advice as much as our money. She can assist with their fund-raising, publicity, and government relations. Further, she proactively searches for innovative ways that the company, our employees, and I can help others. (One such project involving all is our school-painting activity. Through the support of "Publicolor," a New York–based nonprofit, our company buys paint and brushes. Our staff donates their time on weekends to apply color to the walls of an inner-city school building. Together, we transform the learning environment of thousands of kids studying in previously dismal surroundings. Instantly, sweat and cash produce something good you can see.)

We want to be known as a company that not only takes care of our employees, but is also generous to our community. It all helps the bottom line. Companies that don't understand that don't do as well as they could.

Give something back and you'll wind up with more!

Afterword

The question I know you've been pondering is: Why did he write this book? After all, it has taken Matt Winkler and me a lot of time we could have spent elsewhere. We're running a risk, putting down on paper something we can't easily retract. If the reviewers pan it, we'll be thoroughly embarrassed. If the book sells fewer copies than the Pope's, I'll be labeled a literary failure forever (and Kelly MacGown, who has edited and typed Matt's and my revisions so competently and tirelessly, will shoot us both).

The actual writing of this volume has certainly been a humbling experience. I've always been impressed by my friends who fulfill their family obligations, run their own companies, and simultaneously write screenplays, "op-ed" pieces, and serious books. Their literary abilities and self-discipline are vastly superior to mine. They are Renaissance people and I'm a mere dilettante. Rewriting page after page, again and again, has been a challenge. If it wasn't for many friends' constant encouragement and support, I'd never have finished. Of course, they bear no responsibility for the quality. They just pushed me to continue with whatever I could do—and for better or worse, this is what I'm capable of writing.

Matt and our agent, Arthur Klebanoff, mapped out the book's structure and forced me to actually put pen to paper. Then, taking Matt's scribblings and mine and combining them into prose when I'm used to communicating verbally took forever.

Myles Thompson, of John Wiley & Sons, Inc., began it with a call to our marketing guru, Elisabeth DeMarse, soliciting our interest. My initial instinct was *absolutely not!* On a risk/reward basis, what's in it for us? In fact, most friends I mentioned it to said the same thing. Which is probably why I decided to go ahead. Stubborn isn't a word I'd use to describe myself; pigheaded is more appropriate. To a contrarian like me, constant advice *not* to do something almost always starts me quickly down the risky, unpopular path.

Then, there's the desire to see one's name in print. I claim immunity to the ego gratification a self-promoting book provides. After all, with the success of our company, my name on the door worldwide, myself as the company's spokesperson, you'd think I'd be blasé about publicity by now. But the truth is, recognition is heady stuff, and receiving even insincere adulation is a kick.

Let's not forget the business reason to have bookstores globally displaying our logo. Name recognition improves access for our salespeople. Building a widely recognized brand and a favorable image in consumers' minds takes decades and costs zillions. Every bit of publicity helps; you never know which imprint makes the difference. With radio, television, Internet access, and magazines competing for the public's attention, the old adage, "As long as they spell your name right," applies more than ever.

Another thought was more prophylactic. If we don't, someone else will. Having a rogue writer out there taking journalistic liberties to commercialize the truth is dangerous. Glasses can be half empty as well as the reverse. I'd just as soon get in our best shot first.

In the end, though, there was only one compelling reason to go ahead. I wanted to say something. I have strong beliefs as to how young people should prepare themselves for the future. I think I know how to inspire groups to work together, particularly where technology and complexity are introduced by competitive pressures. I know what's great about my country and how I can make it even better. And while many don't contribute to society what they should, I'm sure I can convince them to do so, to share their knowledge, to spread around their wealth, to be more compassionate, and to assist others.

I wanted to help, explain, and change, rather than just complain. If I didn't do my part, then I'm no better than those I accuse of living mediocre, hypocritcal, or selfish lives. I have something to say. This was my opportunity. Why shouldn't I have taken it?

Index

Index

Index

Index

Index

Index

Index

U.S. Ski Team Educational
Foundation Board, 244–245
United States Treasury bonds,
69–70, 72

Vatican, 58
Venture capitalists, impact on
entrepreneurs, 43
Video on Demand (VOD), 108
Vietnam War, 14–15
Vision, 43, 147, 151
Vogelstein, John, 244

Wall Street Journal, 28, 67–71,
74–76, 79, 84, 92, 94, 131
Washington Post, 79
Weinberg, Janet, 114
Weisel, Tom, 219–220

What-if scenarios, 45, 53, 68, 87,
143
Wilson, Margarette, 34
Winkler, Matt, 67–80, 83, 92–95,
97, 100–102, 127, 162, 251
Work ethic, 16–17
Work habits, 163
World Bank, 58
World Wide Web, 109, 121, 128,
197
Wu, Andy, 48

Xerox, 27, 173

Yale University, 239

Zegar, Chuck, 46, 48, 51

261